What Is a Madrasa?

Islamic Civilization and Muslim Networks

CARL W. ERNST AND BRUCE B. LAWRENCE, EDITORS

Highlighting themes with historical as well as contemporary significance, Islamic Civilization and Muslim Networks features works that explore Islamic societies and Muslim peoples from a fresh perspective, drawing on new interpretive frameworks or theoretical strategies in a variety of disciplines. Special emphasis is given to systems of exchange that have promoted the creation and development of Islamic identities—cultural, religious, or geopolitical. The series spans all periods and regions of Islamic civilization.

A complete list of titles published in this series appears at the end of the book.

WHAT IS A

Madrasa?

Ebrahim Moosa

The University of North Carolina Press CHAPEL HILL

Designed by Kimberly Bryant
Set in 10.2/14 Charis by Westchester Publishing Services
Manufactured in the United States of America
The paper in this book meets the guidelines for permanence and durability of the Committee on Production Guidelines for Book Longevity of the Council on Library Resources. The University of North Carolina Press has been a member of the Green Press Initiative since 2003.

Jacket illustration: At Jamiʿa Naeemia, a madrasa in Lahore, Pakistan.
Photograph by Amjad Perez.

Library of Congress Cataloging-in-Publication Data
Moosa, Ebrahim.
What is a madrasa? / Ebrahim Moosa.
pages cm. — (Islamic civilization and Muslim networks)
Includes bibliographical references and index.
ISBN 978-1-4696-2013-8 (cloth : alk. paper) — ISBN 978-1-4696-2014-5 (ebook)
1. Madrasahs. 2. Islamic education. 3. Islamic religious education. I. Title.
LC904.M66 2015
378'.077—dc23

2014034904

Portions of the Prologue and Chapter 1 were first published in the *Boston Review* as "Inside Madrasa: A Personal Story" on January 1, 2007; the author thanks the *Review* for permission to reproduce this material here.

For Muneer Fareed

I have danced before idols and worn the holy thread, so that
The shaykh of the city may become a man of God by calling me a
heretic.

Now they run away from me, now they associate with me;
In this desert, they do not know whether I am hunter or prey.

A heart that lacks warmth can ill profit from the company of a man;
Come with red-hot copper, so that my elixir can work on you.

—Muhammad Iqbal, *Persian Psalms*, trans. Mustansir Mir

But for us existence is still enchanted. It's still
Beginning in a hundred places. A playing
of pure powers no one can touch and not kneel to and marvel.

Faced with the unutterable, words still disintegrate . . .
And ever new, out of the most quivering
stones, music builds her divine house in useless space.

—Rainer Maria Rilke, *The Sonnets to Orpheus*

Contents

Note on Transliteration and Translation, xi

PROLOGUE Inside Madrasas, 1

PART I. LIVED EXPERIENCE

1. A Novice, 15

2. Wake, Wash, Pray, 31

3. Becoming Scholars, 47

PART II. HISTORY AND CONTEXTS

4. Birth of the Contemporary Madrasa, 77

5. Texts and Authors, 108

6. From a Republic of Letters to a Republic of Piety, 122

PART III. POLITICS OF KNOWLEDGE

7. Preserving the Prophet's Legacy, 145

8. Believe, Learn, Know, 176

PART IV. MADRASAS IN GLOBAL CONTEXT

9. Talking about Madrasas, 207

10. The Future of Madrasas, 219

11. Letter to Policy Makers, 233

12. Letters to My Teachers, 241

Epilogue, 250

Glossary, 255

Notes, 259

Bibliography, 269

Acknowledgments, 277

Index, 279

Figures, Illustrations, and Map

FIGURES

Select genealogy of Deobandi scholars from the eighteenth century to the present, 70

Key scholars in the Farangi Mahall school, 80

Scholarly genealogy of the Khairabadi school, 99

Genealogy of the Barelvi school, 101

Periodization of education in India over time, 128

Significant Persian influence impacting the Nizami curriculum, 131

A visual schematization of Islamic moral values, 159

ILLUSTRATIONS

Faculty and students interacting at Jamiʿa Naeemia, Lahore, Pakistan, 4

Young male students memorizing the Qur'an at a mosque in Srirangapatna, in Karnataka State in India, 18

Author making ablutions (*wudu*) prior to ritual prayers at one of the mosques of Darul Uloom Deoband in India, 36

Students working on computers at Darul Uloom Deoband, India, 50

Shah Waliyullah's grave in Delhi, India, 95

Statue of Tamerlane outside Ak-Saray Palace in Shakhrisabz, Uzbekistan, 115

Remnants of a historic madrasa built by Mahmud Gawan in Karnataka State in India today, 116

Students interacting with faculty at Jamiʿa Naeemia, Lahore, Pakistan, 154

Mawlana Anzar Shah Kashmiri, 165

Entrance to the Jamiʿa Naeemia madrasa in Lahore with antiterrorism security precautions, 167

Tomb inside the madrasa of Jamiʿa Naeemia, 168
Children in the town of Deoband in India going to elementary school in traditional clothing, 186
Students in class at Jamiʿa Naeemia, Lahore, Pakistan, 189
New York Times magazine story giving the impression that all madrasas are run by the Taliban and are linked to terrorism, 208
New marble mosque on Darul Uloom Deoband campus, 243
Doors to mosque of Jamiʿa Naeemia, Lahore, Pakistan, 248

MAP

Geographical distribution of the main centers of traditional learning in South Asia, 169

Note on Transliteration and Translation

Arabic transliteration in the text and notes is limited to ʿayn where indicated and ʾhamza only in the middle of a word. Otherwise I have dispensed of hamzas as in ʾAbu and written Abu and used ʿulama instead of ʿulamaʾ. I have used the term "Darul Uloom" without standard transliteration features, since most madrasas transliterate in that form. I have also improvised a convenient form of transliteration for the benefit of nonspecialist readers, such as ʿAbdul ʿAli instead of the ʿAbd al-ʿAli. In the bibliography, however, I have used a detailed transliteration system in the event that specialists wish to track some of my sources.

Qurʾan translations are from Thomas Cleary, *The Qurʾan: A New Translation* and Muhammad Asad, *The Message of the Qurʾan* with occasional amendments.

PROLOGUE

Inside Madrasas

One spring morning a few years ago, I walked through the town of Deoband, home to India's most famous Sunni Muslim seminary. A clean-shaven man, his face glowing with sarcasm, called out to me. "Looking for terrorists?" he asked in Urdu. Swiftly and instinctively I protested and yelled back at him, "I have every right to visit my alma mater." With a sheepish, almost theatrical grin, he turned and walked away.

I shouldn't have been so annoyed. The century-old seminary in Deoband came under intense scrutiny after the Taliban leadership claimed an ideological affiliation with similar institutions in Pakistan and Afghanistan. Since September 11, 2001, journalists, politicians, and diplomats have descended periodically on this town near Delhi in the northern state of Uttar Pradesh. This state is one node, along with the province of Pakistan's Punjab, with Lahore as its capital, in what might be called an extended intellectual and spiritual heartland of Islam that spreads across the Indo-Pakistan subcontinent.

However, Muslim seminaries, or madrasas, everywhere became stigmatized once the Taliban was linked to the terror mastermind Osama bin Laden. Everyone conveniently ignored the history of the special, makeshift madrasas that sprang up on the Pakistani side of the Afghan border. These borderland madrasas served as refugee camps for youth in the aftermath of the Soviet invasion that ravaged Afghanistan during the Cold War. The United States supported the war of the Afghan mujahidin against the Soviets.

Since then, top-level government officials, former heads of state like U.S. president George Bush and British prime minister Tony Blair, along with a chorus of journalists, pundits, and scholars—singled out madrasas as breeding grounds for terrorists. They did this without providing a shred of convincing evidence to warrant the indictment of a large, complex network of religious schools associated with multiple Muslim sects and ideologies.

In popular Western media parlance, the mere mention of the word "madrasa" conjures up an "us versus them" dynamic. This strategy effectively mobilizes unwitting audiences to a mindset that does not advance mutual understanding among civilizations and cultures. Revered by many Muslims but reviled, if not feared, by many non-Muslims, madrasas are the single most widely used educational resource to cultivate religious learning in parts of the Muslim world.

Low-budget, monastery-like Muslim seminaries dot the landscape of South Asia. The schools flourish mainly in India, Pakistan, Afghanistan, and Bangladesh as well as in the South Asian diaspora, but similar institutions are equally visible in different shapes and forms in East Asia, especially Indonesia, Malaysia, southern Thailand, and parts of Africa and the Middle East, especially Iran. Young adult males study in the South Asian institutions, but there is a growth in segregated madrasas dedicated to the education of females.

Madrasas specialize in the study of classical theological and legal texts as well as commentaries on the Muslim scripture, the Qur'an. They place special emphasis on studying the life and teachings of Islam's prophet, Muhammad, and are engrossed in complex details as to how rules and morals should regulate public and private conduct according to religious norms. All the secondary disciplines that are needed to gain proficiency in these primary fields of study are also taught, such as Arabic and Persian grammar and literature, rhetoric, logic, and philosophy, among other subjects.

Noted journalistic voices like Peter Bergen, William Dalrymple and, belatedly, policy experts Rebecca Winthrop and Corinne Graff of the Brookings Institution now acknowledge that not all madrasas can be in-

Meanings of Madrasa

Pronounced "*mud-ra-sa*" and derived from the Arabic root word *d-r-s*, meaning "to study," *madrasa* means the "*place* of study." The most common word is *dars*, meaning a lecture or sermon. *D-r-s* also can be used in the senses of "to train," "to discipline," and "to repeatedly read something until one memorizes it." Given the various shades of *d-r-s* in Arabic, *madrasa* can refer to a *place* where a sermon or lecture is delivered, and hence is applied to old-style schools with an emphasis on memory and discipline like the seminaries of South Asia.

In modern Arabic, "madrasa" generically denotes any educational institution from preschool to high school, so every secular elementary, middle, or high school in a place like Cairo would be called a madrasa. The noun "madrasa" can therefore also mean a modern school, college, or academy where lessons and lectures on various subjects are addressed to students.

In different Muslim cultures, the word "madrasa" is used for the equivalent of Sunday school–types of religious instruction. In villages and towns in South Asia, East Asia, Central Asia, the Middle East, Africa, Europe, and North America, young children attend religious instruction at madrasas in order to learn how to read the Qur'an in Arabic and receive basic instruction on matters of faith. They may attend on a daily basis or only on select days of the week. Some students might also devote time to the memorization of the Qur'an on a full-time or part-time basis parallel to their pursuit of secular education.

The madrasas discussed in this book refer to the institutions of higher Islamic learning in South Asia. They are the equivalent of seminaries, where religious functionaries and experts in Islamic law and theology are trained.

dicted in the war on terror.[1] Yet sympathetic sound bites do not provide an accurate picture of what happens inside madrasas, nor do they humanize the inhabitants of these age-old institutions. The gulf in perception is captured in the disparity of firmly held convictions as portrayed by "insider versus outsider" perspectives on the madrasa-sphere of South Asia.

For Taqi ʿUsmani a prominent figure in Pakistan's madrasa hierarchy and a former Shariʿa court judge, the purpose of a madrasa is a noble

Faculty and students interacting at Jamiʿa Naeemia, Lahore, Pakistan. (Picture: Amjad Pervez)

one. Education, he declares, is "to change people's way of thinking," and it cannot be reduced to merely a means of guaranteeing that graduates are gainfully employed.[2] Few people disagree with him. One of the many noble goals of education is to strengthen one's identity, to internalize excellent human qualities, and to realize one's potential. "These virtues," says ʿUsmani, make "each individual serve not only their own countries and communities but . . . the whole of humanity." Yet former U.S. secretary of state General Colin Powell claimed madrasas are malevolent and a breeding ground "for fundamentalists and terrorists."[3] Former secretary of defense Donald Rumsfeld stated, "There are a number of madrasa schools [in Pakistan] that train people to be suicide killers and—and extremists, violent extremists."[4] How do these incommensurable views about madrasas make sense to readers? One view portrays the graduates of madrasas as pious and thinking exemplars whose goal is to serve humanity, while another perspective regards madrasas as antithetical to humanity.

Instead of being defensive, I should have told the man who taunted me in Deoband that I had lived and studied in several Indian madrasas between 1975 and 1981. A quarter century later, I had returned—not in search of terrorists, but rather serving as a translator between the world inside the walls of the madrasas and those on the outside; to revisit the places I once inhabited and where I was partly formed, in order to accurately report to those on the outside who are curious and eager to know what, exactly, transpires in these institutions. There are many people on the outside, I tell the folks in the madrasas, who are both knowledgeable about Islam's past and curious about its present trajectory.

Consider the gentleman I overheard in a New York sushi restaurant a few years ago talking to his lunch partner about history lectures he heard on his iPod. The prominent medieval Catholic scholar Thomas Aquinas, I overheard the man say, admitted he learned a great deal from Muslim sources. "Muslims in the twelfth century were studying algebra," he said. Then he added, "Look at Islam. Once it was at the cutting edge of science and math. Can you imagine a subject like algebra came from Islam? But look at it [Islam] now," he said with a sigh; "I don't know what went wrong."[5] I resolutely looked down into my plate in an effort to avoid his gaze, presumptuously fearing he would draw me into an awkward conversation.

Some people in the West, like that anonymous diner, are aware of the story of Muslim civilization and its many contributions to knowledge and culture. They know of Muslim service to the humanities—poetry, literature, and philosophy—as well as to science—medicine and anatomy—and technology about 600 to 800 years ago.

But it is not easy to explain what is happening now. How does one explain to that man in the New York restaurant how the wellspring of creative learning in Islamic societies had gradually dried up in a competitive, globalizing world?

WHAT HAPPENED?

It is not sufficient to say colonialism interrupted the flourishing of learning in Muslim societies. It sounds like an apology. Of course, in the eyes of thoughtful people, militant manifestations of Islam do not exhaust the picture. Economic, political, and social transformations, many acknowledge, did disfigure many aspects of Muslim societies, severely impacting their culture, tradition, and religion. Many hope that efficient governance will restore some stability and allow for prosperity.

Some Muslims try to redeem the dysfunctional present by retreating to some glorious past. As the deeply troubled Changez, a character in Mohsen Hamid's novel *The Reluctant Fundamentalist*, boasts of South Asia's great past, "Four thousand years ago we, the people of the Indus

River basin, had cities that were laid out on grids and boasted underground sewers, while the ancestors of those who would invade and colonize America were illiterate barbarians. Now our cities were largely unplanned, unsanitary affairs, and America had universities with individual endowments greater than our national budget for education. To be reminded of this vast disparity was, for me, to be ashamed."[6] Changez refers to the glory of Indic cultures and philosophies long before the advent of Islam. When Islam arrived in India in the eighth century, more cultural diversity was added to this already highly diverse civilization, and it continued to be added well into the seventeenth century. People adhering to native Indian traditions—later identified by terms such as Hindu, Buddhist, and Jain—crossed paths with those who adhered to traditions called Zoroastrianism, Judaism, Christianity, and Islam. Such a multireligious and multicultural civilization governed by an Islamic imperial system is what scholars named an Islamicate civilization.

Words like alchemy, algebra, and alcohol—derived from Arabic roots, a language intimately linked to Islamicate civilization—are all traces of an intellectually robust Muslim past. Historians inform us that Islamicate civilization played a crucial role in the development of mathematics, astronomy, optics, and chemistry in medieval times.

Many decades ago, these linguistic clues and cultural snippets made me aware of the deficits in my own knowledge of Islam as both a faith tradition and a civilization. My cultural illiteracy set me on a path of discovery—of faith and religious learning. Almost impulsively, my voyage began in the madrasas of South Asia, where my personal and intellectual identity was partly forged. My journey took me from my native South Africa to India, with a later detour in Europe. Throughout these voyages, I carried my madrasa learning with me. I still do so in my vocation as a professor of Islamic Studies in America.

THIS BOOK

In many ways *What Is a Madrasa?* is also my own complicated life story. My spiritual and intellectual journeys began in South Asia's madrasas, but they did not end there. I revisited those madrasas between 2004 and 2007 because of the tumultuous events that had rocked the world, most notably al-Qaeda's attacks on the United States on September 11, 2001. In retaliation, the United States and NATO invaded Afghanistan in a bid to unseat the Taliban and al-Qaeda, leaving both groups weakened but unvanquished, and periodically they metastasize to wreak unspeakable havoc. On the heels of that war followed the U.S. invasion of Iraq in order to topple the regime of Iraq's dictator, Saddam Hussain. Both invasions triggered enormous death and destruction. The full impact of the harm done to Afghans, Iraqis, and Pakistanis has yet to be properly assessed. The unpredictable blowback of these occupations will be decided in the decades to come.

When opinions about Islam and Muslims washed up in every conceivable media and public conversation after September 11, I felt assaulted from at least two sides. First, the terrorists assaulted me. They murdered 3,000 innocent fellow citizens in New York, Washington, D.C., and the plains of Pennsylvania in the name of my faith. Several dozen innocent Muslims were among those who died in New York. And the U.S. Congress cited one, Mohammad Salman Hamdani, for his bravery in attempting to rescue others.

Of course, the terrorists invoked a murderous and distorted interpretation of Islam, its ethics, and its values, but there can be no denial that they did it out of a commitment to their version of the faith. Second, a barrage of undisguised Islam-hating media assaults systematically violated and dehumanized me, and millions of other fellow believers, in a reckless, prolonged campaign of guilt by association that has, amazingly, not yet run its course. The death and destruction visited on tens of thousands of human beings in Afghanistan, Iraq, Pakistan, Yemen, and Somalia were further assaults, which continue to be perpetrated in the name of the citizens of the United States and of several European states. These include a wealth of questionable military and paramilitary actions that test the conscience of the world.

Persons with dubious credentials started to talk publicly about me—my history, my culture, and my civilization—in ways that I was unable to recognize. Since the tragic events of 9/11 many people have come to know more about Islam and Muslims, one of the world's largest religions and a major civilization whose representatives play a major role in global economic, political, and cultural affairs. Scholars and public intellectuals have written excellent books and produced helpful documentary films and programs to educate the public.

Yet one area that most people in the West and in the East do not fully grasp is this: September 11 catapulted the term "madrasa" into media currency but without coming to terms with the reality of this important institution. In the political lexicon of the West, the term "madrasa" serves as a diabolical term for everything Islamic. Hopefully, the reader of this book will come to understand the ambiguity underlying the charge that the madrasa is a geopolitical frontier in the so-called clash of civilizations rhetoric.

Many excellent books have been written about madrasas as institutions in Pakistan, India, and Bangladesh and how they might impact security issues and political stability on the Indo-Pak subcontinent.[7]

What Is a Madrasa? is written for general readers, teachers, and students. In one sense it is a primer about the role the madrasas play in the cultural, intellectual, and religious experiences of Muslims in the present and past. Keeping in view the vast geographical and cultural diversity of the madrasa as an institution and notwithstanding such differences, this book keeps its sights on the madrasas of the Indo-Pak subcontinent with special reference to Sunni institutions. Madrasas in Bangladesh mirror their counterparts in India and Pakistan with different local textures, but they are not discussed in this book. Madrasas in the South Asian diaspora in places like the United Kingdom, South Africa, the United States, the Caribbean, and Canada, which are independent from institutions in the Indo-Pak subcontinent, are also not studied in this book, save for the occasional passing reference.

For the most part, I deal with the Deobandi network of madrasas and its representatives. It is the largest and fastest-growing madrasa franchise. While taking into account today's geopolitical realities, *What Is a Madrasa?* takes the reader inside the walls of the madrasa. The reader will journey with me into the madrasa classroom, get an idea of daily life, meet with scholars, and read some texts studied by madrasa students. Hopefully the reader will better appreciate why madrasa communities exist, get a sense of the recent history of those communities, meet some important role players, understand why students study medieval texts, and learn how madrasas support religious life in Muslim societies today.

What Is a Madrasa? tells the story of people who are connected to a classical intellectual and scholarly tradition of Islamdom. Those allied to madrasas revere their distant exemplars, admire shared texts, and fondly recall places that once sparkled with intellectual energies in the Muslim past. People, texts, and places embody the highest aspirations and the most deeply felt needs of inhabitants of the madrasas.

In another sense this book is about the multiple narratives of salvation within madrasa orthodoxy. While salvation does indeed require the performance of practices, it also involves debates over knowledge regu-

Orthodoxy

The term "orthodoxy," meaning "belief in or agreement with doctrines, opinions, or practices currently held to be right or correct," is frequently used in this book. It generally refers to traditional Muslim authorities, but the meaning of the word "traditional" like the term "orthodoxy," can mean different things to different people. Orthodoxy in Islam comes in different stripes. In South Asia, Hanafi-Deobandi orthodoxy would charge the orthodox Ahl-i Hadith or Salafis to hold certain incorrect beliefs or practices, just as the Barelvi school would disagree with both on some specific issues of doctrine or practice. Whenever I use the term "madrasa orthodoxy," I intend to differentiate those religious scholars, ʿulama, who are affiliated to a particular franchise of madrasa. There are also orthodox elements that operate outside the madrasas. Muslim orthodoxy in African countries, in the Middle East, and in East Asia are highly differentiated, and one should look at their specific practices.

lating these practices. At its core it is a debate about power—a politics of knowledge that determines ways of living in the world. Few people recognize that the madrasa is vital to two primary prerequisites in Islamic life. First, it is central to the acquisition and circulation of knowledge, and second, it is vital to the personal spiritual growth or self-formation of the individual. Of course, not all Muslims follow the teachings offered by the madrasas. Yet ordinary Muslims follow certain blends of madrasa orthodoxy, and paradoxically, there is a variety within madrasa orthodoxies, as we shall see.

Learning, teaching, and moral training are and always have been at the core of Islamic life. All knowledge is revered, but knowledge linked to faith occupies a privileged place in the Muslim religious imaginary. When knowledge directs communities to paths of salvation, then it enjoys a particular premium. To undermine such knowledge traditions, to ridicule their bearers and to humiliate students who pursue this hallowed path, is to show utter contempt for what tens of millions regard as sacrosanct. Not only does such behavior elicit febrile condemnation from Muslim religious scholars, namely, the ʿulama, but this contempt for key religious and intellectual figures and their work generates visceral anger among broad swathes of lay Muslims.

In Muslim eyes, madrasas promote the public good in an Islamic register.[8] Thinking of the public good in a religious idiom might, to Western ears, sound strange. But in a cosmopolitan and globalizing world, it is incumbent that one at least begin to comprehend opposing and differing perspectives of the "good." Madrasas advance the public understanding of morality, ethics, and conduct in an Islamic alphabet, which ranges from intimate matters affecting the family to banking practices, national politics, governance, and the most complex questions of international relations, war, and peace. Madrasas also support and maintain the practice of rituals, prayers, meditation, piety, and the remembrance of God. And yes, sometimes the decisions made by madrasa authorities could make one think their authors had stepped out of a medieval time machine. But then all orthodoxies are equally arbitrary, circular, self-fulfilling systems, and all are enclosed within self-defined limits.[9]

Attacks on madrasas by officialdom in the West and secular elites in Muslim-majority countries might turn out to be politically self-defeating. Such provocations only tend to increase resentment within madrasa communities and help to escalate grievances, which could take the form of support for militancy. As long as Western powers attempt to decrease the influence of madrasas in Muslim-majority societies, their efforts will only encourage committed Muslims from the Middle East to South Asia and elsewhere to energetically support these institutions. Ordinary Muslims believe—despite their disagreement with madrasa authorities—madrasas deserve their financial support, because in their eyes they serve the causes of faith and salvation.

In Euro-American policy circles, madrasas are just one factor of the larger post–Cold War security firewall erected against Islamdom. As the Berlin Wall came down, former British prime minister Margaret Thatcher prophesied that the impending danger to the West was the "green peril" of Islam now that the Soviet "red peril" had been laid to rest. A self-fulfilling "green peril" was realized in Euro-American encounters with a host of state and nonstate actors from Muslim-majority regions. The most troubling of such engagements was with the global militant and terrorist network called al-Qaeda.

Apart from a handful of madrasas linked to militancy in Pakistan, to equate madrasas with terror is absurd. Probably no image is harder to dislodge from the collective memory of the world, especially Americans, than the sight of bearded men wearing turbans and loose-fitting tunics with Kalashnikovs slung around their shoulders in the immediate aftermath of September 11, 2001, known as the Taliban. The alliance between the Taliban and the international terrorist group al-Qaeda, led by the late Saudi millionaire Osama bin Laden, only blackened the image of the madrasas. Since then, the Taliban movement in Pakistan has metastasized into a gruesome force, notable for its violence not only against women but also against all Western cultural institutions, especially modern schools. Yet the Taliban are not the representatives of the madrasa network. If anything, they reflect the pathologies produced by the confluence of failing states and highly opportunistic, if not dysfunctional, political theologies.

Not only Westerners but also many Muslims are uninformed about madrasas. Madrasas serve the religious and cultural needs of the largely working and lower middle classes of India, Pakistan, and Bangladesh. Increasingly, even religious-minded middle classes are fostering attachments to madrasas. Yet sections of the modern secular Muslim elite often play the most diabolical game with madrasas. They may pay public lip service to the madrasas for the purposes of political expediency and a fear of being ostracized, as Pakistan's military leadership frequently does. Yet privately they dismiss madrasas as medieval relics and a burden to their societies.

One challenge I faced in writing this book was to speak in a balanced way to deeply skeptical audiences about Islam, a thoroughly maligned faith in the West. Civilized debate about Islam in the aftermath of 9/11 has often been a luxury. How does one explain to doubting audiences that not all madrasas are the malignant institutions they have been led to believe they are by media caricatures?

I believe the best way to deal with this challenge is to talk about the contemporary madrasas in an unvarnished manner, highlighting both positive and negative dimensions. Madrasas are religious institutions, and their scholars are social actors who have opinions about the place of religion in public life, questions of personal religious identity vis-à-vis citizenship, authoritarian governance, economic corruption, and more important, the interpretation of Muslim law, ethics, and theology in a dangerous world where extremism makes its presence felt in countless ways, not all of which are connected to the actions of Muslims. Terrorism is not a problem internal to madrasas, except in a select few, though often it surrounds them in countries like Pakistan.

Readers of this book will note how global events of the past several decades have created an atmosphere of political hostility and suspicion toward the United States. Especially within large sections of madrasa communities, there are strong resentment and criticism of American military conduct in Muslim-majority countries. In a select number of letters at the end of this book, addressed to the U.S. policy makers as well as to my former teachers in the madrasas, I suggest ways for mutual understanding and for the lessening of tensions. I hope remedies laced with compassion, wisdom, and insight will be pursued in order to mend one of the toughest challenges of our times, namely, to improve relations between people in the Muslim world and people in the West, especially the United States.

PART ONE

Lived Experience

Spending six years in the madrasas of India has unalterably shaped my experience of Islam as both an intellectual tradition and a practice. After pursuing journalism, political activism, and academia, I found a deeper appreciation of my complex formation in the madrasas.

CHAPTER ONE

A Novice

Mumbai, still known as Bombay in 1975, was a bewildering city for an eighteen-year-old young adult from Cape Town, South Africa. Nothing prepared me for the intimidating throng of beggars and street urchins outside the airport, the countless people sleeping on sidewalks, and the city's heavy monsoon air and strong odors. At the time, I wasn't aware of the full impact of the "state of emergency" that Prime Minister Indira Gandhi had imposed to silence her critics, but I knew that fear surrounded me: people whispered about danger and secret arrests. But there was a bigger fear that engulfed me. As much as I was enthusiastic to learn about Islam, the faith I had inherited from my parents, my first glimpses of India made me fearful. What was I doing there? I suddenly understood my father's reluctance to let me go to study religion in India.

Deciding to study in India began with a crisis of faith precipitated by an attack on my religion in high school in Cape Town, South Africa. I was barely sixteen when a classmate, a Jehovah's Witness, brought some stinging anti-Islamic literature to class. I still hear my fellow student Gabriel saying, "Muhammad was an impostor, who spread his message by the sword and was unworthy of being a prophet." And he added, "Actually,

Muhammad cribbed his teachings from Jews and Christians whom he met during his travels." At the daily after-school religious sessions—also called "madrasa" in South Africa—I had learned that as a youth, the Prophet Muhammad traveled to Syria with his uncle. During one such journey he met a friendly Christian monk who, in a peculiar way, anointed him as a prophet, according to Muslim tradition. But never did I suspect the Prophet of treachery. This first exposure to the hostility some Christians harbor toward Muslims crushed my innocent and fragile sense of faith. But the encounter also allowed me to think critically about Islam: it changed my life.

A trip to the library in Cape Town did little to reassure me. The refined prose of Western authors like Sir William Muir and Montgomery Watt recycled the same charges against Muhammad and skewered Islam's claims to authenticity. On reflection, it seems rather odd that as devout Christians and rational Scotsmen, Muir and perhaps less so Watt found it plausible that God could be incarnate in a man from Nazareth, but adamantly denied that a seventh-century Arab could proclaim prophecy as did the Jewish prophets.

I found comfort in the circles of a group called the Tablighi Jamaʿat. The Arabic word *tabligh* means "to convey or transmit." The Tablighi Jamaʿat's mission was to remind Muslims of their religious duties and how to be devout. I attended their study circle at my neighborhood mosque in District Six, Cape Town's multiethnic and defiant cultural center where I lived during the school week. Several years later, apartheid's architects would obliterate District Six in order to disprove the possibility of the coexistence of different races. We were assigned to racially segregated ghettoes.

But questions about my faith persisted. My religious doubts—and my existential anxiety as a person of color in a white supremacist world—became unbearable. My plans to become an engineer slowly gave way to another obsession. I wanted to go to India to study the faith of my ancestors, to reconcile that faith with my gnawing demands to understand faith within the idiom of revelation, reason, and science. My mother was sympathetic to my cause, but my father didn't want to see his eldest son turn out to be a poor cleric dependent on the benevolence of the community and with diminished life prospects.

At the time, Dad, who had been born and raised in South Africa, was not really observant, giving priority to his business. He relented to my plans, though, when my aunts cajoled him and reminded him of the noble standing of learned scholars of Islam and the Qur'an and the promise of paradise awaiting their benefactors as well.

In my heart I was following my mother's prayers as I confronted the challenges of student life in India. She had come to South Africa as a nineteen-year-old bride from the state of Gujarat. Far from close relatives and burdened with domestic chores in an extended family with seven children, one of whom died in infancy, she took refuge in religion. In particularly tough times she would share with me, her eldest, the religious lore she learned in her childhood in the village of Dehgaam, of how the Prophet Muhammad's daughter, Fatima, endured life's trials.

My grandiose plan to study Islam, however, was also an escape from the drudgery of life in South Africa: the third-rate segregated schools, where discipline was dictatorial, violence the norm, and education poor, and the weekends and vacations spent in backbreaking work in the family grocery store in the Strand, a seaside town thirty miles (48 km) away from the main metropolitan city, Cape Town. I was aware of the country's segregationist politics. I knew little of the lives of the majority of black South Africans and only fully recognized their plight following the Soweto uprisings of June 16, 1976, after I'd been in India just more than a year.

NINETY DAYS

I had agreed to spend four months in the Tablighi Jamaʿat before entering a madrasa. A brainchild of an Indian cleric, Muhammad Ilyas (d. 1944), who felt the teachings of Islam were not reaching the grassroots faithful in British India, the Tablighi Jamaʿat has no real bureaucratic administration, but its presence is felt in almost every corner of the globe. Resigning from his teaching position at a prestigious madrasa, Ilyas devoted himself, against tremendous odds, to revival work (*daʿwa*) in the Mewat in the 1920s, a region straddling the two states of Rajasthan and Haryana. He used a small mosque, the Banglawali Masjid, as his base in Delhi, where he cultivated his core of loyal associates. On the same site today in the Delhi suburb of Hazrat Nizamuddin, a spartan mosque serves as the international center (*markaz*) of the Tablighi Jamaʿat, an explicitly nonpolitical piety movement that incorporates elements of Islamic spirituality (Sufism). It is important to note that the Tablighi Jamaʿat is broadly affiliated with the Deoband school founded in the late nineteenth century but differs radically from more radical offshoots of

Young male students memorizing the Qur'an at a mosque in Srirangapatna, in Karnataka State in India. Memorizing the Qur'an is done at the elementary level of madrasa education. (Picture: Prakash Subbarao)

this highly diverse Deobandi theological formation that will be discussed later in this book.

Ilyas had a simple but highly effective evangelical message boiled down to "six points" to supplement the observation of Islam's five cardinal pillars of practice: make sure Muslims grasp the true meaning and implications of the creedal statement that "there is no deity, except Allah and that Muhammad is His messenger"; pray conscientiously five times a day; acquire learning and engage in the frequent remembrance of God; honor fellow believers; adopt sincerity in all actions; and participate in missionary work (*daʿwa*) by spreading awareness of Islam. The Tablighi Jamaʿat now hosts some of the largest Muslim gatherings, involving millions of participants on the subcontinent and around the world.

Working with the Tabligh was a grueling ordeal with a steep learning curve, and overcoming the inevitable cultural shock of passing my days in India was daunting. We slept on the floors of mosques, ate simple meals, navigated treacherous roads, and traveled in overcrowded trains. By the lights of my naïve faith, eternal damnation awaited these millions of Hindus apparently devoted to idols. In just weeks, India taught me to ask the first and most enduring question about the workings of divine justice: how was it possible that a just God could promise me paradise . . . and damn all these people who look like me? Years later, I would discover that many thinkers in the monotheistic tradition were confronted by similar questions, including the eleventh-century thinker Abu Hamid al-Ghazali (d. 1111), about whom I would later write a book. Ghazali too struggled to understand why only some people would be saved and not others. In the end, he found solace in spiritual experiences and the intuitive truths of mysticism.

I cut short my planned four months with the Tablighi Jamaʿat to three and headed for the Madrasa Sabilur Rashad in Bangalore along with two other South Africans I met in the Tabligh. At the austere, walled campus, I found dozens of students apart from the majority South Indians and the few from my home country—young men from Trinidad and Tobago, Malaysia, Indonesia, and the United States and a lone Cuban. I occupied the fourth thin mattress in a sparse and cramped dorm room with a West Indian, an African American, and the Cuban. In pursuit of piety, the latter two would rise at 3 A.M. for optional prayers and liturgy, tormenting the rest of us for not doing the same. I already witnessed in the Tablighi Jamaʿat a grating notion of piety, which to my mind was like a "calculator mentality" and now it was even more evident in the attitude of some of my fellow students. Some of my roommates were not only preoccupied with attaining afterworldly rewards for performing certain acts of piety but they also celebrated their outlook.

Daily madrasa routine in Bangalore would begin at least an hour before sunrise with preparation for the early morning prayers. Afterward students remained at the mosque to read designated portions of the Qurʾan. Others used the auspicious early morning hours to memorize the Qurʾan, known as *hifz*. Breakfast would follow in the dining hall, called the mess, a stark reminder that the British once ruled India. Breakfast consisted of South Indian *idli* (steamed savory cakes made of lentils and rice), a crispy roti (baked bread), and *chai* (tea boiled in milk). Most foreign students made breakfast in their rooms with a spread of eggs, some toast, and *chai*.

I had arrived at the madrasa only one month before it closed for the long Ramadan break, the end of the academic year. But in that short time I chafed at the highly regimented and pietistic environment, and worst of all, the abysmal cafeteria food. I took a class on memorizing portions of the Qur'an for liturgical purposes and perfecting my recitation of the holy book. The six-hour day of memorization was tedious, and students would take frequent bathroom breaks, sip lots of tea, and play surreptitiously to pass the time. The memorized passage for the day and the back lessons were recited to an instructor at least twice in a day. It takes two or three full years to memorize the entire Qur'an fluently. Not having budgeted such a length of time, I selected chapters that would be useful in delivering sermons and for liturgical purposes. Later in life it turned out that knowing the Qur'an intimately was an asset for instructional purposes. Since all instruction was in Urdu, I also threw myself into learning both Urdu and Arabic in private lessons.

But after almost four months in India, I had yet to enroll in an *ʿalimiyya* program required for gaining the knowledge and skills of an *ʿalim*, the Arabic word for "a learned person." The plural *ʿulama*, meaning those learned in the religious disciplines, is the generic term used today to refer to Muslim clerics. So while madrasas were on vacation, I spent the Ramadan break with my maternal grandparents, visiting my parents' ancestral villages in Gujarat near Bharuch, a bustling city on the banks of the Narmada River. On the outskirts of Bharuch I fortuitously discovered a small madrasa (seminary), Darul Uloom Matliwala, supported by an affluent South African family, which at the time enrolled some 200 students.

The centerpiece of the seminary was a three-level Parsee bungalow. Parsees are followers of Zoroastrianism, an ancient religion of Persia. They straddle Indian and Anglo cultures and often speak both English and Gujarati. The bungalow was large enough to accommodate several classrooms and administrative space. To the side of the sprawling compound on Eidgah Road was a beautiful mosque of pastel greens surrounded by palms and a well-maintained garden. A student dormitory abutted the tilled fields that ran down to the banks of the Narmada River.

The pace was relaxed and congenial. I decided to enroll. By coincidence, three fellow South Africans came to study as a private cohort with a brilliant teacher, Mawlana Ibrahim Patni, who allowed me to join his group. Mawlana Patni's talents could have led him to success as a lawyer, as a businessman, or in any profession, but he had chosen the life of a teacher in the madrasa. For the first few months we four would spend most of the day at the back of a class with dozens of twelve- to fourteen-year-olds who were taking elementary classes in the pre-*ʿalimiyya* program. We were on average eighteen years old, practicing Arabic and

Urdu writing with dusty white chalk on child-sized black slate boards. At first we hardly understood the day-classes we were auditing, but as the weeks and months progressed, things became clearer. By year-end I had a good handle on Urdu, and my Arabic was coming along.

As I adjusted to my new life, I also learned that my naïve views about madrasas were not immune to contradiction. Puritanism characterized the madrasa environment and sex was taboo. I recall one evening in Bangalore when one student had raised the alarm in the dorms, claiming that he had caught two male students in an embrace in the bathroom. I was scandalized, and the revelations haunted me for weeks. At home and in the madrasa I was taught that heterosexual conduct outside marriage was forbidden and in terms of classical Islamic legal prescriptions had life-threatening consequences; homosexuality, I was taught, was a sin, and I was therefore surprised to find it prevalent in the madrasas.

Within a few months at the Bharuch madrasa I received my second jolt: I learned that it was an open secret that one of the teachers had sexual relations with younger men or perhaps even boys. I was getting a reality check. Challenging as it was, I understood the need to distinguish between the personal lives of teachers and fellow students on the one hand, and if I were to pursue pious learning in the madrasas, on the other. In a matter of a year, I realized that Bharuch was a provincial city and the madrasa I attended lacked the more robust intellectual environment that I sought but that was available in the more reputable North Indian madrasas.

After a year in Gujarat, I headed for Darul Uloom Deoband—the most prominent and prestigious madrasa for those affiliated with the Deobandi interpretation of Sunni Islam. Being a student at Deoband was at first a dizzying experience. I devoured my texts, and they opened up new worlds to me. Madrasa education drives home the sacred nature of knowledge. One is taught to show the utmost respect for the carriers of knowledge—teachers—and the instruments of learning—books. Novices quickly learned that some scholars, such as the anticolonial activist Mawlana Husain Ahmad Madani, could not even tolerate the sight of paper lying in the street. To carelessly discard paper was to desecrate knowledge itself. Texts were not only symbols of learning but markers of progress too. So, for instance, if you ask a student what year of the program he is in, he will cite the text he is studying; only an insider could translate the name of that text into a specific year of the curriculum.

We studied books that had been written in the tenth century and earlier, as well as those composed by authors in the fifteenth to the eighteenth centuries. The beauty of the textual tradition lies precisely in its discordant variety: texts serve as palimpsests, which refract the multiple layers of the ancient world to modern readers. The best professors not only translated and clarified the text; they made an effort to link the ancient world to contemporary realities.

Law, called *fiqh* in Arabic, is the mainstay of the madrasa curriculum. *Fiqh* or Shariʿa, as it is also called, is actually moral discourse that proposes ethical guidelines for society. Learning the classical *fiqh* texts was exciting and an awe-inspiring experience. To be able to navigate texts authored by famous figures in the tradition was a thrilling event and made me feel that I was at last beginning to grasp the crucial issues of the tradition. I was filled with reverence for the learning imparted to me as authoritative and proper practices of the faith. Learning the practices advanced by tradition also conferred on one a certain responsibility and authority. I initially held out the hope that the proper application of *fiqh* would create an ideal Muslim society, only to find out that it would take far more than law to change society. It was a struggle to come to terms with what passes as the execution of Shariʿa practices involving gruesome amputations and floggings. I now believe that norms are culture specific and that there are other ways to deter murder, theft, and sexual violations. There were few teachers with whom one could air such concerns and doubts. Senior professors would try to douse such questions by reminding me of the dire spiritual and theological hazards awaiting the one who was engaged in such thinking. Challenging the authority of a canonical teaching supported by the consensus of past scholars could invite denunciation and charges of anathema (*kufr*). Needless to say, such questions never really left me; rather, they have framed my interrogation of the inherited practices of tradition.

Even as students we would lampoon some of what we were taught, questioning its utility. For instance, in the *fiqh* class there were endless discussions about seven types of water usable to secure ritual purity: rain, sea, river, and well water, followed by water melted from snow and ice, and finally spring water. Most of us had only seen water from the faucets and wells, and few students from rural India would have seen snow or the sea, except for in pictures. But pictures were rare, since images of animate objects were taboo. Thoughtful professors would transform

Fiqh and Shariʿa

Fiqh literally means "understanding" and "discernment." Scholars who devote themselves to the study of the Qurʾan, the statements of the Prophet Muhammad (hadith) and who also give credence to the context in order to find the rules and teachings, are literally called "discerner(s)," *faqih*, plural *fuqaha*, designated as jurist(s) or jurisconsults. Jurists are ranked. The *faqih* is the generic category. A master-jurist is called a *mujtahid*, a recognition of expertise and the effort (*ijtihad*) exerted in writing the procedures of interpretation (hermeneutic) in order to discover the ethical rules from the source texts and how to implement these rules in new social contexts. In the Shiʿa tradition, every practitioner is required to follow a living master-jurist (*mujtahid*), a tradition that exists to this day. In the Sunni tradition, there are medieval interpreters of the law whose teachings laypersons today follow. The writing of the rules of interpretation for individual jurists remains circumscribed among Sunnis. In modern times committees of scholars deliberate the rules of interpretation and the application of these in practice (*ijtihad*) among Sunni scholars.

In popular Muslim usage, Shariʿa is synonymous with *fiqh*. But Shariʿa literally means "a path" and factually refers to what is revealed, which included the Qurʾan and *Sunna*. Revelation is subject to interpretation. Orthodoxy insists on the fixity of Muslim norms; hence the Shariʿa too is increasingly viewed as a fixed set of rules. Muslim modernists, revivalists, and some members of orthodoxy pay greater attention to changing social contexts and hence display a more flexible approach to the application of the Shariʿa.

arcane lessons into broader discussions, for example, about the validity of recycled water for ritual purposes, a possibility unimaginable to the medieval authors of our texts. Critics often charge the madrasa system of anachronism, a claim that is partly true. Defenders of the traditional curriculum, which was devised by the eighteenth-century scholar Mulla Nizamuddin, insist on the supreme pedagogical value of the old texts. In other words, there is a fascination with the classics of the Islamic tradition rather than with contemporary issues. It's like studying the classical texts of Aeschylus, Sophocles, Euripides, the Bible, Augustine's *City of God*, and Aquinas's *Summa Theologica* at a liberal arts college or a university today and nothing else!

After three years in India I started asking questions about the relevance of the texts I studied and how to apply their insights in the modern world, especially how I would fare with my training on my return to South Africa. By now I had become acutely aware of the political challenges of my native country, racism foremost among them. But the Muslim clergy there, I knew, was intransigent in its refusal to speak out against the evils of apartheid. Reading the uncensored Indian press and following political developments at home via literature of Nelson Mandela's party, the African National Congress, which was banned at the time, impressed upon me the challenges I would face whenever I returned to South Africa.

My restlessness drove me to read widely and independently, especially literature written by more contemporary authors. One such author was Mawlana Abul Aʿla Mawdudi (d. 1979), whom most teachers in Deoband censured and for whom only the bravest expressed guarded admiration. Mawdudi was a gadfly among traditional clerics, an iconoclast, as it were, who promoted what is today called "political Islam." Mawdudi rose to prominence during the twilight years of British colonialism. After partition, he moved to the new state of Pakistan. While he had formal credentials, he was not considered to be a member of the clerical elite, being for most of his life an autodidact, a gifted writer and founder of a continent-wide social movement known as the Jamat-i Islami. Mawdudi's prolific writings guaranteed him audiences among modern educated Muslims. As the traditionalist ʿulama bickered with him on petty issues, Mawdudi emphasized the social dimensions of Islam as an ideology. If Muslims conceived of Islam as a social teaching, he advocated, then they could build new and flourishing societies too. Establishing an Islamic state, fully backed with Islamic laws and institutions, was one of Mawdudi's main ideals. Mawdudi was not only an ideologue with a vision and a political program but he also courted international influence. Sayyid Qutb (d. 1966), the prominent Egyptian writer and ideologue of the now banned Muslim Brotherhood in Egypt, was persuaded by Mawdudi's analysis that the contemporary period marked by secular materialism was akin to the days of ignorance, *jahiliyya*, that preceded the birth of Islam. Qutb and others were arrested, tried, and executed by Gamal Abdul Nasser's government for sedition in what appeared to be murky circumstances.

Islamic Revival

A handful of ideologues constitute the mainstay of the contemporary Islamic revival. Abul Aʿla Mawdudi (1903–1979), also spelled Maududi and Maudoodi, was a scholar of Islam who gained renown as a journalist for his insightful style of writing on a range of Islamic topics. He was chiefly an ideologue of Islamic politics in prepartition India and became the founder of the Jamat-i Islami in 1941, a revivalist movement dedicated to organizing society around Islamic norms with a view to create an Islamic state on the subcontinent. He settled in Pakistan after its formation.

Sayyid Qutb (1906–1966) was an Egyptian teacher, literary critic, and enthusiastic proponent of Islamic revival who was executed on charges of conspiracy by the government of President Gamal Abd al-Nasser. Qutb belonged to the Muslim Brotherhood established by Hasan al-Banna in 1928. Qutb was a passionate writer who had a mesmerizing spell on his readers. He underwent greater radicalization during his frequent spells in jail for political views that the secular Egyptian government found threatening.

After the Arab Spring, a party affiliated to the Muslim Brotherhood, the Freedom and Justice Party, led by Mohamed Morsi, won the elections in Egypt in 2012 but was ousted from power by a military coup on July 3, 2013. The Muslim Brotherhood was designated an outlawed group, and many of its members were imprisoned.

As a student I discovered an interpretation of Islam outside the walls of the madrasa where I found heady inspiration and guidance for building society on an Islamic platform. The ancient texts I was studying suddenly seemed musty and stale. Based on personal experience the exaggerated Western media portrayal of political Islam as a universal monolithic menace sounded (and sounds) odd to my ears that were accustomed to hearing the remarkably diverse, often contradictory chorus of voices drawn to put Islamic teachings into practice. Recent post-Arab spring experiences have once again shown how diverse political Islam and its leaders are in places like Tunisia and Turkey when compared to elements in Egypt and Iran. At the furthest end of the spectrum are, of course, the bloodcurdling political Islam of the Taliban in Afghanistan and Pakistan or the militant rebels in Syria and Iraq.

An unexpected three-month vacation to South Africa in 1978 changed everything. An overbearing South African government clerk told my father that my expired passport could not be renewed unless I physically returned home. Later we discovered that this was an error, but by then we had already incurred the expense for my fortuitous homecoming. On arrival in Cape Town, I realized my isolation from the real world in India—just how much I had changed compared to people in the city—and so I began to question everything: my lifestyle, my attire, and my ideas about my future. Up to that point, I had hardly spent any time in Indian cities, nor did I watch television, go to movies, or listen to music because of the strict interpretation I had followed for three years that forbade such activities. I had given away all my Western clothes, vowing to wear only what I then believed was "Islamic dress": the typical loose-fitting, knee-length tunic, called a *kurta*, and loose-fitting pants.

I now knew that if I were to follow the rules of Deoband, not only would my life in South Africa be restricted—I had come to the madrasa to escape such confinement—but so too would be my own emotional and intellectual development.

On my return to India to complete my studies, I stepped into the precincts of Deoband wearing a t-shirt and jeans, a cavalier affront to my immediate friends. Even though the act was largely symbolic—I would still wear the conventional attire—I spurred a debate among close friends about what I thought were the deficiencies in the madrasas. Fellow students and a few teachers predictably labeled me a "modernist," meant to be an egregious insult, but as a rebel I wore the label with pride. Some of my younger teachers, who often gently challenged my views, helped me realize how self-righteous I had been in the past about the superiority of an Islamic dress code and of my claims about the superiority of the interpretations of madrasa authorities over alternate views. I taught myself to learn from my errors, and ever since they have been my best teachers.

I was still determined to complete the *ʿalimiyya* program, but I needed to find a madrasa with less emphasis on texts. I explored opportunities to study in Libya, Iraq, and Egypt, where I thought the education was better, but to little avail. I was less of an idealist by now, and the burden of becoming independent started to weigh on me as I approached twenty-one. Taking over the family business was certainly not an option; I needed to find a vocation.

I decided to transfer to Darul Uloom Nadwatul ʿUlama, a madrasa in the capital of Uttar Pradesh, Lucknow. Nadwa was located on the banks of the Gomti River that flows through this historic Mughal city, reputed for its refined taste, culture, and food and as a place where people still nostalgically hanker after the days of nobility. In Mughal times this region was known as Oudh, and its rulers were mostly those who followed the Shiʿa rite. In my student days there were occasional Sunni-Shiʿa tensions around the beginning of the Islamic month of Muharram, signaling the Muslim New Year, when public exhibitions of Shiʿa passion plays rekindled ancient grievances that underlie the sectarian split within Islam more than a millennium ago. Yet Lucknow was a city that took pride in its Urdu language and civility, always rivaling Lahore. That was before the subcontinent was partitioned into the two nations India and Pakistan, followed by Bangladesh later.

Moving from Deoband to Nadwa is like transferring from a conservative divinity school to a liberal one. Deobandis looked askance at Nadwa as too modern and liberal for their taste when it was founded. Nadwa saw itself as more global and worldly in outlook. Its former president, the late Mawlana Abul Hasan ʿAli Nadvi (d. 1999), was internationally reputed in the Arabic-speaking world. A onetime colleague of Mawdudi (with whom he later had differences), he was clearly enchanted by Sayyid Qutb and the Muslim Brotherhood. He wrote extensively on the plight of Muslims in the twentieth century and mobilized for their welfare and advancement. Nadwa received a great deal of support from foundations and individuals in the Arabian Gulf, and the campus has undergone significant upgrades over the last three decades.

Abul Hasan ʿAli Nadvi was a descendant of the Prophet's family, and therefore known as a sayyid. He wrote mainly in Arabic and strongly believed that a renaissance among the Arabs would have a salutary influence on the rest of the Muslim world. Toward the end of his life he was less sanguine about such an outcome.

Nadwatul ʿUlama was launched in 1898 by a broad spectrum of ʿulama, ranging from traditionalists to modernists, who all believed that the Deoband-type madrasa education did not equip students for the challenges of modern life. Placing a greater emphasis on the liberating message of the Qurʾan, Nadwa favored certain departures from the traditional curriculum and emphasized the study of the Muslim scripture and history. Nadwa's motto was "Synthesizing the profitable past with the useful modern." Nadwa's tolerance for intra-Sunni differences made it attractive. Students adhering to the Barelvi school of thought, a less puritanical strain of Islam that accepts elements of popular religion, and those who adhere to Salafism, a strict scripturalist interpretation, all enroll at Nadwa to pursue different degrees, but they will not find Deobandi madrasas to be welcoming environments. At Nadwa students are allowed to attend class wearing Western dress, although the majority wear *kurtas*.

But while Nadwa offered me space to pursue my own interests, the curriculum was, in the end, not that different from Deoband. Visiting both places recently, I was unable to tell the difference. By that time, the Nizami curriculum to my mind seemed largely redundant. Classes at Nadwa were not very demanding. And I was completely put off by the lifeless study of Islamic law, even though the philosophy and sociology animating law and ethics intrigue me to this day, and I continue to believe that these resources are underutilized. On my own, I frequented the British Library in the Hazratganj area of Lucknow and borrowed widely from Nadwa's excellent library collection to read in subjects including political science, economics, and English literature. I found Alex Haley's biography of Malcolm X inspirational and became totally enchanted by Muhammad Asad (Leopold Weiss), the author of *The Road to Mecca*, an account of an Austrian Jew's discovery of Islam, his fascinating life as an explorer, confidante of king and rulers, scholar, and diplomat. Asad and Malcolm X kindled in me the desire to write. I published an essay in Nadwa's monthly Arabic newspaper and submitted op-ed pieces to the daily *Northern India Patrika* on politics and Islam.

In 1980 several international speakers attended a conference on Arabic literature held at Nadwa. A tall and imposing Egyptian lawyer and Princeton postgraduate, Dr. Mohammed Fathi Osman (d. 2010), impressed me. We had several animated conversations about the Iranian revolution, which had just occurred. Later, when I was about to graduate, I wrote Osman seeking advice. I received no reply, and decided to go to Egypt in order to pursue a master's degree at al-Azhar in Cairo. By then I was thoroughly disabused of my earlier, negative views of Islamic education in the Middle East. But just weeks before I was to leave India, Osman sent a message inviting me to join the staff of a promising new magazine, sponsored by liberal Saudis, that he was launching in London. The choice between studies in Egypt and journalism in the United Kingdom was an easy one for me. I grabbed the journalism offer and set off for London. *Arabia: The Islamic World Review* turned out to be the beginning of my career as a journalist. Even though I moved on from *Arabia* after only eighteen months, its closure a decade later was a great loss to the world of progressive Islamic ideas.

CONCLUSION

Spending six years inside India's madrasas had left deep imprints that over time have become more significant. If I had to do it all again and choose between a madrasa education and a university, I suspect I would opt for a madrasa.

I remain a friendly critic of madrasa education, acknowledging its inability to provide the big picture of Islamic ideas and its failure to effect the intellectual transformation of contemporary Muslim societies, especially in the sphere of religious thought. Yet madrasas can offer something of enormous value—provided they are effectively upgraded in the knowledge stakes. Properly harnessed, they are repositories of classical learning and seeds for intellectual sophistication that might challenge the shallow discourses of fundamentalism and revivalism that too often pass as Islam today.

My experience in the madrasas is an atypical one: I crafted my own program and selected from what was offered, whereas most graduates conform to the syllabus and ideology tendered. Yet as I have continued in my work first as a journalist and a social activist and then as an academic in South Africa and at Duke University and now at the University of Notre Dame in the United States, I have been able to retrieve the layers of my madrasa education: the depth, the subtlety, and the value of what I learned there. Like a scraped ancient scroll on which the previous writing sometimes shines through, the resources I acquired in the madrasa became accessible to me. I am sure the madrasa authorities would not approve of the way I use my madrasa training, since it might not meet their scrupulous standards of piety. Yet now, as I write about human rights, bioethics, Islamic law, and the ethical interpretation of tradition, I can do so with confidence and argue that tradition is not necessarily moribund but organic and open to positive change.

Law Schools

SUNNI LAW SCHOOLS

Hanafi school—founder: Nuʿman bin Thabit (d. 767), better known as Abu Hanifa

Maliki school—founder: Malik b. Anas (d. 795)

Shafiʿi school—founder: Muhammad b. Idris al-Shafiʿi (d. 819)

Hanbali school—founder: Ahmad b. Hanbal (d. 855)

SHIʿI LAW SCHOOLS

Jaʿfari school—founder: Jaʿfar al-Sadiq (d. 765)

Zaydi school—founder: Zayd bin ʿAli (d. 740)

Ismaʿili school—founder: Ismaʿil bin Jaʿfar al-Sadiq (c. ninth century)

In my own thinking, writing, and activism in Islamic thought, I can not only push back against many retrogressive religious forces but also form productive associations with progressive ones. I doubt I would have had the courage to undertake some of this risk-filled work without the burnishing experience inside India's madrasas.

Madrasa life is one of intense observation of religious rituals. The purpose of knowledge is to deepen the practice of faith. Faith and practice go hand in hand, and the one is not independent from the other. A day in the life of a madrasa student is punctuated by learning and the practice of prayers. But the daily routine of life is similar to other educational institutions.

CHAPTER TWO

Wake, Wash, Pray

Wednesday, April 23, 1975: "The start of our four months in India. We slept after reading two *rakʿas* [formal Muslim prayers]. After *fajr* [pre-dawn prayers] and *ishraq* [optional after-sunrise prayers] we slept again. This was at Khar mosque in Bandra, Bombay."

So reads the first entry I made in the diary I kept periodically during my six-year journey in India's madrasas when I was barely eighteen. At the time, this new routine of a prayer-filled life felt very strange, but I was comforted by the thought that I was part of the Tablighi Jamaʿat for only four months. Little did I know that this routine of prayer and religious observation would become my daily habit for the next six years. When I later signed up in a proper madrasa, I realized that part of that discipline of prayer and religious practice was integral to madrasa life. But it was not the only aspect of madrasa life. If the Tablighi Jamaʿat was a kind of mobile madrasa, then it was so mainly in terms of discipline and practice it offered lay Muslims. The other aspect it stressed was that each member of the faith, including scholars, had a duty to share the message of Islam with Muslims first and then with the rest of humanity. Only when Muslims lived a righteous life, the Tablighi Jamaʿat taught, following God's commandments, will they earn the right to give leadership to the world.

But this is where the comparison between the Tablighi Jamaʿat and the madrasa also ends. The madrasa offered a much more robust intellectual and scholarly environment than the ascetic Tabligh program. Infatuated with the aura of deep spirituality available in the Tabligh, I thought at first that spirituality and prayer were the sum total of religious life. Little did I then know that serious scholarship and learning are both integral to a meaningful religious life. Later, I learned that Muslim sages frequently warned that piety without learning can lead to damnation. How? Well, one can with the best of intentions but without proper knowledge perform certain acts that would be unsanctioned in terms of the tradition and they will count as impious deeds.

Grasping the teachings that inform the confessional rhythms of a day in a madrasa gives a particular depth and density to life. A devout engagement with learning is not without its own norms and beauty—its aesthetics. What follows summarizes the inspiration, teachings, and motives that grounded my own madrasa experiences and that were confirmed by my observations of madrasa life three decades later. The account offered are the observations of a participant that are mingled with an interpreter's insights. What does a life of prayer mean to people who inhabit the madrasas?

PRAYERS AT DAWN

When the faintest white of dawn streaks the horizon to signal the impending day, it announces the hour of spiritual plenitude—time to prepare for the morning prayers. Dawn is significant not only for its inspiring calm. It is an hour pregnant with divine epiphany, says Ibn ʿArabi, a fourteenth-century mystic highly esteemed in madrasa circles.[1] Figuratively, the Qurʾan describes the morning prayers as the "dawn recitation," suggestive of the auditory nature of the liturgy, an essential part of the prayer ritual. The Qurʾan alludes to this dawn-hour of plenitude as "a recitation that is witnessed." What is the meaning of this early morning witnessing? Who witnesses the recitation? The holy, tradition teaches, witnesses the devotions of the faithful. As the heart leaps to answer the call to prayers, God listens to whoever seeks the divine light.

Thus, long before most of the inhabitants of a city, town, or village on the Indo-Pak subcontinent wake, apart from Hindu sadhus, Buddhist and Christian monks, bakers and dairymen, there are stirrings in modest, almost hermitic dwellings inhabited by Muslims. Here, young and older Muslim men, and women in strictly segregated locations, rise hours before sunrise in order to prepare for communion with God in a life bounded by prayer, learning, and practice. Some of the professors, a handful of devout students get up much earlier in order to pursue special voluntary devotions before the official prayers.

> *Keep awake in prayer at night—all but a small part*
> *Half, or a little less, or even add more.*
> *Recite the Qurʾan with thoughtful rhythm*
> *For surely, We shall send you a weighty word.*
> *The night vigil is indeed most intense as a discipline*
> *And most appropriate for receptivity to the Word.* (Q 73:2–5)

These verses refer to what might be termed Islam's monasticism-lite without any renunciation of marriage. Divine words invite humanity to participate in a spiritual laboratory in order for individuals to do work on themselves: securing strong connections with the divine and the hidden cosmos. Detailed portraits of the Prophet Muhammad in the tradition present him as a shining exemplar, as an ascetic person who endures long hours of nightly prayer vigil, going to such lengths that his feet would swell from long hours of standing. The Prophet's immediate companions and later pious adherents vigorously adhered to this schedule.

Made rapt by the divine word, the worshipper performs gentle body movements in order to direct the mind, body, and spirit toward sanctity. While modern thought has recently rediscovered and explored the virtues of the body and its senses, the ancient faiths have long valued the centrality of the body to one's personhood. Devotions, *salah*, a set of bodily movements and pauses, are replicated in each prayer session and repeated several times a day. Thus, in a life of devotion, it is repetition and replication that pervade the body. Worshippers partake in what moderns call "embodied" practices: devotions inhabit the corporeal body. It is at the composite site of the body animated by the crucial ingredient, namely what religious folk call the soul, where one could say religion happens.

In their nightly pious meditations the carriers of Islamic learning, the ʿulama, are expected to bear the burden of moral responsibility, prefigured by the expression, a "weighty word." This moral responsibility is elucidated in the Qurʾan and explained in the words of the Prophet.

Lessons of moral responsibility are drawn from the ages: from the ancient memories of the Biblical prophets to ancient lore and wisdom literature to the exemplary life of the Prophet Muhammad and his Companions.

The hearts and minds of Muslim learners are regularly bathed in the stories of a religious humanity over time. These figures from the past serve as exemplars of moral responsibility just as the Prophet Muhammad and the prophets who preceded him did. Since moral responsibility and stewardship are hallmarks of spirituality, thousands of madrasa students train and aspire to reach that high standard. For this reason thousands of students look forward to the day they will graduate in order to seek out spiritual masters at Sufi lodges where they can work on their spiritual repertoire under the guidance of caring spiritual masters. Full-time madrasa students are discouraged from signing up for spiritual training, because it requires a great deal of time and solid traditional learning is a prerequisite.

Depending on the season, around 4 A.M. or 5 A.M., and around 6 A.M. in winter, are the times for the official and compulsory dawn prayers at a typical madrasa in India, Pakistan, or Bangladesh. A faculty member or an employee makes the rounds in the various residences to alert students to get ready for morning (*fajr*) prayers. This specific prayer-hour has a very narrow time frame, to be completed well before actual sunrise. As the students wake, an amplified call to prayer, *adhan*, breaks the morning silence, inviting the faithful at the madrasa and folks in the vicinity of the institution to congregational prayers at the campus mosque. In a melodious voice and in Arabic phrases recognizable around the world, the caller to prayer would chant:

Allahu akbar . . . [said four times]
God is greater than everything . . . God is greater than everything
God is greater than everything, God is greater than everything
I bear witness that there is no deity except God
I bear witness that there is no deity except God
I bear witness that Muhammad is the Messenger of God
I bear witness that Muhammad is the Messenger of God
Hasten to prayer *(salah)*
Hasten to prayer
Hasten to success
Hasten to success
Prayer is better than sleep

Prayer is better than sleep [only said in the call to morning prayers]
God is greater than everything
God is greater than everything
There is no deity except God

As students rise, everyone heads for the bathrooms and the dedicated ablution facilities conveniently located in different parts of the madrasa. The main purpose at this hour is to perform the ritual ablutions. Since all devotional acts in Islam have certain prescribed preliminaries, these also have to be meticulously performed. All Muslims are required to ritually wash specific limbs, known as the "cleansing," *wudu* (see chapter 7), before the act of ritual communion with God. Cleansing is not only about washing body parts; it is also a sign of intentionality performed on the body. "All acts are determined by their intentions," said the Prophet Muhammad, in a saying that captures the heart of Islam's ethical creed.

Ritual cleansing begins with the washing of the hands, then the face, followed by rubbing water on the arms up to the elbows, wiping the forehead with a wet hand, and then washing both feet up to the ankles. Not only is each part of the body washed thrice with ritual solemnity, but tradition also requires the rinsing of the mouth and nose followed by a light wipe of the ears. When all the visible sensory parts of the head and other limbs are refreshed in preparation for prayers, it ought to create a certain sensation within the human psyche. What is the purpose of refreshing? What, according to tradition, does refreshing do to the soul and the self?

The act of cleansing the limbs before prayers is already a performance in the preliminaries of worship. How? Some philosophers say that at one level a human being is also like, say, a chair, at first, merely "a thing." But what makes humans different from a chair is that they are also something more than a "thing." Human beings can navigate from the interior to the exterior, go beyond themselves; in other words, they can "travel" beyond being merely a "thing." This ability of humans to extend beyond the *thing-ness* of themselves, beyond the exterior, is described as an ability to transcend, that is, to go beyond one's self. What enables this capacity to go beyond (transcend) is intentionality. Thus the everyday or quotidian acts of washing, bowing, and prostrating in prayers all gain a different meaning from being just ordinary and mundane acts because of the way humans can *intend* something.

Author making ablutions (*wudu*) prior to ritual prayers at one of the mosques of Darul Uloom Deoband in India. (Picture: Rodrigo Dorfman)

What transforms everyday acts into something more than what they appear to be is intentionality. Specific acts that are accompanied by a wholehearted intention turn into pious acts. The credo of piety cherished by inhabitants of the madrasa-sphere but also by those Muslims beyond this space is captured in this often-studied report of the Prophet.

> Purity is a portion of faith. Praising God tips the scales with good deeds. Glorifying God, while praising God, fills everything between the heavens and the earth. Prayer is a glow; charity is a proof [lit. shield]; patience is radiance. And, the Qur'an is either your ally or adversary. In the struggle of life people transact their lives, either in redemption or perdition.[2]

Lurking behind the apparent simplicity of the ritual of washing before prayers is the profundity of Islam's ethical and moral philosophy, which is centered on the concept of intention. "All actions are determined by their intentions," a famous prophetic report reminds the faithful. Having washed, students ought to be fully cognizant of the virtue of remembering the divine, aware of the sources of guidance and life's many and often risky travails. On entering the sacred space of the mosque or prayer space, a person recites a special liturgy in Arabic, the liturgical language of Islam: "O Allah open for me the doors of your mercy."

Each student first individually performs two sets of genuflections as part of the prescribed prayer set of the morning prayers. Each genuflec-

Salah Formal Islamic Prayers

Salah Formal Islamic prayers, pronounced "*so-laa,*" are divided into defined postures (genuflections) that are patterned on the practice of the Prophet Muhammad. Each genuflection involves a liturgy recited while standing, movements of bowing, and prostration. Some genuflections are recommended by the Prophet and are designated as *Sunna* prayers, while other sets of genuflections are mandatory, called *fard*. Without performing the mandatory parts of one's prayers, the obligation remains incomplete. Scholars differ in minor matters of prayer ritual.

tion is called a *rakʿa*. A *rakʿa* consists of reciting a memorized portion of the Qurʾan that always includes the first chapter (*The Opening*) as well as any other portion as liturgy in prayer, while facing Mecca in a standing posture with the hands folded over the belly or at rest on the side. Qurʾan recitation is followed by the posture of bowing at the waist for a few minutes. After straightening up, the worshipper makes two prostrations by kneeling and placing the forehead on the ground by gently leaning on the palms of the hands. In each of the bowing and kneeling postures, the worshipper whispers liturgical formulae in praise of God. On completing one set of these postures, one genuflection, *rakʿa,* is completed. Each of the five daily prayers is divided into sets of almost universally agreed-upon required genuflections.

Seated on the carpets of the mosque, students and professors waiting for the congregational prayer to begin enjoy the solitude of meditation and contemplation. Some choose to recite portions of the Qurʾan from a copy of the scripture or from memory in a low hymnlike rhythm, careful not to disturb the tranquility of other worshippers.

Congregational prayers proper begin when the person charged with making the call to prayers assembles worshippers in straight rows, in words resembling the call to prayers. This time the announcer adds only the words "Prayer begins." When the prayer-leader, the imam, begins with the recitation of the liturgy, all the worshippers listen intently to his words and follow his instructions as he performs and leads them through the various postures in unison. Since the liturgy in the morning prayers is often longer, a full prayer session could last as long as half an hour.

Reminded to be forever "mindful of the dawn recitation," the Prophet Muhammad lengthened his official dawn prayer, and all conscientious Muslims recognize the significance of this early morning ritual. If, according to traditional accounts, angels of the night and the day witness the devotions of humans, then other interpretations suggest that the supreme witness is the God-given illumination in the human soul. Early morning prayer, explains one modern commentator, heightens the inner perception of a human being at a "time when the darkness and stillness of night begins to give way to the life-giving light of day, so that prayer becomes a means of attaining to deeper insight into the realm of spiritual truths and, thus, of achieving communion with all that is holy."[3] The early morning is endowed with spiritual epiphany, a belief shared by multiple religious traditions, as countless Hindu, Buddhist, and Catholic monks will testify as well as devout worshippers of every stripe.

Liturgy, as well as all pious and good acts, is preceded by the formulaic "In the name of God, the Benevolent, the Merciful." The liturgy in each genuflection will consist of the mandatory recitation of the "Opening" (*al-Fatiha*), the first chapter of the Qur'an, consisting of seven verses.

All praise is due to God alone, the Sustainer of the universe
The Benevolent, the Merciful
Ruler of the Day of Requital.
It is You we serve, to You we turn for help.
Show us the straight path,
The path of those you have favored,
Not of those who are objects of anger, nor of those who wander astray.
(Q 1:1–7)

Thereafter the prayer leader will recite any portion of the Qur'an from memory, which could be a minimum of any three verses or more. In morning prayers a middle-length chapter or a portion of it of some forty to fifty verses will be read to a slow, rhythmic, and melodious chant.

What happens after official morning prayers differs from one madrasa to another. In large madrasas, like the Darul Uloom in Deoband, Misbahul Uloom in Mubarakpur, or Jamiʿa Ashrafiyya in Lahore, students are left to their own devices, and they are expected to manage their own spiritual schedules.

In any day at the main mosque attached to the Deoband madrasa or at the one in Mubarakpur, some students will stay in the mosque after the official prayers for meditation and contemplation. Others will pursue their optional devotions in their rooms. In some smaller madrasas it is a rule of discipline to stay in the mosque for some time in order to inculcate in novices the practice of a contemplative life.

In the town of Deoband students also use the adjacent Chatta mosque, a quaint and historic mosque built in a simple style. This mosque has been thoroughly renovated from its condition three decades ago. On my recent visits, the atmosphere had the impress of a Sufi convent. Faculty, staff, and some senior students who were affiliated to different spiritual orders perform their disciplinary practices in this mosque. Careful low voices punctured by ecstatic, incantatory, and hypnotic repetitions of the phrase *la ilaha illalallah* . . . , "There is no other God other than Allah," or *just Allah-hu*, "He is God," fill the air. Others might chant a different phrase, according to the rule set by their spiritual master. Just above this cacophony is a buzz of individual voices reciting the Qur'an in different rhythms, sounds, and ejaculations, like an orchestra warming its instruments with different sounds booming and shadowing others.

A certain vocal-auditory consciousness pervades the place. Some students and their peers will engage in vocalizing formulaic words that praise God with a palpable ecstasy in their voices and faces. Others will recite portions of the Qur'an, both for devotional purposes and to ensure that they keep fresh those portions of the Qur'an already committed to memory.

DISCIPLINE AND PRACTICE

Representatives of the madrasa-sphere often point to one dimension that sets them apart from other institutions of learning like colleges and universities: theirs is a life of learning that is matched by a life of practice. Learning the theory of Islamic comportment is one thing; to internalize a spiritual discipline in one's life is another. Teaching young people both the knowledge and the practice of a moral life is the fundamental purpose of the madrasas of South Asia and their equivalent institutions around the globe. Madrasa life is centered on one's self-formation. Prayers are an inescapable part of practice and discipline.

Of course, not everyone is equally conscientious about ritual and personal practice. As in every other similar institution across religious traditions, there are a few slackers who might miss prayers. While very few students would openly grouse at performing the rituals, it becomes obvious that some comply in a mechanistic fashion, forfeiting the high ambitions and standards of beauty and integrity in a life dedicated to spiritual practice, which the madrasa environment is designed to inculcate.

For some students, attending the madrasa is a chore; for others, attendance is a choice made for them by parents, family tradition, or necessity because other educational opportunities were beyond their reach or deemed undesirable. For most, however, participating in madrasa life is a personal choice made willingly.

Daily Routine

Between prayers and class, some students get some exercise: some will go for early morning walks or do exercises. Breakfast is a small but vital meal, and drinking Indian tea, *chai*, is almost an obligation.

About two hours after the end of morning prayers, a bell or siren announces the beginning of a class. In larger madrasas, housing a few thousand students, an echoing brass bell or siren sounds the end of class periods and announces the various breaks in the day. In smaller institutions there is no bell, but everyone moves seamlessly between classes. Madrasas are run like schools and colleges in terms of class scheduling. Students at every level follow a strict schedule of classes, which meet daily. Only a select number of classes might not meet daily.

Classrooms in most madrasas are often well-aired and well-lit spaces, designed for students to listen to a lecture, and are not meant to be interactive spaces. Only some of the more recently built classrooms have blackboards, as newer methods of pedagogy require teaching materials to be illustrated.

The most common teaching style is the didactic lecture and commentary on a text. With few exceptions, students sit on carpeted floors and use slightly raised desks on which they place their texts and take notes. The teacher sits on a slightly raised platform with a large, comfortable cushion and a desk. Students sit around the teacher in circles or rectangular formation. Each room has a few fans to cool the air on hot days.

A day at the madrasa, including the academic day, is punctuated by the five gatherings for congregational worship. Class schedules are built around these central devotional acts of Muslim life. This devotional cycle, in turn, reinforces the sanctity of both knowledge and its pursuit.

Similarly, the academic calendar follows the Islamic lunar calendar. The Muslim lunar calendar is known as the *hijri* calendar. Its origins go back to the year 622 C.E., when the Prophet Muhammad went into self-imposed exile (*hijra*) and found refuge in the city of Medina some 210 miles (338 km) from his Meccan birthplace. This calendar passes through all the seasons of the year in a thirty-three-year cycle.

Madrasas have a long recess from mid-Shaʿban, the eighth lunar month in the *hijri* calendar, when students and faculty return home in order to spend the month of Ramadan, a period of intense worship, with their families. During Ramadan, Muslims fast from sunrise to sunset, partaking of no food, water, or sex during daylight hours. It is also a month of strenuous additional acts of piety and nightly vigils. The madrasa academic year begins around the middle of Shawwal, the tenth month of the lunar calendar. Another brief recess is from the eighth to the twelfth day of the twelfth lunar month called Dhul Hijja, coinciding with the annual pilgrimage (hajj) to Mecca. The ninth day is the high point of the pilgrimage, when pilgrims stand in penitence on the plains of ʿArafat near Mecca. Nonpilgrims normally do a voluntary fast on the ninth day and celebrate the end of the pilgrimage the day after as a holiday, called ʿId al-Adha, the Festival of Sacrifice. The holiday is both a celebration and an act of solidarity with pilgrims who had completed the highest religious obligation in performing one of the pillars of Islam, a goal every observant Muslim aspires to accomplish if he or she can afford it.

Most madrasas follow a six-day academic week from Saturday to Thursday. On Fridays there are obligatory congregational prayers that are held just after midday. Friday is also the official rest day. Students normally clean their rooms, do their laundry, or do shopping and other chores.

Visiting families over weekends is possible only to those very few who are able to travel within affordable distance to their homes, since most students come from far away. Travel to their homes during vacations is often subsidized by the madrasa stipend. Most of those who study at madrasas come from families of very modest means.

Acts of Worship

Around noon every day, the madrasa breaks for lunch. Lunch is a modest meal consisting of rice and/or South Asian bread such as roti or naan with a curry made of meat and vegetables. Madrasa life is marked by simplicity and austerity that give it a self-consciously spartan and frugal character. Nowhere else does this express itself more than in the consumption of food. A specific etiquette is followed when eating. Food is considered to be a divine gift (*niʿma*), and thus the engagement with food and its consumption requires a certain ritual.

The etiquette of eating is strictly enforced, and the code is provided by the example of the Prophet. To eat with one's fingers is meritorious. Hands are thus washed before touching any food and after one has completed the meal. Eating begins with a liturgical formula, "In the name of God and with the Blessings of God" in Arabic. Depending on the institution, students often eat in dining halls. Mats are laid in rows and students squat to either eat out of individual plates or share a large-sized plate.

Specific postures of seating are required while eating and are meticulously followed. Sitting in a lotus position while eating is seen as an arrogant posture. Only those with some disability or seniors would be allowed to sit with their legs crossed. Most either sit with one leg folded underneath while the other is held upright in a bent position or sit on their haunches. The idea is to ensure that one bends toward the food, in a mark of humility and appreciation for the gift of nourishment. In the prescribed postures, the belly is compressed in order to ensure a moderate consumption of food. The recommended formula is to fill one-third of the belly with food, fill the second third with water, and leave the rest empty. During meals students are encouraged not to talk much, and if they do talk, it should be about some pious act or scholarship. Otherwise, they are encouraged to give thanks to God throughout the meal. At the completion of a meal, a prayer of thanks is uttered: "*All praise is due to God, Who fed us, provided us with water and made us among those who surrender to His will, Muslims.*" Again, here the body and mind (intentionality) are both fully engaged in the act of eating, which is viewed as an act of worship.

After lunch, students almost immediately seek to enjoy a mandatory siesta rest hour, especially in summer when the heat in certain regions of South Asia is unbearable. And since students rise early in the morning, taking some rest in order to complete the day with sufficient energy is crucial.

The afternoon class sessions begin almost immediately after the post-midday prayer, known as Zuhr prayers. Zuhr and the one that follows, when read in congregation or individually, are silent; the liturgy is not read loudly. Each congregant follows the instructions of the prayer leader in order to move from one posture to another to complete the four genuflections of the obligatory Zuhr prayers.

After prayers, classes resume shortly for another two and a half hours until the late afternoon prayer, called the ʿAsr prayers. That marks the end of the official school day. After ʿAsr prayers, students engage in recreational activities such as playing a range of sports, including soccer, cricket, volleyball, and badminton. Sporting activity is encouraged provided it does not absorb all one's energy and does not distract students from their academic program. Taking long walks remains the most preferred form of exercise. All recreational activities end just before the sunset prayers, known as Maghrib. In summer, students take their dinner before Maghrib prayers, since sunset occurs late; in winter, they take their dinner after those prayers. The next prayer hour, the ʿIsha prayers, are normally held about seventy minutes after the Maghrib prayers.

Study Groups

Depending on the season of the year and the size of a campus, after Maghrib or ʿIsha prayers, madrasas are a hive of student activity. A good number of serious students gather in study groups in order to participate in review sessions of the day's lessons. Attending a study group in most madrasas is not mandatory but is strongly encouraged. Students often meet in classrooms or public spaces like mosques or courtyards of mosques and dedicated spaces in madrasa buildings. Study spots resemble the prototype madrasa that Muslim accounts trace back to the *"Folk of the Portico"* (*Ahl al-Suffa*), who occupied a place of distinction in the Prophet's mosque in Medina. Typifying the ideal of poverty and piety, these ascetic-minded persons engaged in learned discussions about the faith. Today's madrasa students attempt to rekindle their memory.

Study groups normally have a fixed number of students headed by one among them, akin to a prefect. The primary function of study groups is to accomplish two things: one is to review the work most recently covered in class, and the other is to preview materials to be read in the next class. In a typical review session, an advanced student rehearses the day's lectures and the texts read. Often spirited colloquia spontaneously commence among students, and debates about the finer points of interpretation the professor made in class ensue. Students may provide their own interpretations and try to relate what they had learned in class to contemporary themes and issues. Study groups are also a venue for pedagogical training. The group leaders hold a status somewhere between that of teaching assistants (TAs) and adjunct professors in the American university system. This is how the next generation of professors and scholars get an opportunity to refine their skills as teachers.

The noted scholar Ashraf ʿAli Thanvi affiliated to the Deoband school highlighted the merit of student review. One can effortlessly grasp the religious sciences, he said, if students complied with four requirements. First, they had to preview the next day's text. Second, they should listen attentively to the teacher in class. Third, they should proceed to the next lesson only once they fully mastered the previous one. Fourth, they should give lectures and explanations to others of what they had learned.[4]

Over time the performance-based reputations of the study group leaders who follow Thanvi's advice invariably enable the group leaders to secure jobs at other madrasas. Study group leaders are often so talented that on occasion their tutorials surpass the professor's lectures. Some have the astounding ability to repeat verbatim large chunks of the commentary offered in class several hours or days ago. Of course, memory and replication are highly valued skills in this environment since the goal is to sustain a tradition of institutional reasoning.

Students select the subjects that deserve the study group's attention. Often, it is the subject that garners their strongest interest or the one that poses the toughest challenge. Some students do not join study groups and prefer to do solitary preparation and review sessions. After study-group sessions, students will either take a break or go to nearby cafés and vendors, which surround most madrasas, to have tea (*chai*) or other beverages and snacks. Otherwise, they will heat water in their own rooms on portable kerosene-fueled primus stoves before adding tea leaves, sugar, and milk and bringing it to a boil to make a creamy drink, the original "chai latte." After a break individual students will continue to study until they retire for the night.

Living conditions for students in most madrasas are fairly modest, if not ascetic. Students share rooms and facilities. The number of students living in a room varies from one venue to another. In madrasas that have the financial means, four to six students might share a room with bunk beds; those with lesser means might require more students to share rooms. In some places dozens of students share a large hall. Only rarely do institutions provide students with beds and modest furniture in their rooms. Most students sleep on rollout beds or thin mattresses. Those who can afford it purchase their own inexpensive cots. I have also seen madrasas where, because of a shortage of space, younger students slept on rollout beds in their classrooms.

Some administrators are particularly aware of living conditions for students and thus go out of their way to create healthy environments. In most madrasas, resources to improve living conditions are low on the list of priorities. Most madrasa administrators are eager to erect huge dormitories in order to accommodate more students, but the administrators pay very little attention to the quality of living conditions. One can immediately get an idea of the economic resources of a madrasa by inspecting the living condition in its dormitories.

Foreign students are sometimes given privileges in dormitories that local Indian or Pakistani students are not allowed. Often there is an assumption that overseas students come from comparatively affluent economic backgrounds and are thus accustomed to better living conditions. Hence, special hospitality is reserved for them. International dorms may house fewer students to a room. Sometimes, overseas students can also order special meals for a modest fee.

For me, the highlight of dorm life was the sense of community we developed as students. Students cared for each other and supported each other emotionally and, if need be, financially. I frequently engaged in discussions with those who were my seniors in my bid to learn from them, and I often bothered them with my textual queries and the arcane riddles of Arabic grammar or the nuances of an Urdu poem. Especially on Thursday evenings, the start of the weekend, students would hold impromptu poetic symposiums (*mushaʿiras*), where poems are read or sung in a melodious voice with vocal responses of appreciation from members of the audience. We developed camaraderie, as students made one believe that we would remain friends for life, only to realize that only in rare instances do friendships survive in one's life after the madrasa.

CONCLUSION

The practices of ritual, gaining knowledge of the tradition, and engaging in recreational activities are all viewed as part of a seamless pursuit of worship and the inculcation of piety in madrasa life. As long as the student keeps his eye on the goal, which is to cultivate sincerity and satisfy God, the crucial requirements of what it is to be a seeker of knowledge is fulfilled. The madrasa provides the "training wheels" for a student in order to inculcate those rhythms of ritual, learning, and piety into the body through daily practice. When these practices become second nature, one can say that the student has inculcated a life of subservience to God's commandments. Madrasa teachings insist that knowledge can have a proper effect only if the receptacle of knowledge, the human body, especially the heart, is properly conditioned to receive such learning. Abstaining from sin makes it possible for knowledge to illuminate the heart and mind with wisdom and insight based on the book learning the student already acquired. Knowledge and the way it manifests itself in the world is a hotly debated topic within madrasa circles.

Knowledge is a covenant, a performative and a redemptive activity. Knowledge is viewed as an antidote to sin. The debate over whether knowledge has two roles, both for worldly flourishing and afterworldly salvation, remains unresolved in madrasa circles.

CHAPTER THREE

Becoming Scholars

In January of 2011, there was an international media buzz about Darul Uloom Deoband in North India, the first campus of the Deoband movement, which was established in 1867. The buzz arose because Mawlana Ghulam Vastanvi was appointed vice-chancellor (or president) of this influential flagship campus of the Deoband school. Vastanvi's appointment was a bold move on the part of Deoband's leadership. In his previous job, Vastanvi had managed several madrasas in the Indian states of Gujarat and Maharashtra. There he successfully combined madrasa education with secular education up to the college level. Perhaps, some thought, he could bring his innovative approach to enact curricular reform to Deoband, South Asia's most influential and growing madrasa network.

His appointment was greeted with great enthusiasm. Observers speculated that the Advisory Council of Deoband was sending a message: one of the oldest Muslim seminaries on the subcontinent was embarking on a much-awaited program of change. Voices of concern, on the other hand, feared Vastanvi might strip Deoband of its vaunted feature as a place of orthodox learning and traditional Islamic piety. Would the merger of

Islamic and secular education not turn Deoband into a "worldly" institution, the concerned voices wondered? Others asked, Will graduates pay more attention to material gain instead of piety?

Vastanvi's appointment was, however, short-lived. In a newspaper interview on the eve of his appointment, he was quizzed about the tragic 2003 riots in his home state of Gujarat, in which several thousand Muslims died at the hands of right-wing Hindu zealots. Trying to stay above the fray, Vastanvi gave diplomatic and evasive answers that caused a firestorm. He said he did not want Muslims to cultivate a victim mentality and ducked from having to comment on the conduct of Gujarat's controversial governor at the time, Narendra Modi, who was widely alleged to have either masterminded the violence or turned a blind eye to it. Mr Modi had since become India's prime minister.

Public reaction to Vastanvi's answers was one of dismay at what was either an expedient dodge or a monstrous gaffe. At the Deoband campus, students swiftly reacted in anger and protested his appointment. In the summer of 2011 Vastanvi was cashiered from his appointment. The Deobandi fraternity was divided. Some saw Vastanvi's departure as a missed opportunity for much-needed curricular change. Those who rejoiced at his ouster favored the status quo with its ascetic outlook and social conservatism. Once again, the Deoband madrasa retained its pious character and avoided a tryst with modernity. This dance with change and innovation in matters of knowledge and learning is endemic to the history of Islamic orthodoxy.

A TALE OF TWO IMPULSES

Over the centuries two views or impulses of learning in Islamdom sustained a productive tension but often became polarized. In one view, knowledge is rooted in the virtue of human sociability. Worldliness is a strong feature. But this is a worldliness that does not diminish concerns about salvation in the hereafter. In fact, this worldly tradition of learning enjoyed great prestige in the Islamic past. Knowledge fostered understanding among people in a non-faith-specific manner. Its favorite genres were *adab*, belles-lettres, which included poetry and rhetoric but also took seriously the study of philosophy, history, and philology. The disregard and reluctance to adopt a more robust intellectual paradigm in Islamic thought are even more astonishing when one considers that the invitation for critical scholarship was made by none other than the

Types of Madrasas

Modern South Asian madrasa networks can largely be divided into four groups or franchises:

- Deobandi madrasas. The first was the Darul ʿUloom established in the town of Deoband in 1867 by Muhammad Qasim Nanautvi, Rashid Ahmad Gangohi, and Haji Muhammad ʿAbid Husayn.
- Barelwi madrasas. The first in this franchise was Madrasa Manzar-i Islam in 1904 in Bareilly established by Ahmad Raza Khan.
- Ahl-i Hadis or Ahl-i Hadith madrasas. The first Ahl-i Hadith madrasa was al-Madrasa al-Ahmadiyya established in 1880 by Ibrahim al-Arvi in the town of Arrah in the Bhojpur district of Bihar.
- Shiʿa madrasas. The first Shiʿa madrasa was Jamiʿ-i Sultaniyya or Shahi Madrasa in 1843 when Sayyid Muhammad persuaded Nawab Amjad ʿAli Shah of Awadh to establish one in Lucknow. It was abolished in 1857. In 1890 Mawlana Sayyid Abul Hasan Abbu Sahib established Madrasa-i Nazimiyya in Lucknow.

great ʿAbd al-Rahman Ibn Khaldun in the fourteenth century. Without a critical apparatus that includes "a good speculative mind and thoroughness" but also knowledge of custom, political realities, the nature of civilization, sociology (what he calls "human social organization"), and comparative studies, a historian is doomed to err, wrote Ibn Khaldun.[1] And if one did not explore historical contexts with the aid of philosophy and science, what Ibn Khaldun calls the "knowledge of the nature of things," then one can stray "from the truth and [find oneself] lost in the desert of baseless assumptions and errors."[2] Despite its prestige and its obvious benefits, this widely affirmed "worldly" tradition within Islamdom always had to compete with another trend, especially in modern times.

Although there is significant overlap between the "worldly" and "otherworldly" trends, the "otherworldly" trend stresses the virtues of monastic introspection and the desire to acquire the right knowledge in order to gain salvation. Piety inculcated through the study of the prophetic traditions (hadith), exegesis of the Qurʾan, and adherence to the rule-based (deontological ethics) practice of the discipline of law (*fiqh*)

Students working on computers at Darul Uloom Deoband, India. (Picture: Rodrigo Dorfman)

takes precedence, resulting in an impressive and powerful Shariʿa-mindedness and piety. There is, of course, always the possibility that the study of history, rhetoric, and philology can shape the piety-minded to be more receptive to humanistic learning, if only this can be accomplished with efficiency. But the potential to make this "otherworldly" trend more intellectually robust has yet to be realized in the contemporary madrasas. At first I deeply admired this trend, but over time I became disenchanted by its thin intellectual veneer and gradually drifted in search of more vigorous knowledge traditions along the lines Ibn Khaldun advocated.

In modern times the ideological fault lines between the two trends play out differently. Vastanvi, a proponent of the "worldliness" of tradition, advocates a synthesis of modern and traditional knowledge, where science, social science, and the humanities effortlessly mingle with traditional learning. But all experiments to accomplish a modest level of innovation in traditional Muslim educational circles in South Asia for over a century have been largely stillborn. Experiments to integrate multiple knowledge traditions in order to enhance the study of religious discourses have been shockingly incompetent with little to show in tangible outcomes. The best some madrasas have done was to incorporate elements of high school subjects ranging from English to computer literacy, geography, and history into the lower elementary levels of madrasa curricula. While this is an improvement, it has minimal impact in the study of the advanced madrasa curriculum.

In fact, the pietistic tradition of learning, sustained by inertia, has become more strident in its monopoly of religious discourses because the alternatives are weak. Pluralizing knowledge and constructively exposing Muslim religious thought to newer methods of inquiry such as critical readings of history, sociology, theological anthropology, philology, and hermeneutics using a variety of intellectual resources and tools remains an unaccomplished task. Oftentimes, new approaches are dismissed as efforts to undermine or corrupt the Muslim discursive tradition or worse, deemed to be conspiracies hatched by orientalists and implemented by duped and pliant Muslim scholars.

There are several reasons why the opportunity to embrace a cosmopolitan posture in knowledge is still passed over in favor of the inward-looking and pietistic impulses. It is not a form of resistance to innovation as some people might suspect. Rather, the objection to new disciplines and knowledge traditions is associated with a fear and loathing of a materialistic West whose knowledge traditions are viewed as poisonous. Therefore, the purity and piety of Islamic knowledge traditions are hailed and embraced. In times of crisis, with a decline in the moral and political authority of the ʿulama, another explanation goes, the monastic narrative of isolation and reclusiveness enjoys great appeal. Furthermore, when contemporary Muslim scholars of religion are marginalized by society and live in disenchanted contexts, especially when material prosperity is out of their reach, then ascetic approaches are appealing as either a choice or a default mode. More compelling is the explanation that large sectors of the South Asian ʿulama view knowledge itself as an act of piety, which translates as ascetic poverty. Some ideologues envision the madrasa as a model of a counter-utopia, first, in resisting the hostile colonial nation-state and then second, as an alternative to the failing postcolonial state, especially in Pakistan.

By contrast, when Muslims enjoyed power, then one could find scholars like al-Farabi, Ibn Sina, Ibn Haytham, Ghazali, Ibn Khaldun, and countless others who had little compunction in drawing on the knowledge traditions of the Greeks, Indians, and other cultures in order to fortify their own intellectual projects and enhance their comprehension of Islam as a religious tradition.

POST-MADRASA LIFE

At every madrasa I visited in India and Pakistan, I made sure that I spoke to some of the students in order to get a sense of their ambitions and plans after they had graduated. After all, I remember when I was a student at the madrasas decades ago. At some point the idealism of madrasa life fades and real-life questions become more important. I remember frequently thinking, what will I do after I have graduated? Will I serve a mosque-community? That was, for me, the least attractive of options at the time. I was interested in doing advanced studies in Islam, and writing was a foremost passion. Was journalism, then, an option? I thought at the time. At one stage, and for many months, I toyed around with the idea of starting an institution for Islamic learning in South Africa after my return.

So I was curious to know what kinds of career questions preoccupied the students in the madrasas today. Once I introduced myself and told them of my own journey from the madrasa to modern universities, they became quite curious. Many wanted to know how I made the journey out of the madrasa to a modern university. Often students asked about the condition especially of Muslims in America. Queries were couched in their lurking curiosity about a feared and fabled West of their imaginations. "Does the American government allow Muslims to practice their faith?" was a frequent question. "Why would Americans allow Islam to be taught at universities?" many incredulously ask. "Do those who study Islam also convert to Islam?" they ask. Both presidents George W. Bush and Barack H. Obama enjoyed a mixed reception in the madrasa circles of South Asia.

People like myself who teach in American universities come under some suspicion frequently. For it is incomprehensible—nay, illogical—for many to comprehend that an America that wages wars against Muslim-majority countries in Afghanistan and Iraq would also sufficiently respect Islam and adorn its universities with its teachings. Those who teach Islam in America must have a crooked and paradoxical agenda similar to that of the U.S. government, many assume. Attempts to explain to them the difference between the U.S. government and its policies and U.S.-based institutions of civil society like universities do make some dent in their perceptions, but is not compelling to all, and thus remains a difficult conversation for many Muslim scholars who live in the West. The tragic irony is this: the world's greatest superpower has scant access to the hearts and minds of vast Muslim communities in order to correct or engage in mutually rewarding exchanges!

I got a range of responses from the students when I inquired what they would do after graduation. Many inquired about the requirements for study abroad or possibilities to serve Muslim communities in the West. Group dynamics also generate boilerplate questions and answers. Most students gave a standard, if not often rehearsed, response if I asked them what they will do after graduation: "I will consult my teachers on how to serve the faith (*din*)." Service to the faith or practices of salvation, *din*, is a standard expression for the kind of sincere and self-effacing persona one is required to cultivate as a student.

Here is the dilemma about post-madrasa life for virtually every student. Throughout one's years of training, one is taught that not only is the knowledge of the faith sacred but to take compensation for anything related to knowledge is not permissible. To serve the faith-tradition in the sphere of knowledge therefore requires sacrifice. Poverty is the ideal. One should adopt a lifestyle of frugality, self-effacing modesty, and reliance on God and shun materialism if one is to become a devout servant of the faith.

From the get-go students are taught to view knowledge of *din*—knowledge associated with acts of salvation such as faith, dogma, Islamic law, and the Qur'an—as an *end* in itself, not as a *means* to a career as an imam (the equivalent of a clergyman), a writer, a scholar, or a public intellectual. Early Islamic teachings proscribe any compensation for those who advance knowledge of the faith, and this remains the predisposition of the pious today. One often hears of some teachers in madrasas who have a modest subsistence income from agriculture or business, and therefore they return their monthly salary checks to the madrasa in keeping with the pious ascetic ethos.

Over centuries the teachings on compensation for those involved in disseminating knowledge of the faith have changed on the grounds of "necessity" and for advancing the "public good." Hence, special rulings, fatwas, now permit teachers, scholars, imams, and other functionaries associated with disseminating knowledge of the faith to be paid. Without compensation, the fatwas explain, the faith sector will suffer. Yet practitioners have to bear in mind that they are not compensated for their invaluable knowledge but for the dedication of their time to pious pursuits. Knowledge in and of itself cannot be transacted.

"If our students do not study *din* as an end, but only as a means, then surely they pour water on all our efforts," observes Saʿid Ahmad Palanpuri, now a professor of hadith at the Deoband seminary.[3] "If they had studied *din* as an end in itself," he rhetorically asks, "then how is it possible to choose another profession after they had graduated from the madrasas?" Palanpuri's comment epitomizes the ascetic approach to learning and to embrace poverty as an ideal. Given the prevalence of the ascetic ethos, most graduating students are riddled with guilt, paralyzed by ambivalence and insecurity when weighing their options on graduation. Do they go against their madrasa formation and pursue careers in broader society related to their skills, or do they comply with the normative narrative (*maslak*) of their alma maters? The majority comply.

Many madrasas decline the opportunity to have their degrees recognized in the national education system in their respective countries, which would enable their graduates to pursue advanced studies at secular universities. In Pakistan the national educational system recognizes certain madrasas that are certified by a central board. In India madrasa degrees are recognized on an ad hoc basis by the national educational system. The recognition of madrasa degrees, of course, limits students to pursue advanced degrees only in subject areas like Arabic, Persian, Urdu, and Islamic studies at universities. Madrasa authorities are apprehensive to link their degrees to university systems because they fear their graduates will become careerists and give up their calling as pious teachers of the faith.

Several of the students I interviewed said that they planned to engage in the work of *daʿwa*. *Daʿwa* literally means "to invite" or "to call." Every Muslim is required to invite humanity to the path of salvation per the teachings of the Qurʾan. "Invite or call to the path of your Lord," the Qurʾan says, "with wisdom and beautiful speech" (Q 16:125). In another place the Qurʾan says, "Who is better in speech than the one who invites to God, does good works and then announces: 'I am among those who surrender' " (Q 41:33).

Daʿwa takes many forms. The most common type is to engage fellow Muslims and to remind them of their religious obligations and to announce to persons of other faiths, as well as those with no faith, the meaning and purpose of the gospel of Islam. Inviting fellow Muslims to a life of observance, offering guidance in matters of the public good, especially if it involves questions of faith and practice, is what madrasa graduates most often engage in. Face-to-face contact and private visits to individuals is one mode of *daʿwa*. Often madrasa graduates develop astonishing repertoires, combining an eloquent Urdu diction or a local language with the ability to cite verses of the Qurʾan, the speech of the Prophet together with the wise insights of the pious effortlessly in order to become mesmerizing public speakers. Such charismatic and reputed individuals are able to draw large crowds; the more successful ones develop networks of influence both nationally and internationally. The most common format is for a madrasa graduate to be invited to visit a community and give a motivational lecture (*waʿz*) at a mosque or a public facility. The topic is often about faith and salvation in the hereafter and a successful religious life in this world. Others who are more attuned to global affairs will make comments about current affairs in order to make their audiences aware of the fact that a faith-based approach to life is not only necessary but also a viable option.

For a long time, print media was the most common way to reach audiences. Writings by scholars like Ashraf ʿAli Thanvi, for example, gave him an enduring and most influential legacy, just as print brought immense benefits to innumerable other scholars.[4] Often publishing ventures operate as nonprofit organizations to become the source of income for many madrasa graduates. However, the advent of electronic and cyber media has completely altered the landscape of *daʿwa*. Madrasa graduates use a range of media from audio and video recordings to websites and blogging forums in order to offer guidance, inculcate pious practices, and instruct their audiences how to observe the Shariʿa.

Becoming an imam at a mosque in villages, towns, and big cities is perhaps the most common form of employment for a madrasa graduate. Often mosque communities offer an imam a modest salary, free or subsidized housing, and some benefits. In addition to being a prayer leader, the imam often instructs young children in the reading of the Qurʾan. Occasionally, imams offer classes to adults in the basic teachings of Islam.

Some madrasa graduates with excellent language skills in Arabic and Urdu also do work as translators and journalists. Some get absorbed in the lower levels of their respective country's national Foreign Service agencies and embassies, while others are employed in the private sector in the Gulf region. A number of graduates also work in radio and television services, where they render news in Arabic and staff media programs dedicated to religion.

Establishing madrasas has become an opportunity for entrepreneurial graduates. All over India, Pakistan, and Bangladesh, as well as in countries like the United Kingdom and South Africa, madrasas are growing at a rapid rate. In two decades, observes Mawlana Dr. Waris Mazhari, a Delhi-based, madrasa-trained public intellectual and editor of the Deoband Old Boys magazine, *Tarjuman Darul Uloom*, the number of madrasas has possibly trebled in cities like Delhi. The same could be said for big cities like Karachi and Lahore. But often madrasas flourish in regional cities and medium-sized towns. In larger size districts in the state of Gujarat in India, madrasas for men and women cater to a wide variety of audiences. Madrasa graduates are recruited nationally to staff new madrasas, and a good number of South Asian madrasa graduates are recruited at overseas madrasas.

In a few madrasas, such as those at the Jamiʿat al-Hidaya (Jamea Tul Hidaya) in Jaipur in India, administrators have successfully integrated training in computer technology, welding, and electrical training alongside theological training. Administrators anticipate that the technical skills will give madrasa graduates some kind of income independence while allowing them to pursue their religious calling. But no madrasa integrates modern science, social science, and the humanities into a seamless and coherent curriculum in conversation with the core traditional madrasa curriculum and its emphasis on religious teachings.

COSMOLOGY OF ʿULAMA KNOWLEDGE TRADITIONS

If you wish to grasp how the ʿulama view their calling as purveyors of sacred knowledge and their societal role as moral guides, then think in cosmic terms. "Cosmic" here means to think of an ordered universe or a system of thought in metaphysical terms: reality beyond the physical, the measurable—in short, not empirically verifiable—a description of a cosmos supplied by knowledge revealed to selected persons such as prophets, sages, and philosophers. At least in Islamic history, knowledge pertaining to salvation and devotional practices had an empirical dimension and a dimension linked to a cosmic perspective.[5] Therefore, the learned in matters of faith are equal in reverence to the Israelite prophets, according to a tradition attributed to the Prophet Muhammad. In Islam the status of prophecy is an exceptional one: ordinary mortals cannot attain it by their will because prophets are providentially selected for such honors. What the learned in Islam share with their Israelite exemplars is *access* to divinely inspired knowledge, wisdom, and intuition. Prophets and the learned share a commitment to save humanity through learning and by their example during a time of moral decline.

For many orthodox Muslims as well as those of other Islamic orientations too—despite objections from modern historians—belief in a "rise and fall" narrative of Islam's political and moral fortunes is a valid one and serves as a motif for renewal. For the orthodox it is a decline in moral authority—what they deem as spiritual blindness and a lack of observance of religious practice—that precipitates a decline in Islamdom's political fortunes. During an era of decline, only true knowledge of faith, they believe, can rescue communities and help them establish their bonds with God. This is also a view offered by Qari Muhammad Tayyab (d. 1983), a long-standing president of the Deoband seminary. "There is a need to reverse this condition [of decline]," he proposes, with

> education and formation, *taʿlim va tarbiyyat*, as the first [remedial] pillar, be a specific form of education that one receives from devout learned scholars, *ʿulama*. Education is the means whereby the knowledge of the Qurʾan and the Prophetic tradition, *Sunna*, is attained, followed by disciplinary training in order for the knower to act upon such learning. One's aesthetic predisposition or taste, *dhawq*, and understanding are corrected by apprenticeship and the companionship of devout scholars in order realize the appropriate spiritual "colors," "*the coloring of God," sibghatullah* [Q 2:138], [in the learner]. . . . It is insufficient to merely read books and expect the divine "color" to download into one's human persona. In order for the self to absorb this [divine] coloration, it is a precondition to have a healthy path to the heart. Without self-mortification and spiritual self-discipline, [*ascesis*] *mujahada* and *riyadat*, the heart is not healed.[6]

PERFORMING KNOWLEDGE

As heirs of the prophets, the learned scholars, ʿulama, of the madrasas also imitate the ancient prophets, says Karachi-based Mawlana Adnan Kaka Khel, a rising figure in the Pakistani Deobandi madrasa network. The ʿulama do what the ancient prophets did in conveying God's knowledge and wisdom to the hearts of the people they serve. "Certain people dedicate their lives to this task of teaching and make sacrifices in pursuit of this goal in order to transmit the heritage of the Prophet in an uninterrupted chain to the successor generation" is how Kaka Khel explains the purpose of madrasa education.[7] Learning in the madrasas, he eulogizes, is transmitted from one generation to another, not via books, but "from heart to heart," meaning from teacher to student. The distinctive feature of a madrasa education is captured in Kaka Khel's alliterative, if not clichéd, rendering in Urdu: "knowledge is derived from *persons, nufus*, not from *texts/imprints on a page, nuqush*," a point repeatedly made by advocates of the madrasa tradition.[8]

Heart-to-heart transmission of learning is shorthand for personal instruction and authorization (*ijaza*) of knowledge by observing meticulous teacher-student protocols. More specifically, it signifies the esoteric dimension of tradition. Knowledge is transmitted through living narrators who can personally vouch for acquiring their knowledge from a living teacher. "The evidentiary chain of authority for the transmission of knowledge, *isnad*," one ancient authority commented, "is a virtuous trait among the qualities of the community (*umma*) of Muhammad, and it is a practice that enjoys a great deal of attention."[9] Ibn al-Mubarak, another early authority, noted, "An evidentiary chain of authority for the transmission of knowledge is integral to the path of salvation, *din*; were it not for secure transmission, everyone would talk as they pleased." And he also cautioned, "To seek the learning of religion without evidentiary support is like trying to get on to a roof without using a ladder!"[10] Apart from learning from exemplars, the idea of personal face-to-face education was the default position in Islam's oral culture at its founding. Personal education then was the only means to transmit learning and hence enjoys the aura of authenticity in terms of the prewriting and preprint eras of learning.

Based on this model, the study of narrators whose life histories and integrity are crucial to the chain of evidence for knowledge and learning is a highly valued practice among Muslims. In short, traditional Muslim knowledge practices rely heavily on testimonials. Furthermore, authentic face-to-face learning from teachers fulfills the function of embedding knowledge and information into a network of authority, authenticity, and sanctity.

A student who is authorized is also licensed to instruct and induct others into the network of personal learning. By now it should be clear to the reader why physical proximity, personal apprenticeship, and guidance are such highly prized aspects of madrasa education. Cherished is the transfer of knowledge from the heart of one person to that of another. Equally vital is the opportunity to be physically present and to witness the learning process where both erudite activities and the cultivation of spirituality serve as guarantees for the integrity of the education imparted.

Kaka Khel criticizes the prevalent modern modes of autodidactic learning made possible by print and modern electronic media. "You can verify yourselves," he continues, "and you will find that whenever this heart-to-heart or personal transmission of learning is absent, you can be guaranteed that misguidance in matters of religion flourishes."[11] Modern modes of scholarship promoting skepticism, he laments, afflicted the study of Islam. Opinionated modern scholars of Islam do nothing, Kaka Khel rails, but pose as emblems of free thinking and innovation in matters of religious thought and sow doubt about Islam's authentic sources of learning. Reformers claiming to be armed with modern methods of learning and under the pretext to renovate and reform Islam, he complains, actually carry axes in order to demolish the very knowledge that Muslims had preserved for nearly 1,400 years and undo the vaunted system of transmission.

Kaka Khel's siren rhetoric might give the impression that the madrasa brooks neither change nor amendment to the content of learning. Yet terse and difficult texts used in the madrasa syllabi are frequently substituted by other ones, and small changes to the modes of disseminating religious knowledge are tolerated. Kaka Khel, for example, freely uses the Internet and posts his lectures and speeches on YouTube. Ironically, in adopting new technology, he himself no longer personally teaches a distinct group of actual students in real-time. Rather, he addresses an anonymous and "virtual" audience whom he never meets face-to-face except in a cyber-mediated fashion.

Effectively, in his practice, he concedes to a change in the much-vaunted traditional medium of personalized education. His lectures and communications are now digitally preserved and virtually transmitted via Skype and Google. In theory, his spoken words will have an animated afterlife even when he, the lecturer, is no more. This is a break with his precyberspace traditionalist predecessors, whose words had only an inanimate afterlife in books. Today traditional Muslim scholars employ video recordings, live broadcasts, and a myriad of communication technologies in cyberspace that alter the previously prized forms of face-to-face transmission of learning. In other words, they unconsciously invent new modes of attachment to learning that might over time change the centrality of the teacher and where the medium might invariably become more important. With digital learning, knowledge is now largely in the hands of the consumer and end-user whose direct attachment to the teacher is limited but more importantly customized.

COVENANT OF KNOWLEDGE

Acquiring knowledge in the madrasas is like having a contract with knowledge itself or alternatively with the source of all knowledge, namely, God. When teachers in the madrasas talk about the "responsibility of learning," they refer to a covenant one has made with knowledge. And when the light of knowledge reaches the heart of the learner, madrasa authorities explain, learning itself creates a warrant, called convictions. Complying with the warrants of learning takes different shapes. Acquiring knowledge is what modern thinkers call a *performative*: a sincere undertaking to comply with the demands of that learning and act on its imperatives. To *know* means the ability to *act* and to *perform*.

The renowned seventeenth-century Ottoman lexicographer and scholar Abul Baqa al-Kafawi claims the meaning of knowledge is not only "to grasp something in its true essence."[12] In his view, knowledge involves a greater purpose: to attain salvation. "Sometimes," Kafawi continues, "learning is actually used as a figure of speech [metonymy] for deeds."[13] The performance of any worthy deed, it is presumed, is always prefigured by a quality of knowledge that is consciously or intuitively acquired. "For surely any beneficial deed," Kafawi notes, "cannot be *sans* knowledge."[14] When learning itself is imagined as making us perform certain actions, as part of actualizing one's salvation (another way of describing the term "soteriology"), then knowledge does indeed become a sought-after torch.

What douses the torch of knowledge? According to a multitude of Muslim authorities, negative bodily qualities dull the light of knowledge and serve as impediments to proper compliance. How? Sinful acts and impure thoughts extinguish the luminescence of the soul. If knowledge creates a heightened awareness of the larger world around us, then surely sin has the opposite effect. Sin impedes awareness and induces a state of forgetfulness and heedlessness.

Affective Soteriology of Knowledge

Ancient wisdom teaches that knowledge produces spiritual light and prevents a practitioner from committing a sin. This is a conception that persists among madrasa communities today and was reaffirmed in nineteenth-century colonial India by a variety of religious authorities. From his thriving Sufi lodge in the small village of Thana Bhavan, some 119 miles from Delhi, the capital of British India, the mystic and scholar aligned to the Deoband school, Ashraf ʿAli Thanvi, advocated such a view. "Knowledge is the antidote to sin," Thanvi writes. "A sinner does not attain knowledge. If merely enumerating words constitutes knowledge, then it could even co-exist with sin. . . . The inner meaning of knowledge is light, *nur,* as disclosed in the verse of the Qurʾan: '*indeed light has arrived for you from God and a book that is clear.*' And the Qurʾan also refers to knowledge as the 'spirit,' *ruh* as in: '*He assisted them with the spirit.*' "[15]

Thanvi's exegesis of a passage of the Qurʾan lends support to his view. Not everyone should go to war, says the Qurʾan. Instead, a group of believers dedicated to the pursuit of learning must be protected. The verse reads,

> *Believers should not all go forth in battle; why would not a group from every distinct unit among them stay behind, to devote themselves to deep learning of religion* [*how to perform acts of salvation*] *and thus be able to teach their people when they return home from the battlefield, so that they might abstain from wrong?* (Q 9:122)

No scriptural passage, writes Thanvi, captures the significance of knowledge more dramatically than this commandment. For the Qurʾan stresses the duty of learning to continue even when the faith community faces the greatest peril, such as war, jihad, when its very existence is threatened. If anything, the verse underscores the responsibility to continuously configure and refine knowledge for the salvation path (*din*) and its various modalities. *Din* is semantically rich. It shares the sense of, among other things, "habit," "accountability," "judgment," "obedience," "compensation," or "recompense" to "governance" and "informed opinion," and it can also signify revelation.[16] Hence, Muslims often use the term *din* in order to describe a vast life world that is inclusive of revealed morals and daily practice that can lead to salvation.

It is utterly clear to Thanvi why the pursuit of knowledge enjoys such a sanctified position. The quest for knowledge in itself is a redemptive act, he explains. Performing knowledge is an act of obedience. Why? Because it is an answer to a Qurʾanic imperative: *"Recite!"* Hence acting on a divine command is, in Thanvi's view, a testament of obedience. But obedience is not a passive act. Obedience is anchored in intentionality, and when an act is faithfully performed, it gives the practitioner a sense of getting divine approval. Acquiring knowledge about the acts of salvation can turn a mundane act of learning into one that has transcendent dimensions. Knowledge, in the eyes of Muslim traditionalists, acquaints humans with the will of God and is therefore viewed as a highly valued possession.

The Qurʾan with its 6,236 verses introduces Muslims to the will of God as expressed in seventh-century Arabia with its everlasting wisdom. A good portion of the Qurʾan is in a homiletic or sermonic tone. Sometimes an event or a story known to seventh-century audiences of the Qurʾan is turned into a moral lesson. The Qurʾan also frequently recounts different aspects of the experiences and trials and tribulations of the Children of Israel. For instance, an anonymous story of two farmer brothers is related in the Qurʾan. One brother shows gratitude to God and is humble, while the other is arrogant and vain. When a natural catastrophe strikes their harvest, it is the humble brother who has the spiritual resources to deal with his loss. Meanwhile, the arrogant and materialistic brother only laments and loathes himself as a ruined and miserable wretch unable to come to terms with life's challenges. In sermonic parts, the Qurʾan mobilizes the emotions of its audiences with the intention of touching their inner core. Like announcing a result, the God of the Qurʾan proclaims,

> *God has sent down the best story*
> *as a Book of similar refrains*
>
> [*When listening to some parts of it*] *the flesh of those who are in awe of their Lord freeze,*
>
> [*When hearing other parts of it*] *their flesh and hearts soften to the remembrance of God.* (Q 39:23)

Another carefully pitched homily forecasts the Day of Reckoning:

> *The day We will say to hell,*
> *"Are you full?' It will say, 'Are there more?"*
> *And Paradise will be brought near the conscientious,*
> *Not far away*

"This is what is promised to you
For everyone who keeps turning to God, mindful
Who inwardly fears the Benevolent One
And comes with a repentant heart.
Enter therein, in peace.
That is the day of eternity." (Q 50:30–34)

It is the rhetorical force and awe-inspiring images that move readers and listeners of the Qurʾan. Of importance is the mood with which one ought to read the Qurʾan and the horizon one should foster. The reading of the scripture becomes manifest in a reverence that is sensed in the flesh. If the devout reader does not at times feel the goose bumps at some places of the scriptural reading and experiences delight at other places of the narrative, then the exercise might have to be repeated again. In other words, to read the Qurʾan is not merely reading. It is to read with the body.

Both outsiders and insiders experience this at least with the original Arabic recitation of the Qurʾan. Arthur J. Arberry (d. 1969), the doyen of British orientalists who produced an enviable translation of the Qurʾan, writes of his experience in Cairo while working on his translation. He reminisces about a prominent politician who was also his neighbor and at whose home a Qurʾan reciter chanted the scripture during the month of Ramadan. Arberry's enchantment is palpable when he writes,

> I would sit on the veranda of my Gezira house and listen entranced to the old, white-bearded Sheykh who chanted the Koran for the pious delectation of my neighbour. . . . It was then that I, the infidel, learnt to understand and react to the thrilling ryhthms of the Koran, only to be apprehended when listened to at such a time in such a place.[17]

Depending on one's mood, time, and place as well as the passage being recited or heard, many a reader or listener of the Qurʾan is moved to tears, ecstasy, and passion by the pure beauty and meaning of the scripture.

KNOWLEDGE, SIN, COSMOLOGY

Thanvi's observations about knowledge and sin actually channel the teachings of the ancient jurist-theologian, Muhammad bin Idris al-Shafiʿi. Shafiʿi was not only a towering eighth-century Muslim figure and the founder of what is now recognized as a major Sunni school of legal interpretation. Shafiʿi was also a gifted poet and a moralist, who famously said,

Every time life taught me
It exposed my intellect's deficits
The more learning I acquired
Life expanded my ignorance.[18]

Shafiʿi's talents captured in two memorable stanzas also immortalize his memory as an exemplar of "knowledge as salvation." Once, according to legend, Shafiʿi told his teacher Wakiʿ that he was unable to remember the things he had studied. Wakiʿ instinctively diagnosed the flaw in his student's moral profile. Forgetfulness of moral teachings, Wakiʿ explained, is a result of sin. In famous lines Shafiʿi recounts,

I lamented to Wakiʿ the poverty of my memory
He advised me to avoid sin
Knowledge is light, he informed me
Surely God's guiding light
To a sinner is denied outright.[19]

When knowledge turns into light, Wakiʿ says, it becomes a touchstone for the kind of morality and spirituality often fostered in madrasa communities.

The link between knowledge and cosmology made by Wakiʿ in his discussion of memory and forgetfulness is not unusual. North American native myths and Greek myths of religion, anthropologist Claude Levi-Strauss wrote, produced similar anxieties about forgetfulness. Forgetfulness was the result of a failure to communicate with oneself. In early Hindu traditions, forgetfulness was considered to be a metaphysical error. Hence, multiple Hindu stories describe how the powerful Shiva danced on the demon of forgetfulness.

Muslim ritual practices activate memories and narratives in which God, the Prophet Muhammad, his Companions, and the early and pious leaders (imams) of Islam feature prominently. These images, feelings, and sensibilities are made possible by what scholars of religion call cosmology and myth: in short, detailed and meaningful stories. These are the stories that provide the "meaning of meaning" to the lives of people. Cosmology is thus a complex amalgam of things that make up what we understand as the realm of existence or being, in other words, a true picture of reality consisting of fundamental meanings *and* feelings that provide a sense of fullness to all other meanings. In the language of philosophers, this meaning-giving aspect is called "ontology."

Qur'anic motifs too liken the instances when humans forget God to be equal to a scenario of forgetting oneself. In the Greek tradition, forgetfulness was part of an indiscretion which, in turn, results in giving false testimony or neglecting a duty, in other words, committing a sin. All this points to how knowledge and salvation in Islam inhabit a complex mythical substrate, as described by the term "cosmology." Thus Muslim cosmology shares deep and profound features with the mythical systems of other faith and cultural traditions.

What makes forgetfulness such an exorbitant lapse, according to traditional worldviews, is the intimate connection remembrance makes with ritual. For, if one forgets, then one can also neglect one's duty, the obligation to perform rituals. And the allure of ritual lies in the way it sustains a sense of continuity and belonging to a community. Yes, it is both knowledge and ritual that cement the individual to bodily practices. Yet the meanings of practices make sense only when a frame larger than the practitioners themselves, namely, the cosmos, is invoked. If forgetfulness becomes a permanent condition, then it sunders the bodily practices, disrupts meanings, and severs one's link with the cosmos.

KNOWLEDGE, NOMOS, NARRATIVE

Madrasas adhere to a *maslak*. What is a *maslak*? The word derives from the term "virtuous conduct" (*suluk*)—an expression frequently used by Muslim mystics. Virtuous conduct, at least one sense of it, means to act according to certain rules or standards (normativity). Madrasas lay down exhausting benchmarks in order to seamlessly connect religious beliefs to behavior. It is the requirement of conduct that differentiates madrasas from liberal and secular educational institutions.

Secular institutions do not require compliance to exacting standards in matters of personal conduct. Apart from pledging to shun sexual harassment, to abide by rules regulating alcohol consumption, and not to cheat, most modern public universities do not require students to comply to any other moral strictures of a religious kind, except voluntarily. Denominational colleges with a church or religious affiliation around the world and in the United States, of course, like madrasas, require adherence to a code of ethical living.

Madrasa students are required to adhere to a full regimen of moral teachings, ethical living, and pious practice. Madrasa students, in turn, follow the intellectual line of their respective schools on vital doctrinal issues. They attend daily prayers. They conform to the dress code in ways that almost resemble that of a holy order. Applying the knowledge acquired in one's daily life is at the heart of the madrasa enterprise. Similarly, scholarly interpretations remain within the boundaries of the madrasa's ideals, preferences, and values; advocacy of practices also comply with the standards of the *maslak*.

Another sense of a *maslak* is that of a story: a compelling narrative justifies the religious practices adopted. And this story is further validated because it conforms to the correct version of Islamic history. In other words, *maslak* is a keyword that describes how an institutional memory of virtuous conduct is constructed, sustained, and cherished by folk who follow tradition.

Counterpoint too is an essential element of a tradition-based life. The *maslak* as a narrative continuously harmonizes and realigns the present with some continuous logic of the past. Traditional practitioners see it as their highest goal to find a precedent or analogy—no matter how slender—in past practices or in the lives of the pious ancestors, in order to thread the continuity of reasoning from the past with new conditions.

Every madrasa franchise narrates its own version of institutional memory and showcases its theological goods of authenticity. Representatives of the Deoband school, for instance, explain their *maslak* as

> not merely devotion to principles or the worship of personalities; neither do they [adherents to the Deoband *maslak*] view literature on religion and religious instruction as sufficient on their own, nor do they regard role models on their own, or individual research or personal opinion and ideas as sufficient, nor do they place reliance and trust in the views and acts of role-models alone. *Rather, it is an amalgam of principles, rules, individual stories and personal biographies.* In short, literature on religion is only acceptable on condition that it involves the lived companionship of the righteous and allows for the formation of a virtuous temperament (*maslak*). To ignore any specific aspect of this is impermissible. The essence of this virtuous code is comprehensiveness, moderation, caution and a middle of the road approach. Hence, the distinctive feature of this virtuous code is that wisdom and moderation manifest in all di-

Master-Disciple Relations

In Sufism the master-disciple relationship is the essence of the spiritual development of a disciple. Similarly, apprenticeship with a master-teacher during one's education and training is equally essential to one's success to acquire not only book knowledge but also the wisdom that is associated with learning. The master-disciple or teacher-student model is derived from the example of the Prophet Muhammad and his relations with his Companions.

> mensions of religious and intellectual arguments, and these features are reflected in the most minute aspects of the study of the Qur'an and hadith, the study of law and theology, the discipline of spirituality and moral philosophy, etc. Wisdom and moderation is the operational model.[20] (Italics for emphasis mine.)

Accounts of the role models revered within a *maslak* would often start with how such a figure from childhood to adulthood endured hardships and received divine favors in order to attain piety and performed God's work as part of a narrative of sacred history. These stories thus construe an exemplary person whom others feel compelled to imitate.

The *maslak*-narrative is able to convey the message that the madrasa leadership also trains students in exactly the same way the Prophet Muhammad taught his Companions, namely, through the indispensable role of apprenticeship. And imitating the Prophet is an equally critical aspect of the *maslak*. The student–teacher relationship is a sacred one, like the relationship between Sufi master and disciple or the Prophet and his Companions. For the Deobandis this apprenticeship (*sohbat*), discussed later, is absolutely crucial just as it is in madrasas belonging to the Barelvi and Ahl-i Hadith madrasa franchises.

NARRATIVE FRAMINGS

The *maslak* also frames the larger interpretative paradigm. A whole set of nuanced doctrinal propositions are involved in the elaboration of the *maslak* by drawing on elements of the past tradition. Prefiguring future events based on pious and mystical insights is a vital element of the *maslak*-narrative. For instance, the death of Qasim Nanautvi, one of the founders of Deoband, is prefigured by one of his close associates. Yet note how the prediction in this style of religious thought is carefully construed with attention to an interpretation laden with tradition or received opinion.

The occasion is around 1876, when Nanautvi participated in the second of two highly publicized debates held in Chandapur in the North Indian district of Shahjahanpur billed as "The Festival of Recognizing the True God," an event sponsored by the British authorities.[21] In that town Nanautvi debated, among others, the Hindu leader Swami Dayanand Sarasvati and a European Christian by the name of Father Samuel Knowles.

After the Muslim side thought it had triumphed in the public debate, one of Qasim Nanautvi's associates, a relative and associate called Yaʿqub Nanautvi, made a prediction: "I got the feeling," Yaʿqub said, "that the time for the departure of our revered master [Qasim Nanautvi] from this world is imminent. God used him as a means to accomplish an important task. Thus, in a gathering of multiple faiths [the debate at Shahjahanpur] one of Islam's representatives announced God's truth to His creatures."[22]

Ashraf ʿAli Thanvi provides a clarification of this prediction. Yaʿqub Nanautvi was also Thanvi's teacher. His teacher's interpretation, says Thanvi, was "intuitive."[23] Its parallel, Thanvi writes, can be found in the predictions made by two Companions of the Prophet Muhammad, namely, ʿAbdullah Ibn ʿAbbas and ʿUmar bin al-Khattab, when they too sensed the imminent death of the Prophet Muhammad. They shared their predictions with their contemporaries soon after the revelation of the chapter in the Qurʾan called "The Triumph."[24] Here is a compelling example of how traditionalists employ counterpoint to authenticate their practices as part of their narrative. In doing so, it casts them as loyal followers of the Prophet as well as following in the footsteps of the Prophet's Companions, who are viewed as revered exemplars.

A nuanced understanding of the *maslak* can also result in fairly bold and unexpected interpretations. Ponder the interpretation offered by a prominent early twentieth-century figure, the inveterate anticolonial activist Mahmud Hasan (d. 1920), fondly known in Deobandi circles as "Shaykhul Hind" (Master Teacher of all India). The issue at hand is the fervent Muslim response to any criticism or satire leveled at the person of the Prophet Muhammad. Mahmud Hasan offered a different view. Muslim protests against blasphemous utterances directed at the Prophet,

The Triumph

When you see God's help and victory arrive
And you see people follow the path of salvation [*din*] in numbers
Then praise your Sustainer
And seek his forgiveness
For He always accepts repentance.
(Q 110:1–3)

he reasoned, for the better part, reflected the wounded psychology of the Muslim community more than a fulfillment of any theological imperative!

One of Mahmud Hasan's students, Manazir Ahsan Gilani (d. 1956), recalls his teacher's view during a class discussion on the commandment requiring Muslims to show undivided love and devotion to the Prophet Muhammad. "None of you truly believe," the Prophet Muhammad declared, "until I am more beloved to him than his kin, his wealth, and when I am more preferred to all other persons [in love]."[25]

Muslims had so fully internalized this commandment, Gilani told his teacher, Mahmud Hasan, that even the slightest contempt shown to the person or memory of the Prophet Muhammad would be intolerable. Indignant Muslims, he added, will not hesitate to sacrifice their lives in defense of the honor of the Prophet. Mahmud Hasan, Gilani explains, treated his student's comment as a teaching moment. Mahmud Hasan confirms that Muslims do indeed display their passion in response to blasphemous assaults on the honor of the Prophet. Yet, ironically, Mahmud Hasan questions whether Gilani had accurately diagnosed the motives behind such protests.

"Love," Mahmud Hasan explains, "requires that one sacrifice everything in order to please the beloved."[26] Then with biting wit he asks, did the religious conduct of the ordinary protesting Muslims really please the Prophet? Does the indignation Muslims display, he asks, truly symbolize their love for the Prophet? "Think about it," Mahmud Hasan then astutely remarks:

> contempt shown the Prophet, on whom be peace, unconsciously hides our own experience of that attempted scorn; actually it is the collective ego and self-esteem of the Muslims that feels wounded.

Select genealogy of Deobandi scholars from the eighteenth century to the present.

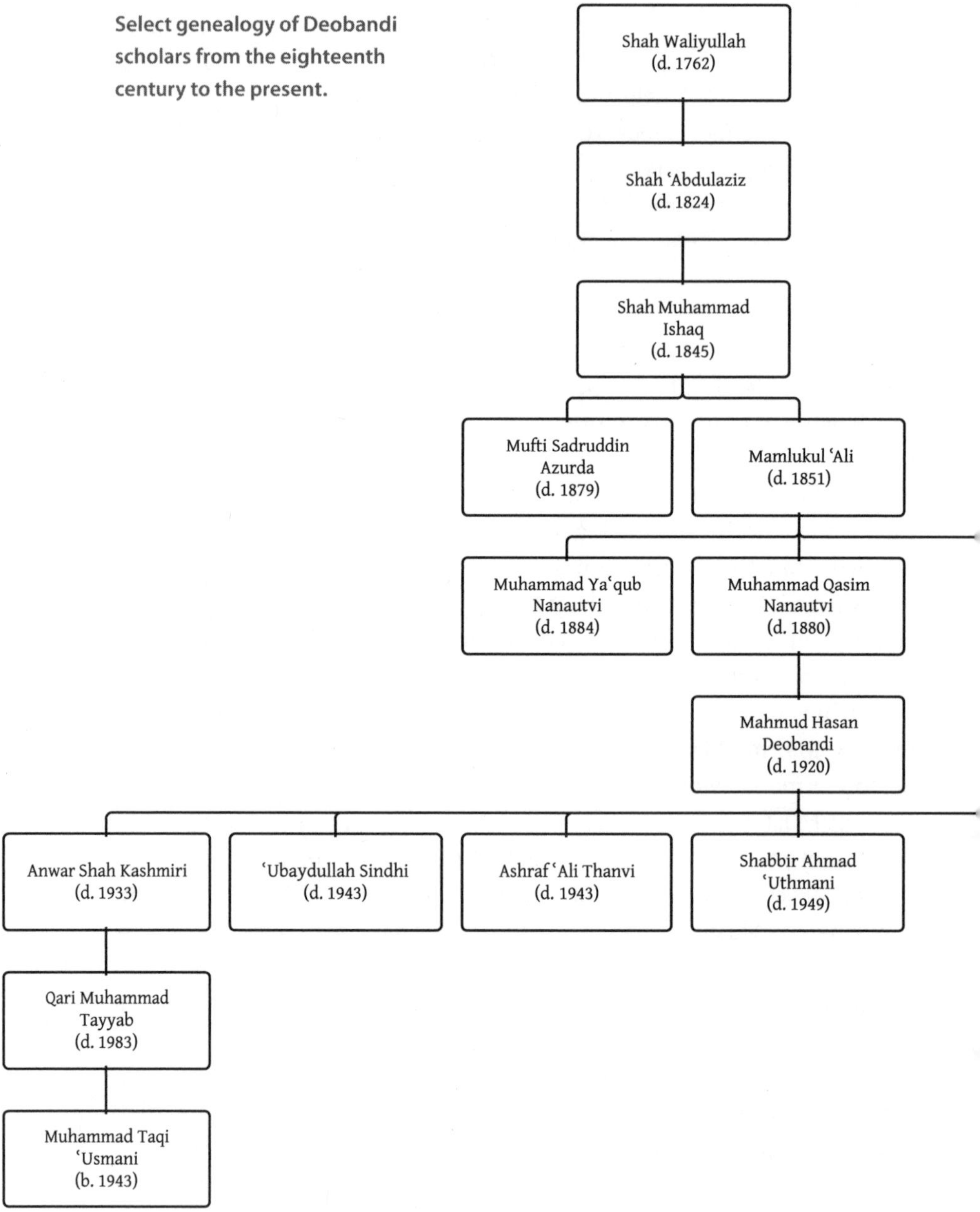

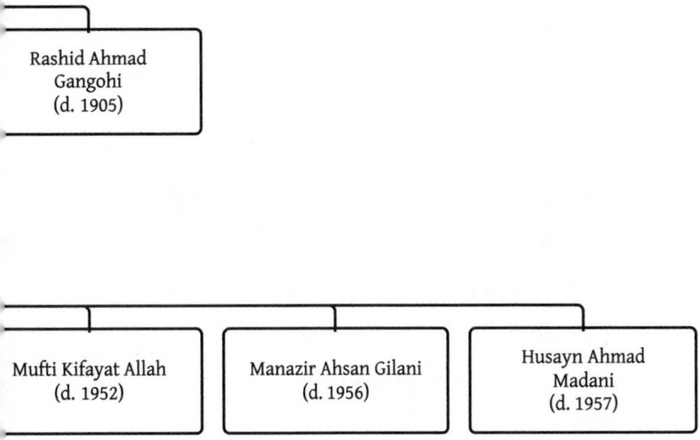
Rashid Ahmad Gangohi (d. 1905)
Mufti Kifayat Allah (d. 1952)
Manazir Ahsan Gilani (d. 1956)
Husayn Ahmad Madani (d. 1957)

Mahmud Hasan

Mahmud Hasan (1851–1920) is among the first generation of graduates of the Deoband seminary. He rose to become the highest authority, Shaykh, for the study of hadith at Deoband. His fine cohort of students later gained renown in the madrasa network and made a contribution to public life in South Asia in fields as diverse as religious scholarship, politics, and institution building. A scholar-activist, he furthered his anticolonial campaign by collaborating with Mahatma Gandhi and the Indian National Congress. Known as the "Master Teacher of all-India" Shaykhul Hind, he organized the "Silk Handkerchief Movement," a secret communication network, with the help of his students and activists to mobilize Muslims in order to undermine British rule. He was active in the Khilafat Movement, a campaign to support the Ottoman caliphate's anti-British stance during World War I. As a result of his revolutionary activities he was arrested by a pro-British governor while on pilgrimage in Mecca and then imprisoned on the island of Malta for three years and released in 1920. He was instrumental in the founding of a modern secular Muslim university called the Jamiʿa Millia Islamia, which is now based in Delhi. His noteworthy students include the following:

- Anwar Shah Kashmiri (1875–1933), a virtuoso hadith scholar at the Deoband seminary
- ʿUbaydullah Sindhi (1872–1944), a Sikh convert to Islam, a cosmopolitan scholar par excellence and an international political activist
- Manazir Ahsan Gilani (1892–1956), who prolifically recorded the history of Deoband's founders and served as a professor of Islamic Studies at Osmania University in Hyderabad
- Husayn Ahmad Madani (1879–1957), a hadith scholar at the Deoband seminary and a vocal anticolonial activist who was also imprisoned in Malta with his teacher

> Yet, whom we regard as Prophet and Messenger is not someone you can possibly humiliate. It is the collective ego, "we," that experiences the lash of contempt. To claim that love for the Prophet, on whom be peace, drives the desire to avenge such an offence is to only further a serious misunderstanding. Self-delusion is possibly the best description. Whoever contemplates this matter calmly will surely recognize their inconsistent conduct and will reach a similar conclusion [to mine]. Yet, people will go on claiming that their actions please their beloved, irrespective of the consequences. In the meanwhile, the daily calls to prayers go unanswered while the multitude indulge in futile and useless conversation and thus fail to hasten to the muezzin's invitation to pray. In all fairness: how appropriate is the proclamation of love for the Prophet made by the mouths of such people?[27]

Such a counterintuitive explanation from a pioneer of the Deoband school exhibits the intellectual confidence, sophistication, and maturity of a traditionalist interpretation. At their best, traditionalist discourses give priority to the big picture of Islam's ethical values rather than merely following the simplistic application of rules. Mahmud Hasan's point is a thoughtful one: to qualify as a serious defender of the Prophet Muhammad's honor requires a protagonist to make a prior commitment to the Prophet's basic teachings, an obligation that many frenzied protesters often ignore with impunity.

CONCLUSION

Muslim traditionalists in South Asia struggle to hold on to both the imperative of piety and the modern challenge to have the broadest grounding in knowledge. But the aspiration to integrate the full panoply of knowledge remains a struggle. A minority of voices have questioned whether madrasas should exclusively focus on knowledge of salvation as a priority, which remains the default position.

The absence of modern knowledge from madrasa curricula results in intellectual deficits. A theologian or an ethicist with a deep understanding of history or sociobiology will appreciate the development and evolution of values formed within religious systems and discourses much better than someone who lacks such training and expertise. Complexity and the interweaving of disciplines mark the world of knowledge today. Yet traditional madrasa scholars are still very much committed to a linear understanding of knowledge, with an appetite for hierarchies and dated taxonomies of knowledge. Often, an interdisciplinary approach does not make sense to many traditionalists and they dismiss it as a confusion of categories.

Robust internal debate about the future of the madrasa curriculum and the shape of knowledge that is required in order to produce meaningful Islamic discourses compatible with the emerging world Muslims live in will in all likelihood continue. Yet the phenomenal growth of madrasas defies all predictions about the secularization of Muslim societies. To the contrary, it shows that communities are increasingly invested in madrasa education for a variety of reasons. The power and influence of the ʿulama as religious authorities for Muslim communities are among the premier reasons for the growth in madrasas.[28] Even the modern educated sector of Muslim societies in South Asia concede that the Muslim community support the ʿulama, give them financial support, and entrust them with the religious education of their children.

PART TWO

History and Contexts

Madrasas in modern South Asia cannot be understood outside two powerful narratives: family franchises and theological disagreement over Islamic reform. Both of these narratives have contributed to the making of the contemporary albeit contested madrasa orthodoxies or traditions. Understanding the roots of the conflict is essential to configuring the different "franchises" or "brands" of Islam in South Asia, with each tradition competing for a share of the religious "market." Crucial eighteenth- and nineteenth-century orthodox figures staked their positions, giving rise to subsequent theological divisions known as the Deobandi, Barelvi, and Ahl- al-Hadith schools.

CHAPTER FOUR

Birth of the Contemporary Madrasa

"Whoever resides in India and ties the sacramental robes of learning will inevitably head for the Farangi Mahall," the noted scholar and historian Shibli Nuʿmani writes romantically after a visit to the great North Indian city of Lucknow in 1896. "When I paid a visit to the shrine of Mulla Nizamuddin and saw his modest upper story institution, to my utter surprise," he exclaims prayerfully, "I saw—God is greater than everything, *allahu akbar*, that this is India's own Cambridge [University]!"[1]

Nuʿmani exalts the accomplishments of one stellar family franchise known as the madrasa at Farangi Mahall, "The European's Mansion," named after the European merchant who once occupied the house in which the madrasa was founded. Three centuries ago, many family franchises and networks of individual scholars dotted the geography of precolonial and colonial India. Itinerant students received specialized training in different disciplines at these institutions. What held them together was a common but complex religious and cultural tradition.

From the middle of the eighteenth century up to the twenty-first century, competition between loosely organized madrasa networks remained intense. Scholarly rivalry driven by interfamily contestations and theologically driven ideologies were the prime movers. Families, scholars, students, and their supporters were the main actors in an unfolding drama of Muslim intellectual, political, and theological dueling that continues to play out today.

Individuals are indispensable to madrasa orthodoxy: their lives and accomplishments are formative. Without appreciating how individual scholars shape the tradition in order to become its mainstay is to forfeit a vital aspect of the madrasa orthodoxy in general and the modern South Asian madrasa tradition in particular. Madrasa orthodoxy curiously fuses personal charisma with institution-building measures in order to give certain individuals unprecedented visibility and influence. In turn, their institutions enjoy efficacy and longevity. A selection of scholarly personalities discussed in this chapter will demonstrate how these figures formed the backbone of the late modern or contemporary madrasa project and how they manufacture a variety of madrasa franchises. The nineteenth-century madrasa at Deoband and its mushrooming network across South Asia for over a century is the culmination of an evolutionary madrasa tradition and is discussed in what follows.

Two locales that could hardly be more different—the remote village of Sihali and the swarming metropolis of Delhi—are the sites where these dramas begin, but they radiate throughout the subcontinent, and later, beyond. As claimants to distinguished pedigrees and intellectual legacies, scholarly families from the eighteenth century onward achieved the aura of religious aristocracies in India. The events that besiege them are a combination of serendipity, tragedy, labor, and luck; they lead to jihad, to death, and to theological showdowns that still reverberate today.

SIHALI AND LUCKNOW: THE FARANGI MAHALL SCHOOL

In the winter of 1692, on or around March 27, the peace of Sihali was shattered by lawlessness and murder. Sihali, a large village known as a *qasba*, some nineteen miles (29 km) from Lucknow, the principal city of what is now the state of Uttar Pradesh in Mughal India, was where the prominent patrician of the pious Ansari family, Qutbuddin, resided. Malcontents torched his home, killing him and others in a cascading inferno.

Abu Ayyub al-Ansari

Abu Ayyub was a distinguished Companion of the Prophet Muhammad, a famed warrior-evangelist. According to legend he died during an unsuccessful Muslim siege of Constantinople, modern-day Istanbul, in the seventh century, although some modern historians question this claim. He is known as an *ansari* because he was among the Medinan Muslims who gave hospitality to their "migrant," *muhajir*, brethren. He was buried under the city walls of Istanbul. Today a huge mosque complex stands in his memory in one of that city's suburbs.

Qutbuddin was a renowned and distinguished scholar whose achievements had brought recognition from the Mughal emperor Aurangzeb (d. 1707) with whom he frequently corresponded. Qutbuddin's family roots go back to Herat, in Afghanistan. He carried a special badge of honor as a member of the Ansari lineage, descendants of a prominent Companion of the Prophet Muhammad, called Abu Ayyub al-Ansari.[2]

Qutbuddin's mastery of the rational humanistic tradition (*ʿaql*) together with the textual tradition (*naql*) enabled him to excel over his peers. Combinations of both rational and textual interpretative strategies in Muslim theology and moral philosophy are like points on a continuum rather than fundamental opposites. Muslim traditionalists often showcase their intellectual preferences in one or more stylistic registers.

One style makes its arguments in writings, lectures, and teachings by hewing closely to the utterances and formulations of the early generations of Islam. With copious use of proof-texts drawn from prophetic reports (hadith) and citations from the Qurʾan, this cohort of traditional scholars relies on ancient materials to persuade audiences of their positions. Another outcome is that they burnish their reputations as representatives of an authentic version of Islam.

Another cohort of traditionalists prefers the rhetoric of philosophy, logic, and rationalist theology as their style in arguments. In other words, they translate the messages of scripture into a reason-based discursive tradition and do little by way of "chapter and verse" citation and argumentation.

Perhaps the most accomplished traditionalists, the third style, are those who fuse both methods: they rely on the citation of authority

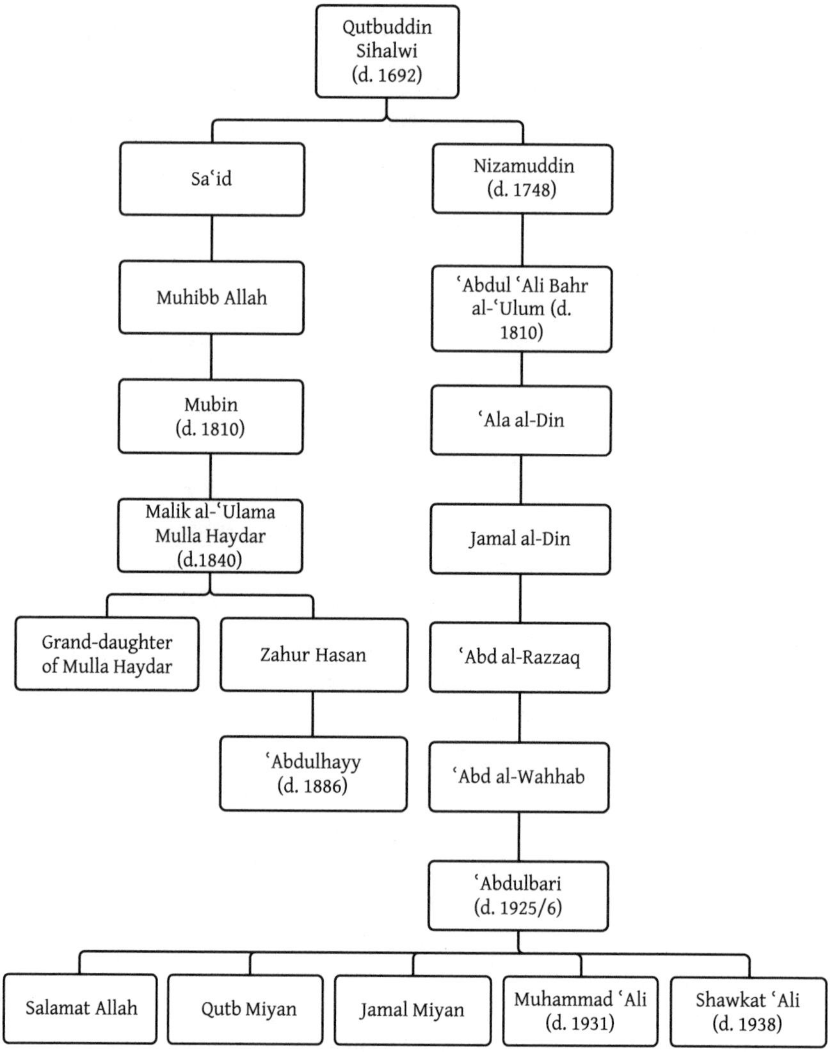

Key scholars in the Farangi Mahall school, whose founder produced the Nizami curriculum.

together with reason-based arguments in order to convince a range of audiences. Qutbuddin, like many of his contemporaries, established his credentials as one of these "ambidextrous" scholars: he mastered the art of citing ancient textual sources along with using the tools of logic and philosophy with generous doses of grammar, literature, rhetoric, poetry, theories of exegesis, and historiography. Men with high social aspirations, and some women too, mastered these disciplines.

Despite Qutbuddin's academic flair, one's reputation is not just based on style. If today a graduate's cache is measured by the prestige of the university or college he or she attended, then in madrasa circles the prestige of one's teacher and, later, one's spiritual master became, and remain, the marketing badges of a given scholar's reputation. On completing his formal studies at the late age of thirty, Qutbuddin went to seek a spiritual master.[3]

He found Qadi Sadruddin Ilahabadi, better known as Qadi Gahasi, of the Chishti Sufi order. Qadi Gahasi was the disciple of the renowned Muhibbullah Ilahabadi, one of India's most extraordinary figures in Muslim mysticism.[4]

What drew Qutbuddin to these kinds of figures? His teachers showed a strong commitment to the Akbari tradition. Members of the Akbari tradition follow the much-rhapsodized thirteenth-century mystic and intellectual Muhiyuddin Ibn ʿArabi from Muslim Spain.[5] Ibn ʿArabi imagined a world in the tranquil colors that marked the coexistence of all being; all reality reflected one God, and in many forms—from spiritual, animal, and human to vegetative and mineral. Qutbuddin's scholarly descendants, along with scores of other traditionalist scholars in South Asia, admired the exuberant metaphysics of Ibn ʿArabi, not least because during its best moments, it sponsored a spirit of tolerance and inclusion of all creation.

Such was the intellectual lineage of the man whose death precipitated the founding of a new institution in the modern period. The exact cause of Qutbuddin's death in 1692 remains shrouded in mystery. Some say he was the victim of a bitter rivalry between his own family and other landholders.[6] Others say the cause of Qutbuddin's death was jealousy and fear that his regular correspondence with the Emperor Aurangzeb might report the unlawful activities happening in the vicinity of Sihali.

Whatever the cause, the murder itself was a gory, traumatic business that was seared into his family's memory for generations. The casualties, beyond the death of the sixty-three-year-old scholar himself, included several wounded or deceased persons, and, significantly, Qutbuddin's precious library, containing some 700 books.[7] For the indignity he suffered at the hands of evil, posterity remembered him as a "martyr" (*shahid*), the highest honor accorded to one who dies in the service of knowledge and learning. Qutbuddin's fourteen-year-old son, Nizamuddin, was at first held captive by the malcontents but was later released.

Ibn ʿArabi

Muhiyuddin (Muhi al-Din) Ibn ʿArabi (1165–1240) is an unrivaled genius in the annals of Muslim history. His vatic thought is memorialized in his birthplace of Murcia in Muslim Spain to his resting place in Damascus and every place he traversed in between and beyond. His literary and intellectual marvel, *The Meccan Unveilings/Openings or Inrushes* (*al-Futuhat al-Makkiya*) is a virtual encyclopedia of religious thought in Islam. Together with *Bezels of Wisdom* (*Fusus al-Hikam*) and other works, Ibn ʿArabi's writings astounded generations of scholars for their insightful teachings, which hold that all of existence is interconnected and forms a singular unity. Many theologians generated controversy over his ideas, fearing they challenged existing theological doctrines. They were concerned that Ibn ʿArabi might erase the distinction between transcendence and immanence, the barrier between Creator and the created. Ibn ʿArabi did not conflate these perspectives; rather, he pointed to the complexity of being and proposed a better narrative for existence. Ibn ʿArabi has, over the centuries, maintained a steadfast audience on the Indian subcontinent. Most madrasa scholars revere his ideas and the mystical traditions he embodied. Of course, there are always a few detractors.

As we shall see, he would go on to emblazon the family name in his own career as a great scholar.

Shocked, outraged, and petrified by the violation this Ansari family suffered at the hands of Sihali's criminals, Qutbuddin's eldest son, Muhammad Saʿid, fled with his extended family and siblings to the safety of the city of Lucknow. Later, he traveled south to Hyderabad to lodge a personal complaint with Emperor Aurangzeb about the injustice and loss inflicted on his family. In a sign of support and sympathy for the deceased Qutbuddin, the emperor took immediate action against the murderers. As further consolation he awarded Qutbuddin's surviving family luxurious quarters in Lucknow that had recently been vacated by a European trader.

Indians thought of Europeans as the descendants of the ancient Franks, and hence they were known as the *franks* or *firangis* in Persian, a description that was retained in the Urdu language. The educational institution founded by Qutbuddin's children in the new quarters and sustained by several generations of his heirs until its demise in the early twentieth century became known as the Farangi Mahall school. The building still survives today.

Mulla Nizamuddin

Though some of the family sought and achieved distinction in Mughal India, the man most responsible for the rise of the Farangi Mahall school was none other than Nizamuddin (d. 1748), the youngest son of Qutbuddin, who became the legatee of this tragedy-marred family. Were it not for Nizamuddin's efforts, the star-studded scholarly lineup that bedecked the Farangi Mahall school might not have been possible. Nizamuddin inaugurated a rigorous scholarly tradition—later a curricular franchise for all madrasas—a task he dispatched with unsurpassed excellence. Not only was Nizamuddin an extraordinary scholar in his own right; he was a teacher's teacher, if not an outright intellectual giant. Later generations remembered him with the honorific of *Ustadh al-Hind*, "Teacher of Hindustan," in appreciation for his curricular innovations and writings.[8]

Nizamuddin, like his father, was exposed to and excelled in both the rational humanistic disciplines and the textual tradition. As soon as Nizamuddin became a professor at the age of twenty-five, his star rose rapidly. He attracted scores of students to his classes, which were held in a modest upper-level room in what is today Lucknow's old city. There, according to Shibli Nuʿmani, he singlehandedly established "India's Cambridge."[9]

Indeed, Nizamuddin's reputation as a pious and devout figure did not lag far behind his talents as a scholar par excellence. Different from his father's Sufi order, he affiliated to the Qadiri mystical order, one of the earliest Sufi brotherhoods dating back to the twelfth century. Nizamuddin made a statement about his own moral thinking when at the age of forty he chose the extraordinary and famed mystic Shaykh ʿAbdurrazzaq bin ʿAbdurrahim al-Husayni of Bansa (d. 1724) as his spiritual master. Like several other Sufi masters, Shaykh ʿAbdurrazzaq had little formal training in the disciplines of religious thought. But he was said to have reached a very high rung in mystical and spiritual sophistication. Guided by him, Nizamuddin carried himself with an impeccable reputation and became renowned for his generosity, intense devotions, and extraordinarily high moral conduct. As a sign of humility, he avoided wearing a large turban and the customary scholarly gown that sported extravagantly wide sleeves, even though that was the fashion among the scholarly elites of his day.

Posterity remembers Nizamuddin for his ability to select classical texts for an educational syllabus that produced highly skilled and literate scholars, bureaucrats, writers, and intellectuals in his day. At the time, the beauty of the Nizami curriculum, *Dars-i Nizami* (see chapter 6), named after its author Nizamuddin, was that each text was carefully selected for its pedagogical merits commensurate with the level of development of a student. Despite many mutations over the centuries, the curriculum still carries his imprint and is to this day taught in thousands of madrasas in South Asia and beyond. From the outset Nizamuddin's goal was to produce a graduate who would think logically, acquire excellent writing and linguistic skills, and above all know enough about Islam as a religious tradition to address issues beyond basic questions of religious practice.

A student who completed the Nizami curriculum, for instance, would not immediately be proficient or equipped to issue legal opinions (fatwas) or speak too authoritatively about the Qur'an. In order to reach advanced levels in these subjects, students today, as in the past, are required to pursue higher studies through apprenticeships in order to demonstrate their expertise in Islamic law, Qur'anic exegesis, or any specialty interest. If anything, the Nizami syllabus—in the madrasa-sphere of education—fulfills the equivalent of what we today would call a basic college education, where a student selects a range of subjects and acquires a range of crucial skills. The only difference is that students in the basic Nizami curriculum do not choose a major. The curriculum has a default major that has changed focus over time.

The early iteration of the Nizami curriculum centered on subjects like philosophy, logic, and theology, features that also became the trademark of the Farangi Mahall school. In the twentieth and twenty-first centuries the emphasis in madrasa education has shifted to prophetic traditions and Islamic law in almost all the theological denominations of Sunnism. Shiʿa madrasas have followed a different path.

Like his father, Nizamuddin believed in grounding students in the rational disciplines, making this the foundation on which to build

Sufi Orders

All Sufi orders trace the origins of the pious and contemplative practices to the Prophet Muhammad and some of his Companions. Each Sufi order or path (*tariqa*) has networked connections, called a *silsila*, literally meaning a chain, which allows initiates to identify with the complex tree of Sufi masters and their disciples. Sub-branches within each order abound, as do hybrids like the Sabri-Chisti orders. Each mystical order has its own practices, teachings, and peculiarities, which are documented in handbooks. Some might permit the use of music for spiritual elevation, whereas others will forbid it; some will encourage vocal chanting of the divine names and prayers, while others will prefer silent vigils. Some Sufis will, over a lifetime, be affiliated with one or more Sufi masters, *shaykh*, plural *shuyukh*, each belonging to a different order. Several Sufi orders flourish in South Asia, a few of which are the following:

- *Qadiri*, named after ʿAbd al-Qadir al-Jilani (d. 1166), one of the oldest formal Sufi orders in Islamdom. He hailed from the region of Daylam on the southwest coast of the Caspian Sea. In Mughal India, several influential Qadiri masters shaped the religious landscape, such as Makhdum Muhammad Gilani Halabi (d. 1516), ʿAli Muttaqi al-Hindi (d. 1568), Shaykh Dawud Kirmani Shergarhi (d. 1574), Shaykh Musa Pak Shahid (d. 1592), and Abd al-Haqq Muhaddith Dihlawi (1642), among others.
- *Chishti* order, named after Muʿinuddin Muhammad Chishti (d. 1236), who came to India in 1193 from Sistan and died in Ajmer, India. This order has widespread presence in India, Pakistan, and Bangladesh and beyond. One of the most renowned members of this order is Nizamuddin Awliya, buried in a suburb of Delhi after his name.
- *Naqshbandi*, named after Bahaʾuddin Muhammad Naqshband (d. 1389), who originated from Bukhara in Central Asia. Towering Indian figures in this order were Khwaja Baqibillah (d. 1603), Ahmad Sirhindi (d. 1624), and Shah Waliyullah (d. 1762).

FURTHER READING

Carl W. Ernst and Bruce B. Lawrence, *Sufi Martyrs of Love*, 2002.
Riazul Islam, *Sufism in South Asia*, 2002.
Robert Rozehnal, *Islamic Sufism Unbound*, 2007.

subsequent specialties, be it law, civil service, or perhaps a career as a writer or a teacher of theology or philosophy, among other professions. Designed around texts, the curriculum helped the student to grasp the essentials of a subject. Puzzle-like, these texts are terse and enigmatic, even for qualified scholars. To challenge the student and instill a set of forensic skills—the ability to analyze and solve textual and literary puzzles—was the goal of the curriculum.[10]

The Farangi Mahall school continued its tradition for at least a century and a half. It lost its luster only in the early part of the twentieth century when other institutions like the Deoband school surpassed it. Many of Nizamuddin's nephews (whom he personally trained) and their offspring gained high visibility, status, and distinction in scholarly circles throughout the eighteenth century and continued to serve as intellectual beacons for the Muslims of India and beyond.

Portrait of a Scholarly Life: ʿAbdul ʿAli (d. 1810)

Nizamuddin also trained his own son, the remarkable ʿAbdul ʿAli, who became a renowned scholar and enjoyed such honorifics as "the Ocean of Learning," while others called him "the King of Scholars."[11]

If rivals stereotyped the Farangi Mahall school as a one-trick pony institution which only excelled at teaching the rationalist disciplines and lacked expertise in religious learning, then the genius of ʿAbdul ʿAli defied such critics. His talent in Islamic law and legal theory was unmatched and was equal to his impressive accomplishments in philosophy, logic, and theology.[12]

Distracted from scholarship at first by the malaise of adolescence and quail-fighting, ʿAbdul ʿAli eventually became inspired to pursue his father's footsteps. As an adult, he often went to his father's graveside for inspiration.[13] "Whenever he found textual passages difficult to solve," one biographer writes, "he retreated to the spiritual aura of his father and finally reached such intellectual heights that he became an unsurpassed virtuoso in both the rational disciplines and tradition-based learning, equally adept at discursive and spiritual learning."[14]

Tuition with the esteemed Kamaluddin Fatehpuri, a distant relative and his father's brightest student, sharpened ʿAbdul ʿAli's debating skills in legal polemics.[15] Fatehpuri in his carefree style believed in his student's talent and predicted his name would be emblazoned in the same pantheon as the famous Persian thinkers Mulla Sadra and Jalaluddin Dawwani. Sadra and Dawwani not only excelled in mystical theology, but both Persian scholars owned transcendent reputations for their mastery in philosophy.

For some years ʿAbdul ʿAli taught at his father's school in Lucknow, from where his scholarly reputation spread far and wide. He wrote prolifically, compiling insightful commentaries on legal and philosophical texts. Unlike his cloistered and saintlike father, ʿAbdul ʿAli was profoundly confident in the public realm. He basked in the pageantry of public life associated with scholarship and frequently indulged in debates and exacting polemics with rivals. Intellectually astute, he wrote an unparalleled commentary on a major text in theoretical jurisprudence authored by his grandfather's star student, the acclaimed Muhibullah al-Ansari (d. 1706), also known as Bihari, a reference to his origins in the state of Bihar. Much of ʿAbdul ʿAli's work remains authoritative in the Hanafi legal school after nearly two centuries.

ʿAbdul ʿAli's exit from Lucknow was prompted by Shiʿa anger during one Muharram, the first month in the Islamic calendar, and a time of mourning during which passion-play (*taʿziya*) processions are staged to commemorate a major tragedy in the history of Islam. A wooden baldachin—a portable canopy resembling a mausoleum representing the grave of the martyred Husayn, the Prophet's grandson—was vandalized while it was paraded in public in the Farangi Mahall neighborhood. ʿAbdul ʿAli, reports say, was busy offering a benediction. He surmised the procession lost its way into his neighborhood when he heard the racket produced by the multitude. In order not to interrupt his own ritual, he made a gesture intended to tell his students to redirect the procession from his alley. For some reason, his students interpreted his hand gesture as a sign of disapproval of the event. In turn, they promptly disrupted the procession and shattered the *taʿziya*. Sectarian Sunni-versus-Shiʿa tensions escalated. His learned cousins among the Ansari clan were reticent to support him, thanks to preexisting rivalries, petty jealousies, and family squabbles. All this left a bitter taste in ʿAbdul ʿAli's mouth; in disgust he parted with his extended family and the city of his birth, never to return.

From Lucknow he moved to Shahjahanpur, a city just over 100 miles (168 km) away where the amir, Nawab Hafizul Mulk, his new patron, warmly received him. For two decades he taught large numbers of students while compiling books in relative comfort. But once political rivals ousted Hafizul Mulk, then ʿAbdul ʿAli had little choice but to find a patron in Rampur.

Some 100 miles from Shahjahanpur, Nawab Fayzullah Khan of Rampur became his new patron. Now ʿAbdul ʿAli and his entourage of students moved into Rampur's renowned and established institutions. But soaring enrollments and student stipends put a strain on the nawab's budget. Fortuitously, another royal from West Bengal called Sadruddin Burduwani invited ʿAbdul ʿAli to teach at his institute of higher learning located in a village called Buhar, in the district of Burdwan, known as Bardhaman today. Here ʿAbdul ʿAli spent a few years and lived on a princely monthly salary of 400 rupees, earning more than the beginning salary of physicians at the time.[16] However, when his relations with Sadruddin deteriorated for some unknown reason, he made the critical decision to move to the southern city of Madras.

Facing the Bay of Bengal, Madras in the eighteenth century, renamed Chennai today, was one of India's finest cities. Ranked then as the second largest thriving metropolitan city with a population of over 300,000 people, it was only to be surpassed by Calcutta. Its tropical climate, copious palms, and a window onto the ocean made Madras attractive for Indians, as well as for foreigners increasingly drawn to the east. By the eighteenth century the East India Company made Madras one of its most important centers.

Today Chennai is the capital of the state of Tamil Nadu. Once it was part of a large region called Carnatic. Muhammad ʿAli Khan Wala Jah, the Anglophile nawab of Arcot (d. 1795), became the ruler of the region in 1749, settling generations of conflicts with decisive force. A descendant of the caliph ʿUmar, the second leader to succeed the Prophet Muhammad, the nawab was a man of high literary taste, dignity, and courtesy who gave generously to churches and temples. Despite a stable, five-decade-long rule from the city of Arcot, near Vellore, some eighty miles west of Madras, he fatefully bankrolled the proxy conflicts between the French and the British in Mysore and Hyderabad, wars that ultimately unraveled his power. His need for cash to support his extravagant military adventures forced him to make more territorial concessions to the British. It was around this time of declining power that the nawab was keen to patronize a great scholar who could lend him both legitimacy and visibility. ʿAbdul ʿAli became the perfect candidate.

East India Company

The East India Company was an English and later British joint-stock company, which received a royal charter from Queen Elizabeth in 1600. The company was dissolved in 1874. It was meant to trade with the East Indies but ended up trading with the Indian subcontinent. The company came to rule India with its private armies. Company rule began in 1757 and ended in 1858 when the British Crown assumed direct control over India in the British Raj. Links and access to India were established during the reign of the Mughal ruler Jahangir (r. 1605–1627).

BRITISH INDIA (1612–1947)
East India Company, 1612–1757
Company rule in India, 1757–1858
British Raj, 1858–1947
British rule in Burma, 1824–1948
Princely states, 1721–1949
Partition of India, 1947

When in 1780 ʿAbdul ʿAli, the son of the renowned Mulla Nizamuddin, arrived in Madras, with some 600 students and scholars in tow, the nawab fêted him with a lavish reception rarely offered to scholars. All the ministers of state were required to be in attendance as he entered the nawab's palace. In an unusual gesture, the nawab refused to let the scholar walk unaided into his palace and personally lent his shoulder to carry the palanquin in which ʿAbdul ʿAli was traveling into the royal reception hall. After seating him in the throne room, the nawab showed the utmost reverence to ʿAbdul ʿAli, kissing his feet in a symbolic gesture to honor the stature of scholars over even royalty. ʿAbdul ʿAli must have relished the moment in Madras with both humility and pride after enduring humiliation in Lucknow over the passion-play (*taʿzia*) debacle several decades earlier.

The nawab of Arcot appointed special cooks and assistants to provide for ʿAbdul ʿAli's every need and built a new madrasa for him to teach, where all students were provided with generous stipends. All the subsequent rulers of Carnatic treated him with high honors, and at times

ʿAbdul ʿAli played the role of kingmaker among the nawab's warring successors. When the Wala Jahis lost Madras to the British East India Company, even the English provided him with gifts and a monthly stipend until he died in 1810. He is buried in the courtyard of the mosque of the Wala Jahis in Chennai.[17]

Genius at Twilight: ʿAbdulhayy of Lucknow (1848–1886)

Closing the era of internationally renowned scholars among the Ansaris of Farangi Mahall was ʿAbdulhayy (d. 1886), better known in scholarly circles as ʿAbdulhayy of Lucknow (al-Laknawi).[18] ʿAbdulhayy was a descendant of Nizamuddin's less well-known brother, Muhammad Saʿid. Within a short lifespan of thirty-nine years, ʿAbdulhayy wrote nearly 107 works ranging from epistles and reflections on special topics to commentaries and books on the major Hanafi law texts. He had a profound command of the study of prophetic traditions (hadith), to which several works testify. He too in his youth showed little interest in scholarship. Once when thousands flocked to hear him give a public talk, a friend reminded ʿAbdulhayy of his youthful truancy. He replied, in all modesty, "It is only thanks to the generosity of God that I came to know something."[19] In recent years, leading Arab scholars have enthusiastically embraced ʿAbdulhayy's scholarly legacy. Some have dedicated their lives to the republication and circulation of his writings.[20]

The study of history, ʿAbdulhayy believed, was a crucial component to the study of tradition. He led by example, penning biographical dictionaries of Hanafi scholars. He is regarded as the last of the major Hanafi authorities in the modern era. At the same time, he did not lag behind in the Farangi Mahall trademark of mastery of the rational tradition, and he challenged several contemporaries on their readings of classical logic.

ʿAbdulhayy maintained exacting academic standards, which led to frequent cavils with fellow scholars. He engaged in robust intellectual exchange with Nawab Siddiq Hasan Khan Qannawji (d. 1890), who was affiliated with the Ahl-i Hadith tradition, nowadays known as the Salafis, which rivaled the Hanafi school. For the Salafis, only the authority of the Qurʾan and the prophetic tradition mattered in terms of Islamic teachings; they showed disdain for the historical law schools. No love is lost between the Ahl-i Hadith and the Hanafis, and plenty of polemical shards fly between the two groups to this very day. ʿAbdulhayy confessed to be a moderate Hanafi, and he held the authority of the prophetic traditions to be sacrosanct and authoritative if they contradicted the opinions of the Hanafi school. Despite that overture to the Ahl-i Hadith, ʿAbdulhayy and Qannawji still found much to disagree about.

Intellectual differences apart, the two men had great mutual respect for each other. When Qannawji heard of ʿAbdulhayy's passing, he was grief-stricken by the loss of an intellectual soul mate. On hearing of ʿAbdulhayy's death, in grief he refused to eat dinner, and as head of the government of Bhopal, he ordered that a three-day mourning period be observed.

For a short while ʿAbdulhayy pursued a career in judgeship in Hyderabad, a vocation his father had pursued for most of his life. Despite the promise of promotion in the profession, he decided to return to Lucknow in order to pursue teaching and writing. He twice made the pilgrimage to Arabia and earned scholarly affiliations from such reputed figures as the Meccan scholar Shaykh Sayyid Ahmad Zayni Dahlan (d. 1886). From the latter he received the validation to report hadith, a major endorsement of his stature as a scholar.

A married man, ʿAbdulhayy had no offspring for several years. On the advice of his mother, he undertook a forty-day prayer vigil for benefaction at the holy tomb and shrine of the saint Shaykh ʿAbdurrazzaq of Bansa, who was the spiritual master of his famous granduncle, Nizamuddin. A few months after this vigil, his wife was blessed with a child. Several more children followed, but only one daughter survived to continue the family name.

A few days before his death, reports say, ʿAbdulhayy attended a *mawlid* ceremony, a feast at which odes and praise poetry are sung to commemorate the birth of the Prophet Muhammad. He seemed to approve of the religious topography prevalent in North India at the time, and its popular festivities and rituals. In the early part of the nineteenth century, an emerging trend discredited such popular practices as both superstitious and doctrinally harmful. His decision to undertake the vigil and participate in this celebratory feast suggests that in ʿAbdulhayy, an Erasmus-like theological disposition subscribed to a traditional cosmology in which sainthood and saintly charisma counted as religiously valid practices that allowed for a complicated transference between the living and their dead forebears. Devout religious scholars were allowed all manner of ontological assumptions about themselves in relation to both their pious ancestors and the Prophet Muhammad. This approach would have been much to the chagrin of his puritan contemporaries; the Ahl-i Hadith was not the only group that opposed such practices.

In the same period that some of the celebrity scholars of the Farangi Mahall school flourished, new theological stirrings challenged this old-style religiosity. The resulting conflict created a fresh social and intellectual wave that would propel one wing of traditional Islam in India onto another path.

DELHI: NEW WAVE OF THEOLOGICAL RENEWAL

In India, stirrings of religious and social reform began in the eighteenth century. But reformist efforts intensified after the English consolidated power in Delhi and its surrounds, in the first quarter of the nineteenth century. At that moment a group of Delhi-based divines agonized over how to secure Muslim interests in the face of waning Mughal political influence. Connected to vintage Sufi networks, these Delhi-based scholars renamed their spiritual order as the Muhammadan Path, Tariqa Muhammadiyya. They did this for at least two reasons: to highlight their loyalty to the teachings of the founder of Islam and to distance themselves from what they viewed as the corrupting deviations in popular Muslim religious practices.

Two well-placed religious figures, Sayyid Ahmad of Rae Bareli (d. 1831), hereafter referred to as Sayyid Ahmad, and Shah Muhammad Isma'il (d. 1831) of Delhi, hereafter referred to as Shah Isma'il, were the public faces of the movement. They preached movingly to large audiences, telling the faithful that gross superstition distorted Muslim beliefs and by implication it imperiled their religious practices and relationship with God.

Many Muslims in early colonial India found solace, as many Muslims do today, in directing their spiritual attention to the tombs of saints. They believe in the curative powers of amulets and make requests for prayers as well as seek the help of saints to intercede on their behalf with God. Ornate and ecstatic anniversary celebrations of saints attended by hundreds of thousands of the faithful are commemorated all over the Indo-Pak subcontinent, as well as in other parts of the Muslim world.

In his writings, Shah Isma'il and his Tariqa Muhammadiyya followers strongly condemned these popular practices. Determined to break the spell of personality cults that he believed mesmerized illiterate Muslims and robbed them of their agency, Shah Isma'il turned out to be the theorist-scholar of the movement and copiously wrote popular treatises in the emerging Urdu language. To honor God and to revere the Prophet Muhammad, in his view, could only take place along lines approved by scriptural tradition. Unauthorized rituals, he preached, were unmistakable paths to heresy. He railed against ecstatic festivities celebrating the birthday of the Prophet Muhammad and declared the anniversaries of saints as unlawful. As a revolutionary reformer, he held that only correct beliefs could transform humanity and enable society to reach its highest moral and social aspirations. This model of societal reform, he believed, replicated the model of the Prophet Muhammad devised in seventh-century Arabia.

Shah Ismaʿil occasionally garnished his prose with polemical phrases that turned out, for his critics, to be proverbial theological lightning rods. He chafed at claims that prophets, saints, martyrs, and spiritual masters could make special pleadings to God in order to save their devotees in the afterlife. Only the Prophet Muhammad, he conceded, could intercede on behalf of his followers, and that could be done with the permission of God alone. His clarification was meant to counter popular beliefs that God was in some sense indebted to the Prophet Muhammad, and therefore He allowed him to intercede. Shah Ismaʿil's theological push-back was a delicate matter, since certain interpretations of Islam put the Prophet Muhammad at the apex of the human-God relationship and endowed the Prophet with special privileges.

To believe that God was indebted to certain eminent human beings was, for Shah Ismaʿil, nothing but a backhanded version of anthropomorphism. "Whoever believes that any prophet, saint, divinely guided leader, martyr, angel, and spiritual master can intercede in the divine court in such a fashion," Shah Ismaʿil exploded, "is actually a polytheist."[21] "Such a person is nothing but an incurable ignoramus who did not even possess an iota of understanding what the term 'God' meant," he warned. "Nor did he recognize the power of this 'master of the universe,'" he added.[22]

Saturated with liturgical and Qurʿanic allusions to God's unmatched majesty and sovereignty, Shah Ismaʿil's most highly proclaimed book, *Sustaining Faith*, contained lusty polemical duels and caricatures of popular beliefs in violation of Islamic doctrines. His anxiety centered on reverence for prophets and saints that could lead unsuspecting laypeople on the perilous path of deification. Stepping up the rhetorical pitch in a citation that continues to haunt his legacy with controversy is the line where Shah Ismaʿil intended to explain God's inimitable power.

"The status of this sovereign of kings [God] is such that in a single moment He could deploy the command, '*be*,' if He so desired, in order to create millions of prophets, saints, jinns, and angels, even the equivalent of the archangel Gabriel and Muhammad, on whom be prayers and peace," Shah Ismāʿīl writes. "With a single breath, God can destroy both the heavenly throne and the earth, if only to replace them with another universe. It only requires for God to will it and anything happens," he adds. "God does not require any means or instruments to realize any act. And, if the entirety of humanity—those preceding us and those to follow—were to turn into paragons of virtue like the archangel Gabriel and the Prophet [Muhammad] then not a thing will supplement God's grandeur nor His dominion as the 'master of the universe'; and, if all of humanity turned into devils and the anti-Christ, they would be incapable of diminishing anything of His grandeur. He remains under all circumstances the most supreme of the supreme and the sovereign of kings."[23]

With these words Shah Ismaʿil seeded theological spores that would fertilize conflicts among Sunni Muslims on the subcontinent for nearly two centuries. His critics ignore his arguments about divine sovereignty and instead claim his words make it thinkable that another Muhammad is somehow possible. Such a thought in itself, they argue, is theologically offensive.

Virtuoso Scholar and Mystic: Shah Waliyullah of Delhi (1703–1762)

The man at the center of these disputes, Shah Ismaʿil, was the grandson of the much-rhapsodized Shah Waliyullah (d. 1762) of Delhi, a virtuoso scholar and mystic whose inspiration touched a cross section of Islamic ideologies on the subcontinent. As a contemporary of Mulla Nizamuddin, Waliyullah's broad-spectrum legacy had profoundly shaped Muslim religious discourse in India. His prolific and influential writings apart, he was a part-time political activist and a Sufi who cultivated a transnational audience. He was affiliated to the Naqshbandi Sufi order but maintained an ecumenical approach to the other Sufi orders.

Enigmatic yet crucial instances of divine inspiration are central to Waliyullah's teachings. In Waliyullah's visions the Prophet Muhammad

Shah Waliyullah's grave in Delhi, India. (Picture: Kashif-ul-Huda, TwoCircles.net)

validated his plans to articulate religious knowledge in the rational discourse of his time. In Mecca he dreamed the Prophet Muhammad's grandsons, Hasan and Husayn, gave him a pen with a message: "This is the pen of our grandfather, the Messenger of Allah, on whom be peace and blessings."[24] On the evidence of these esoteric communiqués, Waliyullah, in his magisterial work *God's Conclusive Proof*, persuasively casts Muslim moral philosophy (Shariʿa) in a rational and analytical framework. While Shariʿa teachings are based on revelatory inspiration, he explains, they are also equally subject to rational discourse. Most decisive and to his credit, Waliyullah's most influential contribution was to refresh the debate on the need to engage in independent reasoning (*ijtihad*) in the realm of moral philosophy in order to lessen the reliance on anachronistic models of authority (*taqlid*).

He was equally astute in politics. As the Mughals were reduced to chessboard kings, Waliyullah felt the portents of looming danger in Delhi. The city had a growing population of just over 100,000 residents, and the Hindu Marathas had gained greater power and surpassed the Muslims in military might. Corresponding with warlords in neighboring Afghanistan, Waliyullah welcomed periodic raids on Delhi by Afghan warlords in order to weaken the increasingly growing power of the menacing Marathas. But these incursions and instability also angered many of Delhi's elites, earning him some notoriety too.

Sayyid Ahmad of Rae Bareli: Jihad for Salvation

The person who perhaps felt most compelled to decisively fill the power vacuum Muslims in Delhi faced as Mughal power declined was the warrior and ascetic figure Sayyid Ahmad. He hailed from a village near the city of Rae Bareli called Takia Kalan, home to a Sufi lodge. Sayyid Ahmad was a student and, later, a spiritual disciple of Waliyullah's most distinguished scholarly son, Shah ʿAbdulaziz. He moved to the principality of Tonk in Rajasthan, where he trained as a soldier, showing remarkable talents in self-discipline. He found his métier and passion in mysticism and its teachings on self-formation. His military persona, together with his spiritual orientation, turned out to be a life-transforming event. Seven years after leaving Delhi, Sayyid Ahmad returned as both a highly accomplished spiritual magnet and a gallant soldier, charming both the city's laity and its elite circles with his immense charisma.

His martial virtues demonstrated a certain kind of masculinity—the traits of bravery and willingness to sacrifice—in courageous leadership at a time of turbulence and declining native political fortunes in colonial India. Among the influential people he recruited to his cause was none other than Shah Ismaʿil (Shah Waliyullah's grandson) for his jihad plans in order to protect Muslim interests in India. If Shah Ismaʿil is cast as the intellectual of the jihad movement, then Sayyid Ahmad turns out to be the warrior-monk.

These two leaders from North India struck alliances with fiercely independent Pashtun tribes near Khyber, offering them help to regain their independence from Ranjit Singh, who had annexed their territories to the Punjab in 1818. As the antislavery advocate Frederick Douglass began his freedom campaigns in America, in India around the same time Sayyid

Ahmad and Shah Isma'il prepared to wage religiously sanctioned military efforts (jihad) in a bid to establish an Islamic emirate in this far outpost of the Indian subcontinent. The Sikh rulers' forces, however, proved superior, and in 1831 Sayyid Ahmad and Shah Isma'il were killed together with hundreds of their followers, in a place called Balakot in today's Pakistan.

Yet their defeat never really extinguished the ambition that soaked the faith of their many admirers. The goal was to one day establish a legitimate Islamic political order on the subcontinent. A quarter century after the martyrdom of Sayyid Ahmad and Shah Isma'il, when Indians of different faiths revolted against British dominance in 1857, the aspiration to wage a military struggle (jihad) against the colonizers under the banner of Islam was again briefly fanned and rekindled by a respectable sector of Muslim religious leaders in India. Eventually, the ambition to create an Islamic order of some sort was curated in two political contexts: in the ethos of a new madrasa founded in 1867 in the town of Deoband, some 100 miles from Delhi and its satellites on the subcontinent and beyond; and in the twentieth century the founding of Pakistan, which embodied a political order directed by a Muslim majority.

Ironically, the theological views of the founders of the Muhammadan Path were incorporated in two distinct threads of the madrasa-sphere, namely, the Deoband seminary and the schools of their bitter rivals, the Ahl-i Hadith (known in Urdu as Ahl-i Hadis) franchise of seminaries, who favored a strictly scriptural interpretation of faith. Not unlike the ideology of the American Puritan figure Jonathan Edwards in the eighteenth century, the ideology of Sayyid Ahmad and Shah Isma'il was a coherent narrative where God, polity, religion, and tradition were all components of a single recipe for salvation on earth as a precondition for similar honors in the afterlife. If it was necessary to pick up arms and wage war in order to defend God's cause, then that was a sacrifice that these two men and their followers were prepared to make.

It remains a subject of debate whether the ideas of Muhammad ibn Abdulwahhab (d. 1792), the Arabian religious reformer and the author of starchy puritan doctrines known as Wahhabism, inspired the leadership of the Muhammadan Path. It is, however, libelous to say that Waliyullah was a fan of Wahhabism or was a "fundamentalist," as some authors erroneously do, when both men were contemporaries and Abdulwahhab outlived Waliyullah by three decades.[25] Two men of religion could not be more different in their theological and religious outlooks as Waliyullah and Abdulwahhab were. Waliyullah's grandson Shah Ismaʿil could plausibly have been influenced by Abdulwahhab's ideas amid some scholarly controversy.

The Khairabadis: The Rational Counterpunch of Fazl-i Haqq Khairabadi (1796–1861)

Shah Ismaʿil's theological views met with resistance from a not unfamiliar quarter. Fazl-i Haqq Khairabadi (d. 1861) was the star student of Shah ʿAbdulaziz, who was in turn Shah Ismaʿil's uncle. Fazl-i Haqq felt sufficiently indignant to take on his teacher's nephew over a complex theological issue. As Fazl-i Haqq was internationally acclaimed for his mastery of Islamic philosophy and logic, students from abroad traveled to Delhi in order to study under his guidance. His reputation was bolstered thanks to his affiliation to a line of scholars whose hometown was Khairabad in North India and whose mastery in logic, philosophy, and literature was legendary.

Fazl-i Haqq was an iconoclast of sorts. Noted for his sartorial taste, he refused to wear the standard attire donned by religious scholars: a modest long-shirt and a head covering or turban of some sort. Rather, he flaunted the accoutrements of the Delhi elites and aristocracy. His literary expertise in Arabic was impressive. He crafted a dazzling 4,000 lines of Arabic verse—not a negligible benchmark for a poet, even in a native language.

Like his father, he also worked for the English residency. But Fazl-i Haqq's fate with the British would change when he was arrested and tried for sedition in the uprisings of 1857. He was charged for being among the signatories of the religious ruling (fatwa) that permitted the armed rising against the English colonial power. He escaped death by accepting imprisonment on the Andaman Islands, where he died four years into his life sentence.

The theological juggernaut that Fazl-i Haqq unleashed took on a life of its own in the decades following his own demise and that of his adversary Shah Ismaʿil. The theological puzzle is the following: is it possible for God to create another person identical to Muhammad?[26] In his rebuttal of Shah Ismaʿil's theological errors, Fazl-i Haqq argues that it is impossible for God to create someone similar or even one who resembles Muhammad, once a being with the attributes of the Prophet Mu-

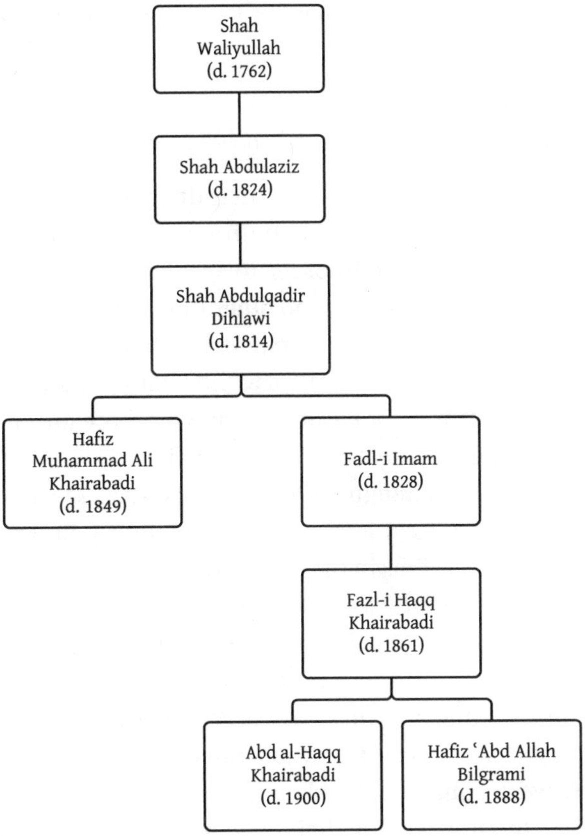

Scholarly genealogy of the Khairabadi school.

hammad was created. Muhammad, in his view, was unique and occupied a preeminent place in an eternal cosmological design. Muhammad was so special, even God would not offer a simulacrum or contemplate to substitute Muhammad. To stress that the Prophet Muhammad was peerless, Fazl-i Haqq named his doctrine "the impossibility of a peer."

More earnestly, Fazl-i Haqq argued, the claim Shah Ismaʿil made was tantamount to refuting the very knowledge the Prophet himself had provided. In established Sunni doctrine, anyone who refutes what the Prophet authoritatively taught deserves to be anathematized. Fazl-i Haqq's primary objection to Shah Ismaiʿl's theological imaginary is that his opponent paints God in capricious and unpredictable colors. If left unchecked, this kind of theology can potentially drain religion of rational content and open the door to moral anarchy. An unpredictable God, Fazl-i Haqq feared, could randomly turn good into bad and vice versa. From there it was a short distance into a moral morass.

Knight of Indignation: Ahmad Raza Khan (1856–1921)

From the city of Bareili in today's Uttar Pradesh in India, a theological fusillade was unleashed on Deoband and all admirers of Shah Ismaʿil and his theology. The person who rose in order to systematically continue the assault initiated by Fazl-i Haqq was no other than a man called Ahmad Raza Khan. Ahmad Riza is his proper name, but he is colloquially remembered as Ahmad Raza, a man who saw himself as the true representative of canonical Sunnism. Of Pashtun heritage, whose ancestors generations ago had settled in the North Indian plains, he was, by all accounts, a knight of theological indignation. On Ahmad Raza's watch the dispute reached furious rhetorical levels and fomented fragmentation and division among Sunni Muslims in the twentieth century in India, Pakistan, Bangladesh, and communities of the South Asian diaspora.

Ahmad Raza was determined to expose the theological error of the Deoband scholars for their wrongful admiration of Shah Ismaʿil and his views.[27] Some Deobandis enthusiastically, and others cautiously, defended Shah Ismaʿil's views. Because the Deobandis endorsed Shah Ismaʿil's theology, they were equally culpable and deserving of anathema for straying into the territory of unbelief. Labeling the Deobandis as Wahhabis, followers of the eighteenth-century Arabian reformist figure, Ahmad Raza declared that their doctrines amounted to denying that Muhammad was the final prophet, and as such they violated a fundamental doctrine of Islam. As apologists for unbelief, in Ahmad Raza's view, the Deobandis were even worse. Invoking an early doctrine, he maintained, "Toleration of unbelief is tantamount to subscribing to unbelief." Several prominent authorities in Arabia endorsed his verdict on the Deobandis, an event that generated countless Deobandi responses and ongoing polemical and theological rows pitting Deobandi followers and scholars against their Barelvi counterparts for a good part of the twentieth century.

In Ahmad Raza's view, Islam is equal to a canonical orthodox tradition and any molestation of tradition is tantamount to heresy. Predictably, Ahmad Raza also opposed anything resembling a contextual theology, since in his view any departure from normative doctrine was just unthinkable. In that sense he was ultraorthodox, holding out little hope

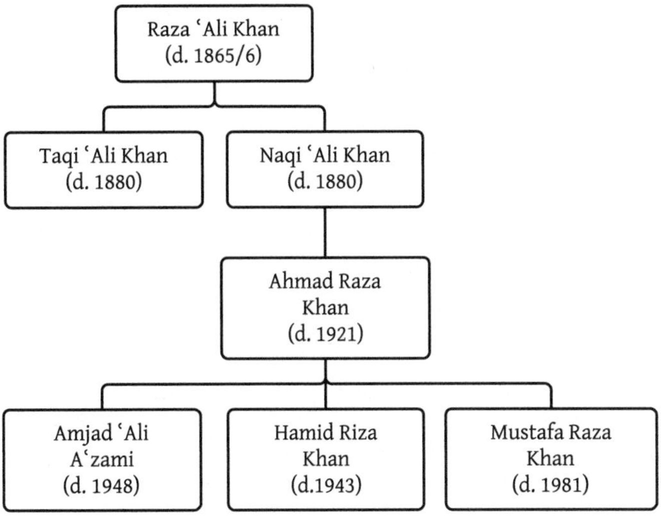

Genealogy of the Barelvi school.

for the reconciliation of doctrine with social change. To this day the vigorous Barelvi madrasa network remains fervently committed to furthering his theological ideals. Throughout the twentieth century, representatives of both the Deobandi and Barelvi schools, their graduates and foot soldiers, all made it their goal to counter each other's views in public debates and religious mobilization. At times these polemics spilled over into violent conflict, causing death and injury.

Deobandis as Orthodox Reformers: Qasim Nanautvi (1832–1880) and Rashid Ahmad Gangohi (1829–1905)

The theological skirmishes between Fazl-i Haqq Khairabadi and Shah Ismaʿil cooked into a perfect sectarian storm after their deaths. Intra-Sunni theological controversies also shaped the multiple emergent madrasa networks. The ideas of Shah Ismaʿil were embedded in the intellectual agendas of the two men who shaped the Deoband madrasa in 1867 and gave rise to the most powerful madrasa network on the subcontinent.

Muhammad Qasim Nanautvi and Rashid Ahmad Gangohi were born in villages within roughly a twenty-eight-mile (45 km) radius from the key city of Saharanpur in Uttar Pradesh. Muhammad Qasim hailed from the village of Nanauta and Rashid Ahmad from Gangoh. As they were accomplished and self-made men, their reputations were catapulted into a transregional discourse of Islam, and once-anonymous North Indian rural villages were emblazoned in the minds of their followers. Over time, with the aid of their successors, these rural men seeded a religious aristocracy of sorts that bequeathed durable scholarly and spiritual legacies.

Two very influential charismatic masters shaped Muhammad Qasim Nanautvi and Rashid Ahmad Gangohi. The two men could not be more different. One was a scholar, Mamlukul ʿAli (d. 1851), and the other was a distinguished Sufi master, Haji Imdadullah Faruqi Thanvi (d. 1899), popularly known as Haji Imdadullah.

Mamlukul ʿAli prided himself as an intellectual first and foremost, with a talent for juridical-theology, mastery of the rational sciences, and his reputable knowledge of both Arabic and Persian literature.[28] "In his persona and profile he was certainly not an ascetic," one eyewitness wrote, adding that "his mannerisms were those of worldly folk."[29] Fired by an inexhaustible passion for teaching, he had the uncanny gift to identify talented students whose abilities he could mold, the way a jeweler cut diamonds. He trained students in the vernacular division of Delhi College founded by the British, offered private instruction at his home, and also taught at the Madrasa Dar al-Baqa, Abode of Permanence Madrasa, in the old part of Delhi, a place of which there remains no trace today.

Visiting his village of Nanauta around December of 1843 during the ʿId al-Adha holiday, Mamlukul ʿAli took his own son Muhammad Yaʿqub and Muhammad Qasim Nanautvi, the son of a relative, with him to Delhi. Muhammad Qasim in his early teens was already something of a prodigy. Family troubles necessitated moving him between nearby towns.[30] Childhood education by private teachers in his native village of Nanauta and in the nearby town of Deoband were followed by lessons from teachers in the regional city of Saharanpur with which he honed his skills.[31]

Rashid Ahmad also left his village of Gangoh to continue his studies in Delhi around 1844, ending up in Mamlukul ʿAli's study circle.[32] He also studied with the pious Delhi-based figure Shah ʿAbdulghani, a leading authority on hadith and a descendant of the renowned seventeenth-century Indian reformer Shaykh Ahmad Sirhindi (d. 1624). Shah Abdulghani left a decisive imprint on Rashid Ahmad's pious rigor of *imitatio Muhammadi*—to emulate the Prophet Muhammad.

At Mamlukul ʿAli's study circle, Rashid Ahmad established a lifelong friendship with Muhammad Qasim despite their differences in temperament. Muhammad Qasim was self-effacing, ascetic, and nonassertive in temperament, whereas Rashid Ahmad was known for both his assertiveness and hyperascetic qualities. Mamlukul ʿAli was confident of their talents and quashed rumors that the two were moving through their texts without comprehension. He gently rebuked such critics, saying, "Son, a student studying with me cannot proceed in his lessons without showing a proper comprehension of the text!"[33]

As young men in Delhi, Muhammad Qasim and Rashid Ahmad frequently met Haji Imdadullah from the village of Thana Bhavan at Mamlukul ʿAli's place. Even though Haji Imdadullah was not trained in theology and law, he nevertheless was regarded as Sufi master par excellence, one who altered the destinies of his disciples. After they graduated, first Muhammad Qasim and then Rashid Ahmad took Haji Imdadullah as their Sufi master (*shaykh*) in a program of spiritual development. For scholars entrenched in orthodox teachings to adopt a Sufi master who is not himself entrenched in Shariʿa is a risky venture. Imdadullah was a Magus-like figure—an extraordinary wise man who directed the spiritual lives of his disciples. He, in turn, authorized his two top disciples and others to induct seekers into the Sabri-Chishti Sufi order. At first Muhammad Qasim and Rashid Ahmad were determined to oust the British from India through armed rebellion. The British jailed Rashid Ahmad for six months for his political activism. Muhammad Qasim, although he was a fugitive, was never apprehended. Muhammad Qasim worked for several presses where he edited and provided brief commentaries on classical Arabic texts of mainly canonical hadith books. But over the years of his career he was also in touch with a notable from the town of Deoband, Haji Abid Husayn, with whom he broached the need to establish an institution of religious learning. Once Haji Abid Husayn raised the money for such an institution, he invited Muhammad Qasim to become the first teacher at the school. Instead, Muhammad Qasim recommended another local person from the town itself to be the first instructor. Around April 14, 1866, the madrasa opened with a single teacher in the Chatta mosque, a landmark that survives to this day. Gradually Muhammad Qasim became more involved in finding a permanent building for the madrasa and oversaw its construction. As the intellectual pioneer, he wrote the mission statement and drafted the founding articles for the institution that would later gain renown as Darul Uloom Deoband. Muhammad Qasim never taught at the madrasa but was part of a troika of founders along with Rashid Ahmad and Haji ʿAbid Husayn. He preferred to write books and engage in public debates with Hindu and Christian leaders about matters of faith and defended charges made by rival faiths against Islam. He only witnessed the first fourteen years of the institution he cofounded and died at the early age of forty-nine. After him, Rashid Ahmad became the executive patron of the madrasa.

Muhammad Qasim Nanautvi and Rashid Ahmad Gangohi proudly embodied a *maslak*, a virtuous temperament embedded in an elaborate narrative, one that etched on their madrasa franchise a distinctive blend of theological convictions, intellectual style, and ascetic pious practice derived from eighteenth- and nineteenth-century predecessors.

The creative thrust of Shah Waliyullah's synthesis of theology, law, philosophy, piety, and mysticism appealed to them, albeit in a new intellectual idiom. Yet they ardently admired Waliyullah's grandson, Shah Ismaʿil, and his unrealized cause of social reform, much to the chagrin of critics. In many ways Deoband saw itself as a theological cum spiritual fortress wherein generations would be prepared in the spirit of Shah Waliyullah's formulation of orthodox teachings in order to defend Muslim interests in modern India.

Deoband's commitment to a reformist blend of orthodox theology was a centerpiece of controversy for nearly a century. It started with the theological dust-up Shah Ismaʿil had with Fazl-i Haqq Khairabadi and a cause that was later fueled by Ahmad Raza Khan. The granular theological debates centered on the modes of honoring the Prophet Muhammad. Sure, the theological polemics centered around forms of allowed and disallowed prayers honoring the Messenger of God. But what these debates obscured was this: two very different orientations and visions of the place and role of Islam in society.

Behind the theological flamethrowing lurked the larger questions of how Muslims vary in their understanding of the nexus between God, humans, and the nature of human agency in history. Today scholars discuss these issues under the rubric of political theology. The Barelvi school, in contradistinction to the Deobandi school, subscribes to a doctrinaire version of Sunni theology that requires Muslims to work within the status quo and the inherited tradition. This political theology *capitulates* to social reality, especially political reality, and fosters a realist vision of tradition. Barelvis prefer stability to change, continuity to discontinuity. Conservatism in political theology is their creed, for God acts in the world through the given conditions of the world. Radical alteration to the world always carries the risk of unleashing unpredictable harm, tumult, and anarchy.

The theology of the Deoband school, in turn, fosters social change and nurtures the ideals of political activism. Such change and ideals, they say, must accord with the teachings of the Prophet Muhammad and as laid out by the early exemplars of Islam. Their signature tropes are Waliyullah's blend of piety, devotions, and politics—conditions that must inspire in humans a restlessness to become the instruments of God in the world and not to accept the fallen state of humans but rather to revive them for higher ends. Yet graduates associated with the Deoband franchise are fairly diverse in their orientations. Some turn out to be social reformers—moderate-minded activists and organizers who operate within the framework of the law of the nation-state—who are cautious about all kinds of excessive behavior. And they also harbor political quietists. Deobandi piety can range from the cerebral and intellectually stunning version of Ashraf ʿAli Thanvi's Sufi teachings and Muhammad Ilyas's model of popular Sufi piety in order to advance social reform in the guise of the Tabligh Movement to the politically active Deobandi scholars who joined Mahatma Gandhi in a nonviolent anticolonial struggle against British colonialism. Others, in turn, adopt an absolutist, if not nihilist, political position irrespective of consequences, of which the Pakistani and Afghan Taliban are certainly the most depressing examples. Even if some despise the Taliban's affiliation to Deobandism, it is nevertheless a version of Deobandi theology on steroids.

These two versions of political theology occur on a spectrum and are not only limited to orthodox practices of Islam on the Indian subcontinent. In other parts of the Muslim world variants of this theology also become manifest and was very much in evidence during the Arab spring and its aftermath.

CONCLUSION

The multiple networks of madrasas that dot the Indian subcontinent today are the cumulative product of a madrasa tradition fed from two streams. One stream was the Farangi Mahall school with its tolerant cosmopolitan tradition that bequeathed a core curriculum to all madrasas and charted a middle-of-the road outlook on practice and politics. The

Ashʿari and Maturidi

Two theological schools arose in response to the Muʿtazila to form the core of Sunni theological doctrine. Both these schools viewed the Muʿtazila to be doctrinally errant. The Ashʿari school is named after Abul Hasan al-Ashʿari (d. 935–36), who once belonged to the Muʿtazila but then became a defender of a traditional interpretation of faith. Ashʿari held that some of God's attributes, like speech, are eternal, and hence the Qurʾan as God's speech is uncreated. God's omnipotence, His power over all things, is the paramount emphasis of this theology; hence good and evil are created by God. God creates the deeds of humans by creating in them the power to act. Later Ashʿaris explained that humans also acquire certain power, to introduce some notion of human agency. No matter how serious a believer sinned, the believer remained within the faith. Contrary to Muʿtazila doctrine, Ashʿaris hold that believers will see God on the Day of Judgment. Abu Mansur al-Maturidi (d. 944) advanced the teachings of the jurist Abu Hanifa. Like the Muʿtazila, he believed humans had the obligation to gain knowledge of God and to thank God on the grounds of reason, independent of revelation. He allowed for metaphorical interpretations of the anthropomorphic verses of the Qurʾan. Divine attributes are eternal, he held. Human acts are created by God, and from that perspective they are subject to God's will; but from another perspective they are also subject to acts of humans and their free will. This stance makes the Maturidis intermediate between the Ashʿaris and Muʿtazila.

other stream was the nineteenth-century reform movement linked to the family of Shah Waliyullah, which generated sufficient theological tinder and diversified madrasa networks along discrete theological lines. In the late nineteenth century the Deoband school became the hegemonic player in madrasa franchises. Throughout the twentieth century it evoked theological partisanship, which in turn spawned the rapid growth of diverse madrasa networks. Each theological camp now fostered its own mission for social outreach, religious authority, and most important their distinct brands of political theology.

Contrary to popular belief, the dominant Deobandi and Barelvi madrasa networks actually have no major structural differences beyond their core disagreement over reformist theology and some aspects of practice involving the authority of intercession by saints. The dictum that cousins fight more savagely than strangers is borne out in the history of these divergent exponents of madrasa education.

What they share, against the Ahl-i Hadith or Salafis, is their commitment to a combination of Ashʿari and Maturidi theological doctrines, the Hanafi law school, and a core curriculum for their graduates, to which we now turn.

Studying classical texts is a strength of the madrasa curriculum. A selection of texts and authors provides a quick glance at the breadth and depth of this tradition and its history.

CHAPTER FIVE

Texts and Authors

TIMELESS TIMELINES

In the course of one day, a student would read a grammar text authored by an Egyptian author of the seventeenth century, a logic text written by an Indian author in the eighteenth century, and a book on prophetic traditions prepared by a central Asian scholar in the ninth century. Indeed, the madrasa tradition cultivates a commitment to scholasticism. The madrasa reveres tradition by preserving the knowledge of prominent scholars and celebrating their intellectual labors from all parts of the Muslim world in the form of texts and scholarship.

Authors from distant lands and bygone eras are networked into the life world of the contemporary Muslim community of scholars by means of the knowledge tradition. All this goes back to the genius of the Nizami curriculum. Students in South Asian madrasas closely study the writings of authors who once lived in Muslim Spain, Egypt, and Greater Syria, a region today known by names such as Lebanon, Palestine/Israel, and Syria, as well as many from Iran, Central Asia, and India between the thirteenth and sixteenth centuries and even earlier.

This networked structure of learning and scholarly communication is the reason why, in my view, South Asia's Muslim traditionalism is so resilient and coherent when compared with that of other regions. This is notwithstanding its internal diversity. The curriculum, with its stable core of subjects and texts, gives it uniformity. In fact, the texts obtain such canonical status among the community of scholars that teachers are not free to change texts at their discretion.

SNAPSHOTS OF SCHOLARS, TEXTS, AND SUBJECTS

I still vividly recall the day I debuted my first reading of an Arabic curricular text. After spending a year learning Arabic grammar and morphology, cramming Urdu and Arabic vocabularies, I was sufficiently eager to begin the Nizami curriculum proper. When I managed to read the first Arabic lines of the primer in Islamic law called *Light of Clarification and the Salvation of Souls-Nur al-Idah wa Najat al-Arwah* by Abul Ikhlas al-Shurrunbulali (1585–1659), I felt a deep satisfaction of making a connection with an extraordinary tradition of learning. In reading the set of prescribed texts, I felt certain that I had joined the company of a distinguished group of scholars whose knowledge and reputation elicited awe and admiration among their peers over centuries. "There are seven types of water that are permissible for use in ritual purification . . . ," wrote Shurrunbulali. Parsing the first lines of this Hanafi law text gave me such a thrill that I can still recall those sensations. In class we spent some time with the introductory prayer of the author, and throughout the year we read the entire book with a teacher who offered commentary and explanation.

While studying the text gave me a thrill, for decades Shurrunbulali was an anonymous figure. I had no idea in which country he lived and worked. It was only after I graduated that I discovered that he was an Egyptian from the region of Manoufia, at a distance of forty-nine miles (80 kms) from Cairo. More importantly, I came to learn that he studied at the famous al-Azhar University and became one of its most renowned and influential teachers. Apart from his writings on law and Islamic mysticism, he was noted for his piety. A historical sketch of his universe would have helped me gain a better understanding of this scholar.

Disciplines studied in the madrasas are divided into two kinds. Some subjects are designated as the "higher sciences" or "transmitted sciences," terms used for received opinion and knowledge. The goal of students in madrasas is to master the "transmitted sciences," namely, knowledge of the word of God, the Qur'an, and to understand the meaning and message of the teachings of the Arabian prophet, Muhammad, the son of Abdullah. Yet, in order to study these primary sources of the faith tradition, students require certain tools. Therefore they study a whole range of other disciplines designated as the "instrumental sciences." This includes the study of the Arabic language and its ancillary disciplines like grammar, literature, poetry, and rhetoric as well as other languages like Persian and Urdu. Disciplines aiding students with modes of reasoning and coherence like logic, philosophy, and a range of other skills in order to gain mastery of the primary sources fall into this category. However, the distinction between the "transmitted sciences" and the "instrumental sciences" is somewhat superficial, since they are interdependent. If one has a poor command of grammar or language, then one's understanding of the transmitted teachings will surely be deficient.

Logic and philosophy, especially classical philosophy and logic, derived from the Greeks, enjoyed widespread currency in the madrasas. Sound reasoning gives impeccable coherence to a theological argument. Therefore, both logic and philosophy are crucial tools for discursive thinking. Early Arab philosophers studied Greek texts, translated them, and then utilized those insights to leaven and deepen their scholarship of Islam as a religious and cultural tradition. And many of the earliest Muslim theological texts used in the madrasas are written in styles that rely on the assumptions of Greek philosophy and logic, with some minor and major amendments.

Among the most prominent philosophy texts circulating among Muslim scholastics is *Guide to Wisdom* (*Hidayatul Hikma*), a primer authored by the Persian scholar Athir al-Din al-Abhari (d. 1263–65). Philosophy is better known as "wisdom" (*hikma*). Abhari also wrote a text called *Isagoge* on logic. Abhari's *Isagoge* is different from Porphyry's book by the same title but nevertheless addresses categories like species, genus, difference, particular accident, and common accident. He also indulges in detailed discussions of syllogisms, a topic that made most students yawn with boredom.[1]

Students in madrasas do read Abhari's *Guide to Wisdom* but as part of a very popular text called the *Commentary on the Guide to Wisdom* by the Persian scholar Husayn al-Maybudhi (d. 904/1498 or 909/1503–4) but who is also referred to as Maybudi in encyclopedias. He was from

Maybudh, a village near the Iranian city of Yazd; became a distinguished scholar; and was appointed as a judge. His strongly held Sunni views clashed with those of the founder of the Safawid dynasty, the ruler Shah Isma'il (d. 1524). Shah Isma'il zealously favored Shi'i interpretations of Islam. Sensing Maybudhi's opposition to his views, the shah decreed that Maybudhi be executed, another piece of history I came to learn afterward.

Often madrasa students refer to a text by taking the name of the author. It is like saying, "I am reading Aristotle." Similarly, a madrasa student will say, "I am reading Maybudhi." However, this author's name is often distorted in Indian madrasas and is commonly referred to as "Mefzi"! When a student studying the Nizami curriculum says he is reading Maybudhi, you almost instinctively know that he is in the sixth year of the advanced madrasa program.

Maybudhi, as all authors of classical Arabic texts, begins his text with a formulaic praise of God and salutations on the Prophet, his family, and all his Companions. It is important to note that when authors send salutations to "all the Companions," they reveal their Sunni identity. If a book is authored by Shi'i authors, they will specify the "select and pure among the Companions," signaling the important doctrinal differences between the two sects over the status of the Companions of the Prophet Muhammad.

Thereafter, Maybudhi, like other authors, lets the reader know why he wrote the book and what motivated him to pen the work, which also signals his favorable attitude toward philosophy. "I finally grasped that the perfect substance of all concrete things is a species of humans who evolve in order to become some of the most sagacious people and are guided to multiple types of wisdom," he asserts. "Surely, the one who contemplates gets insight into the truth of all things via wisdom (*hikma*)," he explains.[2] Then Maybudhi cites a verse of the Qur'an that endorses the pursuit of philosophy, as wisdom. "And whoever is given wisdom, is indeed endowed with an enormous amount of good" (Q 2:269).

Some classical authors and their modern successors despise the study of philosophy, arguing it corrupts Islam's purity. Yet there were equally large cohorts of scholars who were very enthusiastic about the study of philosophy. The curriculum of the South Asian madrasas is aligned to the cohort of philosophy enthusiasts, even though opposition to the study of philosophy from some madrasa scholars does arise from time to time. The teaching of Maybudhi's commentary, among other texts, should dispel the misperception that madrasas are monolithic and entirely driven by a scripture-based intellectual agenda. At the same time, I must concede that a shift toward scripturalism is occurring, and the rationalist thread faces challenges within madrasa discourses.

The first primer in logic that students read is *The Ladder* (*Mirqat*), by the Indian scholar Fazl-i Imam Khairabadi (d. 1828), whose virtuoso son Fazl-i Haqq the reader already met. Then students move on to read *Hierarchy of the Sciences* (*Sullam al-ʿUlum*) by the prolific Indian scholar Muhibullah al-Ansari (d. 1706). He was a judge and a major authority on Hanafi moral philosophy or legal theory. Not only was Muhibullah al-Ansari a tutor for Shah ʿAlam, the son of Emperor Aurangzeb, but he was also a distinguished adviser who moved with the emperor's heir apparent to Kabul and other major regions of India and reached distinguished positions in government.

No one can study Arabic grammar and not hear of Sibawayhi (d. 796), the Persian grammarian who was a paragon of Islam's classical age. Sibawayhi's writings on grammar and his vast erudition are the gold standard of grammatical excellence. When one scholar asks another, "Did you ride the ocean?" the addressee automatically knows the question is, "Did you read Sibawayhi?" After the sack of Baghdad in 1258, the vast Asian Muslim domain attuned to Persian literary and cultural norms took a more prominent role in advancing the Muslim Republic of Letters. Wounded and reduced by the Mongol devastation, learned communities gradually recovered their prestige by building on their earlier reputations.

Arabic enjoys pride of place in the curriculum of any respectable madrasa. Anyone interested in Arabic grammar and lexicography cannot ignore the work of one Abul Qasim Mahmud al-Zamakhshari (d. 1144). Zamakhshari is controversial because of his theological allegiance to the rationalist Muʿtazila creed, but that controversy is only half of the story. In addition to his writings on grammar and lexicography, Zamakhshari is the author of a highly prized exegesis of the Qurʾan, and he undertook a meticulous study of prophetic sayings. Pious scholars often caricature scholars with a rationalist bent to be worldly oriented. Zamakhshari was different; despite his fascination with rationality and contrary to parody he was a deeply pious man. His five-year stay at Islam's holiest shrine in Mecca bears testimony to his piety. There he taught, wrote, and studied grammar and Qurʾan exegesis. His long stay in the holy city earned him the honorific "Neighbor of God" (*Jarullah*), making him a paragon of Muslim learning, piety, and pilgrimage.

Muʿtazila

The Muʿtazila were a group of theologians who propagated their brand of faith in eighth-century Basra and later spread to other cities. The uniqueness of God and divine justice were the cornerstones of their belief. Individuals were responsible for their own transgressions; evil, they held, was not the work of God. God, the Muʿtazila believed, did only that which was the best for humans. God acts according to His promises of reward and threats for disobedience. The quandary for them was the sinful believer who could neither be called a believer nor unbeliever but rather occupied a place in between those polarities. All humans have the obligation to advance the moral cause of commanding the good and forbidding evil. What made them infamous was a belief that the Qurʾan, as God's speech, was created, not eternal.

Even though scholars belonging to the Ashʿari and Maturidi theological schools were uncomfortable with some of Zamakhshari's theological views, they nevertheless valued his intellectual labors. To his credit, Nizamuddin embedded a tolerant intellectual predisposition in his curriculum allowing for diversity. In the madrasas of South Asia, Zamakhshari's highly extolled exegesis of the Qurʾan exegesis, *The Searchlight* (*Kashshaf*), remains a crucial reference work.

Nizamuddin's father, Qutbuddin, boasted an impressive intellectual genealogy that could be traced back to Persia. Several of those distant intellectual teacher-ancestors feature prominently in the Nizami curriculum with the adoption of their texts. One such towering figure is Mir Sayyid Sharif al-Jurjani (d. 1413). Born in Astarabad, he is better known as "*Mir* Sayyid Sharif" or simply as "Sayyid Sharif." A consummate traveler, Jurjani visited Egypt and Constantinople (known as Istanbul today) and is renowned as a teacher's teacher. Posterity remembers him as being punctilious in designing textbooks, writing commentaries, providing learned explanatory notes to texts, and, more importantly, training generations of students.

Jurjani wrote a valuable commentary on a book authored by the distinguished Persian scholar ʿAdud al-Din al-Iji (d. c. 1356) called *Book of Stations* (*Kitab al-Mawaqif*) on theology. Not only is Jurjani's *Commentary on Stations* distinctive for leading the reader by the hand into the nuances of theology, but it also serves as a landmark summary of Sunni Muslim theology up to the fifteenth century. But Jurjani's Persian primers on Arabic grammar and morphology are still used in madrasas today in Urdu translation, known as *The Grammar of Mir* (*Nahv Mir*) or *Morphology of Mir* (*Sarf-i Mir*) following his popular name as *Mir* Sayyid Sharif. Two of his primers in logic, called *Minor* and *Major* (*Sughra* and *Kubra*), are also taught in some madrasas, although interest in both texts is fading. Jurjani earns the greatest mark of distinction in Muslim intellectual circles and is known as "*The Touchstone for the Verification of the Truth* (*sayyid al-muhaqqiqin*)" for his dedication to meticulous investigation and thorough research on every topic.

A contemporary and rival of Jurjani was the equally prodigious polymath Saʿd al-Din al-Taftazani (d. 1390). A number of texts on rhetoric, theology, and legal theory emblazoned his scholarly credentials and are taught in today's madrasas. During the late fourteenth century, the great Tamerlane, the conquering Central Asian chieftain, was fond of hosting scholars at his court. So the conqueror recruited both Taftazani and Jurjani and brought both men to his capital in Samarqand in today's Uzbekistan. Even if Taftazani may have been reluctant to join, declining Tamerlane's invitation would have counted as lèse-majesté.

Though Tamerlane at first treated Taftazani with great honor, rivalry soon broke out between Taftazani and the younger Jurjani, whom Tamerlane favored. He then arranged for a series of public debates at his court between the two scholars. They were each asked to address a number of linguistic questions related to Qurʾan exegesis raised by none other than the invincible Zamakhshari. Another Muʿtazili scholar refereed the debate, and after several public sessions, he declared Jurjani to be the victor. Taftazani was so shattered and inconsolable at his defeat that he died within weeks of the event. Scholars in the madrasas of the Ottoman Empire often studied this debate and boldly took sides on the famous Taftazani-versus-Jurjani debate, signaling their own intellectual tastes. Taftazani's memory, along with the work of his rival Jurjani, lives on in the madrasas of South Asia. Students diligently study Taftazani's text on rhetoric called *Abridgement in Rhetoric* (*Mukhtasar al-Maʿani*) and another, *Commentary on the Dogmatics of Nasafi* (*Sharh al-ʿAqaʾid al-Nasafiyya*).

A work by a jurist and grammarian hailing from Egypt, ʿUthman b. ʿUmar ibn al-Hajib (d. 1249), has a fascinating backstory. Born in Isna in Upper Egypt, a town lying on the left bank of the Nile halfway between

Statue of Tamerlane outside Ak-Saray Palace in Shakhrisabz, Uzbekistan. (Picture: Adam Jones, https://creativecommons.org/licenses/by-sa/2.0/)

Luxor and Edfu, Ibn al-Hajib is the author of *The Sufficient* (*al-Kafiya*), a grammar text taught in the madrasas of India and Central Asia until very recently. Ibn al-Hajib is also a renowned jurist and is counted among the most eminent scholars of his generation in the Maliki school of law. A polymath, he was captivated by his love for Arabic grammar, with many debts to the celebrated Zamakhshari.

As Ibn al-Hajib was renowned as a pious man, it is possible that his esoteric or mystical interests might have bled into his grammar. More than one scholar observed that parts of Ibn al-Hajib's grammar book

Remnants of a historic madrasa built by Mahmud Gawan, who became prime minister of the Bahmanid dynasty in the fifteenth century in Bidar, in Karnataka State in India today. (Picture: Leela Prasad)

encodes a deep and deliberate ambiguity with double meanings of esoteric and mystical reflections.[3]

It took a few centuries for the Indian scholar ʿAbd al-Wahid Bilgrami (d. 1608) to show that Ibn al-Hajib's *The Sufficient* brimmed with mystical insights.[4] Bilgrami latched on to the thirteenth-century Egyptian grammarian's definition of "word" known as a *kalima* in Arabic. But in Muslim theology the term *kalima* also denotes the believer's confession or testimony of faith. So if you address a confessing Muslim and say to him or her, "Recite the *kalima*!" then he or she will promptly declare in Arabic, *la ilaha illallah, Muhammadur rasulullah,* which means, "There is no other god, than God, and Muhammad is His Messenger."

So in both a playful and serious mien, Bilgrami provides an exegesis of Ibn al-Hajib's text that says, "A word (*kalima*) is a name assigned to a solitary meaning [intention]."[5] Bilgrami's interest in grammatical exposition was clearly overshadowed by his obsession with the theological meaning of the testimonial "word" (*kalima*). After wondering out loudly why Ibn al-Hajib did not highlight the moral and spiritual implications of the Muslim article of faith, Bilgrami went on to resolve his own query with speculative arguments. "A word," he writes, "is an utterance, declared by our tongues, observable to our hearts but flourishing in our inner selves." "In other words," the testimonial of divine unity (*tawhid*), he writes, "uttered by our tongues is an *affirmation*; when it is prominent in our hearts it turns into *assent*, but only when it is internalized does it *enrich* the depth of our being."[6]

It is not entirely strange for Bilgrami, proud of his intellectual pirouette, to rehearse in a grammar text themes related to one's self-formation, one's humility, and how to lead a life of righteousness on earth. Attaining faith by declaring the testimonial "word or *kalima*" makes a believer immune to unbelief, he explains, just as enjoining and performing ritual practices immunize one from hypocrisy, since striving for spiritual perfection and integrity is antithetical to sin. Bilgrami, like other predecessors, tried to put Ibn al-Hajib's book to uses beyond grammar. He shows that an "instrumental science" like grammar serves as no barrier for him to also delve into the "transmitted sciences" dealing in substantive discussions of faith and practice.

After *Kafiya,* madrasa students read a text popularly called a commentary by Jamiʿ (*Sharh Jamiʿ*) though its official title is *Luminous Insights (al-Fawaʾid al-diyaʾiyya)*.[7] Who is this commentator called Jamiʿ? He is a mystical giant. Renowned as a child prodigy, Mulla ʿAbd al-Rahman al- Jamiʿ (d. 1492) hailed from Herat, which in the fifteenth century was part of Eastern Iran. Located in modern Afghanistan, this city had strong cultural connections to Iran. Jamiʿ's grammar commentary reflected and perpetuated his lofty reputation: as an extraordinary scholar who was also a poet and a mystic.[8]

Luminous Insights was, until recently, widely taught in the madrasas. For philosophy enthusiasts, this work was prized for its deep appreciation of the philosophy of Arabic grammar and its subtleties. Other readers despised it: students and faculty complained that Jamiʿ's style was arcane, concealing more than it revealed; studying it is a drudgery that does not cultivate proficiency in Arabic as a language and is a waste of time.

As a student, I too was among those who poured scorn on the teaching of this grammar text. I became frustrated because I was inadequately prepared to appreciate Jamiʿ's intellectual subtleties. Many professors only got through a few pages of teaching this text in class. Most get stuck for days at an impenetrable discussion codenamed "self-contained meanings and meanings attained via accessories" (*al- hasil wa al-mahsul*), which to us students was a very complicated debate.

At the time, I had no idea what this debate meant, nor did I appreciate its value. But as a graduate student affected by the linguistic turn in philosophy during the nineties, I started to read the work of the Swiss linguist Ferdinand de Saussure and the French philosopher Jacques Derrida. With that came a newfound respect for the philosophy of language. On rereading the difficult section in Jamiʿ's *Luminous Insights,* I discovered, to my surprise, that this was actually a debate on semiotics: how words, which are really "signs," do their work. "Sign" processes are actually meaning processes. What is the relation between a "sign" that says the word "boy" and the act of "standing" in the sentence "The boy is standing"? Well, it says that the person we are talking about is one among an indefinite number of boys. In semiotics, this process of referring is called *denoting,* and what it refers to is called *meaning.* But the word "boy" can also do something more. It can *connote* certain attributes such as corporeity, animal life, rationality, and certain external features of the boy, which makes the process of meaning-making more complex.[9]

In his convoluted and overphilosophized prose, Jamiʿ elaborates a point made by Ibn al-Hajib, who in his equally terse writing tried to distinguish why in terms of linguistic philosophy an Arabic noun was different from a particle. A noun "signifies a self-existing meaning or intention" with no connection to anything outside the utterance, Ibn al-Hajib explained. A particle, in turn, derived its meaning out of its relationships with other utterances and did not have independent meaning. But Jamiʿ uses highly philosophical language and says that nouns *denote* "the existence of meaning" but they can also *connote* certain attributes inherent to the word. Since this medieval discussion in linguistics and language philosophy has not been updated by modern madrasa scholarship on these topics, the subtleties of these debates remain elusive to most students. Thanks to my reading of modern language philosophy, I think I can now say I have a modest grasp of aspects of this debate.

The goal of all of these "instrumental disciplines" is, as already mentioned, to understand the Qurʾan and the hadith and to know the obligations of Islamic practice. The discipline at the core of Muslim practice is *fiqh,* often translated as Islamic law. Another term frequently used is Shariʿa. In chapter 7 there will be more discussions of *fiqh* debates. But, if anything, madrasa students are often proficient and knowledgeable about the rules of moral practice that do sometimes take the form of laws and rules. Under the rubric of *fiqh,* students master rules, such as those relating to dietary practices, how to pray and do one's rituals, and, more generally, the rules of conduct in public life, whether it is in politics, in economics, or during war and peace. *Fiqh* is taught throughout the entire madrasa curriculum.

The study of *fiqh* is associated with founders who centuries ago devised the interpretive framework as to how one mined the primary sources like the Qurʾan and the hadith. In the Sunni tradition, four schools of interpretation, named after their founders, namely, the Hanafi, Maliki, Shafiʿi, and Hanbali, prevail today. Among the Shiʿa creed, they go by the names of the Jaʿfari, Zaydi, and Ismaiʿili schools. In North Indian madrasas, the Hanafi school is the dominant one, while the Shafiʿi school is prevalent in South India.

One of the texts a student will read on law is called *The Treasure of Subtleties, Kanz al-Daqaʾiq*. It is an elegant text written by Abul Barakat al-Nasafi (d. 1310) that could be taught only with the help of marginalia and commentaries that were written by distinguished Hanafi jurists.

Among all the topics that are studied in *fiqh,* the debates on ritual cleanliness are frequently repeated, year after year, class after class, with gradations of advancement, since all classical authors begin their books with the chapters on purity, with some exceptions. Another oft-repeated topic is the chapter on marriage and divorce. Given his economy of language, Nasafi, in his *Book of Marriage,* often provides every class some reason for chatter and joviality.

Imagine the reaction of young adult boys when Nasafi writes that marriage is "a contract over the right to sexual enjoyment with earnest intent." Of course, a topic like this will be treated with earnestness only when the hormones of young adults peak. For young men in the madrasas, sexual enjoyment at this age is mostly imaginary. Then Nasafi, in an attempt to explain when marriage is voluntary and when it becomes a necessity, writes, "It [marriage] is *sunna*." *Sunna* means that it is a precedent established by the Prophet Muhammad. But the prophetic precedent can vary in its prescriptive authority ranging from being optional to mandatory, an outcome that is highly dependent on interpretation. Marriage, Nasafi explains, by default has an optional legal status; it is not mandatory. Marriage is surely encouraged, but one is not a sinner if one stays single. But it could under certain circumstance be mandatory. And so Nasafi goes on to write a memorable sentence that sounds better in Arabic than in translation: "And if sexual desire is unbearable, then marriage becomes mandatory." He uses an elegant four-word Arabic phrase to express this: "*wa ʿinda ʾl-tawqan wajib,*" literally, "and when [desire] surges, it [marriage] is mandatory." The professor then explains that the word *tawqan* means a serious and unbearable surge in sexual desire to the point that one fears losing the ability to maintain one's chastity. Indulging in unlawful sex is, of course, for students of theology morally unthinkable.

At this point in the reading most male students are pondering their own sexual desires amid giggles and suppressed laughter. For a few days after the lesson, the *tawqan* phrase trends among students. They try to find any pretext to squeeze the newly acquired pithy phrase into their conversations, evoking hilarity and possibly yearning. And pity the soul who, after a nocturnal emission during sleep, requires an obligatory early morning shower before morning prayers. Of course, fellow students will tease the unlucky student on his way to the bathroom. "And when desire surges, marriage is mandatory!" someone will shout, repeating the pithy Arabic line. At reunions, madrasa graduates will humorously recall this phrase of Nasafi, even if they had forgotten all serious topics broached by the great Nasafi. A pithy phrase can often immortalize an author.

Two Egyptians, Jalaluddin Mahalli and Jalaluddin Suyuti, wrote a no-frills exegesis of the Qur'an, known as *The Exegesis of the Two Jalals* because both had identical first names. Jalaluddin Mahalli (d. 1459) was the less famous teacher of the highly reputed Jalaluddin Suyuti (d. 1505). Mahalli wrote the exegesis on the first chapter, called "The Opening," and then from chapter 18, "The Cave," to the last chapter, 114, "The People." Suyuti provided the exegesis of chapters 2 to 17, "The Cow" to "The Night Journey," otherwise titled "The Children of Israel." *The Exegesis of the Two Jalals* is an accessible text, avoiding controversial material that might be slanted to a mystical or philosophical interpretation. The two Jalals adopted only teachings supported by the orthodox Sunni canon of Qur'an exegesis. However, they have been criticized by contemporary scholars for uncritically adopting biblical lore, known as Isra'iliyat, materials that have for centuries been viewed as part of the Muslim canon but are now excised by revisionist commentators of the Qur'an.

Like the growing push-back against biblical lore in Qur'an exegesis with an exclusive focus on canonically approved exegesis, the emphasis on hadith studies too coincides with minimizing the philosophical edge of the curriculum. A form of exclusive Islamic or Islamized knowledge is prized over cosmopolitan resources of intelligible discourse. These shifts all signal a trend to cultivate a different kind of scholarly outlook among the madrasa graduates. This is a far cry from the kind of cultivation of religious scholars at the founding of the Nizami curriculum. In the early years, the ideal scholar was one whose rational and literary skills were honed by his education and who could function in the world as a humanist intellectual. Specialized professional apprenticeship in the bureaucracy, law, theology, teaching, and literature could provide him with a vocation. The new emphasis and shift, in my view, suggest that the madrasa graduate now has a narrower training, suitable only for the vocation as a Muslim religious functionary or a cleric.

CONCLUSION

The contemporary South Asian madrasa retains some features of an ancient scholastic tradition that values the role of a master-teacher, embraces didactic texts, fosters hermeneutical skills, and imparts a core of knowledge of foundational teachings in every discipline. Teaching antique texts seem to yield a diminishing harvest for students today given the gap between the style and presentation of classical authors and the contemporary sensibilities of readers. A history of the authors, their texts, and social contexts as well as the features of the texts might instill a greater appreciation. The motivations of scholarly rivalry and varieties of scholarship only enhance and deepen an understanding of the various disciplines. Snapshots and thumbnail sketches of texts, predispositions, and idiosyncrasies of a select number of authors I provided might serve as one way of beginning a deeper conversation of the history of texts, authors, and disciplines, all important features that are lacking in today's madrasa education.

The Nizami curriculum taught in South Asia's madrasas center on texts on multiple disciplines. Texts, after all, form the backbone of a surviving Islamic tradition narrowly conceived: the Muslim Republic of Letters. This scholarly tradition connects contemporary learning communities to their ancient forebears: noted figures in the Arab and the later Indo-Persian networks of scholars. Ideological divisions within discrete madrasa networks hamstring ongoing debates about curriculum reform. The debates pit reform-minded scholars against ultratraditionalists. The unacknowledged outcome of this tug-of-war manifests itself in a pathology where the cultivation of piety becomes the goal at the expense of rigorous scholarship.

CHAPTER SIX

From a Republic of Letters to a Republic of Piety

NETWORKED REPUBLICS

The eighteenth-century scholar Mulla Nizamuddin did far more than just provide a curriculum to train Muslim scholars in colonial India. He reinvigorated a learned community, and his efforts birthed, for modern India, a new iteration of what I call a Muslim Republic of Letters.

Nizamuddin's curriculum—stitched together as it was by nets of texts, by networks of teachers and students, by written commentaries and glosses on texts, by the exchange of letters, and above all by the circulation of the juridical *responsa* known as fatwas within discrete legal and theological schools formed a community of learning that served as a bridge from the past to his own time.[1] Graduates who studied his curriculum become "citizens" *avant la lettre*, of what we would today call a "virtual community." Scholars writing in Arabic and Persian participated in this community of the learned that crossed multiple geographic boundaries connecting India, Persia, and Central Asia to other Arabic-speaking regions of the Near East, North Africa, and Muslim Spain (Andalus).

Robust Islamic scholarly networks dating back to the tenth century gave rise to a proto-Muslim Republic of Letters. It possibly predates the European Republic of Letters, even though Muslims never called it a "republic." Scholars in different parts of a contiguous Muslim political and cultural landmass remained connected over time via this imagined community of scholars. This network of learned communities could be said to constitute an effective Muslim "public sphere," albeit of the learned and not necessarily of lay members of the public, as envisaged in Europe in modern times by Immanuel Kant. Yet the developments in eighteenth-century Muslim India mark an important turning point.

COUNTERPOINTS AND ECHOES

What were the genealogies and features of Nizamuddin's Muslim Republic of Letters? If the fifteenth-century European Republic of Letters took shape under the impetus of humanism and connected back to the Middle Ages, then Nizamuddin's network of scholarship in the eighteenth century connected to the emergence of Muslim learned communities dating back to the ninth century. In addition to the study of biblical languages, the European Republic of Letters placed its focus on Latin grammar, rhetoric, and poetry, combining attention to the humanities along with ethics and history. In the Muslim Republic of Letters, Arabic was the scholarly lingua franca, in addition to Persian. But what cemented at least these two communities of the learned was a uniform curriculum. One crucial difference, though, is that in Europe the study of nature was excluded, while in the Muslim world the study of nature was critical to the constitution of learned communities. In both locales—Europe and the geographically diverse Muslim Republic of Letters—the imagined communities of the learned were intent on generating consensus, fostering scholarly cooperation, and maintaining an exchange of information.[2] Scholars at first authored books and later published them with the aid of technology, traveled, and regularly corresponded with each other. Above all, they nurtured younger scholars and inducted them into the profession and calling of teaching.

Resilient in its continuity over time and space, the Muslim Republic of Letters differed significantly in other respects from its European counterpart. It was a much more exhaustive knowledge enterprise than its

Western counterpart. While Europeans studied what in Latin was known as the *trivium*—grammar, logic, and rhetoric—Muslim students in addition studied mathematics, philosophy, astronomy, literature, and a dizzying array of subjects related to specialized learning in theology and the exegesis of scriptural sources. These ranged from Qur'anic exegesis to prophetic traditions, theology, and mysticism. Philosophy and logic were especially important, as we will see in this chapter.

Yet something more elemental, a flourishing tradition of learning as a vital part of the human experience, held people together. The great Ibn Khaldun writes that human beings are obliged to cooperate with each other, not just for the sake of knowledge but also for their very survival. The critical basis for learning and shaping disciplines, he notes, is "an organized community" (*al-ijtimaʿ al-muhayya'*), itself contingent on political stability and social continuity.

History, however, emphasizes the elusiveness of both stability and continuity at different stages of Islamdom's growth and expansion. The mid-thirteenth-century sack of Baghdad by the Mongol hordes of Chengiz Khan devastated the heart of the Muslim world. And yet a number of nodes outside Iraq held the intellectual network together. In fact, Cairo actually benefited from the catastrophe in Iraq: for centuries thereafter, it stood as the primary Muslim intellectual center. The Muslim community's great gamble was one of dispersion, and it paid off: even if one node in the network suffered a setback, as happened in Baghdad, the community of scholars was sufficiently robust to absorb such shocks and then painstakingly to rebuild its institutions over time.

THE ʿULAMA

Muslim scholars gave various names to the concrete communities of people that united behind different knowledge purposes. The most common term used early on to refer to a community of the learned was the "learned" (ʿulama), individuals who are prized for their learning. Communities of learning were also known by other terms such as "folk of knowledge" (*ahl al-ʿilm*) and "scholarly cohort" (*mashaykha*). Specialists in law gradually founded their own academies or guilds known as the *madhahib* (sing. *madhhab*).[3]

The sole purpose of the academies was to advance the study of practical and theoretical jurisprudence and to ensure the continuity of that jurisprudence over time and space. Travel in search of learning became a well-established tradition; accounts by itinerant students, well-traveled teachers, and biographical dictionaries all contain a wealth of information of how scholarly communities were formed over time.

Indeed, Abu Ishaq al-Shatibi, a fourteenth-century scholar from Muslim Spain, best describes the community of learning. "Indeed knowledge was at first in the hearts of men," he writes; "then it was transferred to books; now the keys to knowledge are in the hands of scholars."[4] Mulla Nizamuddin, along with others, revived such a community of scholars in India who were entrusted the keys to Islamic knowledge.

BEYOND THE AUTODIDACT

While knowledge must be acquired through a personal commitment to learning, the Republic of Letters also includes—indeed requires—apprenticeship with a master. Apprenticeship is a crucial component of both the ancient and contemporary traditional Muslim communities of learning. Apprenticeship is such a crucial aspect that often a shortage of master-teachers, caused by mortality or increased demand, is itself seen as a sign of a decline in learning. That decline, in turn, is interpreted as a sign of providential displeasure. However, if a community repents and returns to rectitude, it will flourish with the aid of knowledge.

A master-teacher must show passion for his work; the master-teacher is reputed as a serious truth-seeker (*muhaqqiq*)—fallible, to be sure, but also adept in his or her professional expertise. Three distinctive characteristics set a master-teacher apart from others. First, the master-teacher acts on the imperatives of his knowledge and serves as an exemplar. Second, the master-teacher trains his disciples in the same manner that the Prophet Muhammad provided intimate, persistent guidance to his Companions. An apprentice experiences the challenges that the master-teacher encounters every day in the existential and scholarly life. Over time the apprentice develops a deep intuition, becoming attuned to the imperatives of learning to the point that he or she can "behold the proof [of the truth] with their eyes." Third, notes Shatibi, a student must imitate and internalize the exemplary conduct of the master-teacher. Every generation strives to imitate its predecessor and does so collectively, through team effort. An autodidact is an outlier to the orthodox tradition. Therefore, despite the brilliance and phenomenal scholarship of the tenth-century scholar Ibn Hazm of Muslim Spain, madrasa teachers often pointed to him as a prime exhibit of an autodidact who offended interlocutors and courted controversy. Why? Because it is alleged he lacked a master-teacher to instill in him the etiquette and the ethics of learning.

Every madrasa novice is saturated with the hagiography surrounding the importance of having master-teachers and then searches for opportunities for apprenticeship. I recall how I was taught that reverence for the master-teacher was more important than the acquisition of book learning itself. Whereas anyone can have access to books, my advisers reasoned, only the elect have the honor of being an apprentice to a master-teacher. Serving a master-teacher will ultimately let the light of learning enter the heart. In other words, knowledge will turn into practice. Of course, this element is often exaggerated; there is a dissonance between ideals and realities. Despite Shatibi's sage advice, as I later learned, the scholar from Muslim Spain himself challenged his most distinguished teacher, Abu Saʿid Ibn Lubb (d. 1380–81), and evoked the ire of his contemporaries! Over time, I too learned to be judicious in structuring working relationships with a master-teacher.

Attending a salon-like gathering (*majlis*) of senior professors at madrasas can be most illuminating learning opportunities. Mufti Mahmood Gangohi, the senior juristic authority at Deoband when I was a student at that institution in the 1980s, was also a Sufi master, so he daily received many visitors and traveled frequently. His late afternoon salon was often filled with visitors, faculty, and students. Visitors would share interesting reports or ask questions to which Mufti Mahmood would skillfully, humorously, and pithily reply. Attending the salon of Qari Muhammad Tayyab, the vice-chancellor of Deoband, often meant an hour-long intellectual treat of eloquent Urdu laced with philosophical insights and theological nuggets on any question posed to him or a topic raised in discussion. Despite the importance of finding a master-teacher, texts written by distinguished master-teachers in their own times are equally valued and play an important role in the scholarly formation of students.

SNAPSHOTS OF THE NIZAMI CURRICULUM

The significance of the eighteenth-century Nizami curriculum is its mobility: it points to something far larger and more diffuse than one person, one place, or one time. The curriculum not only fosters intellectual exchange between Indian scholars and their contemporaries; it also links them to a historical memory of predecessors across multiple ideological orientations, diverse spaces, and temporalities. During periods of great upheaval, this imagined community of scholars is able to give stability to the community of letters. The Nizami curriculum gives Muslims encountering the juggernaut of modernity a sense of their roots and a trace of their belonging.

The inception of the Nizami curriculum coincides, fatefully, with the political shocks and unstable transitions in Mughal rule. The dismemberment of the Mughal empire was followed by British colonial rule and then, by the mid-twentieth century, the creation of two independent and later, rival nation-states: Pakistan and India. Political uncertainty fosters religious imagination; during this same period, the community of religious scholars also nurtured some of the great minds of Muslim India. It endured for more than two centuries until it was surpassed and marginalized by the growing secular systems and the institutions of knowledge modern education spawned.

For all its diversity and range, the goal of Mulla Nizamuddin's curriculum was simple: to make students proficient in studying (*mutalaʿa*) classical texts in several disciplines. Even though the pedagogy involves a penchant for polemics, the texts are not merely an object of study. Rather, they are treated as carriers of knowledge that link their readers to a chain of authorized scholars in the past.

Argument and debate, far from being eschewed, are encouraged and rehearsed, in the manner of Socratic debates or polemics between adversarial points of view. Students gain a sense of the juristic and theological differences among scholars from a variety of schools within Islamdom. They also gain confidence in themselves as worthy successors to their scholarly mentors. And at its inception, the Nizami curriculum promoted logic and philosophy as tools meant to sharpen a student's skills in argumentation and debate. But the Nizami curriculum is one link in a long chain of curriculum developments associated with Muslims in premodern India that can be summarized in five phases.

PHASES OF EDUCATION IN THE SUBCONTINENT

From the beginning of Islamic education on the Indian subcontinent to the present day, the madrasa curriculum underwent alteration during five phases. Each phase is distinguished by the addition or subtraction of texts and changes in the focus of curricular design.

By this historical reckoning, Mulla Nizamuddin's curriculum in the eighteenth century fits into the fourth stage of a venerable trajectory of

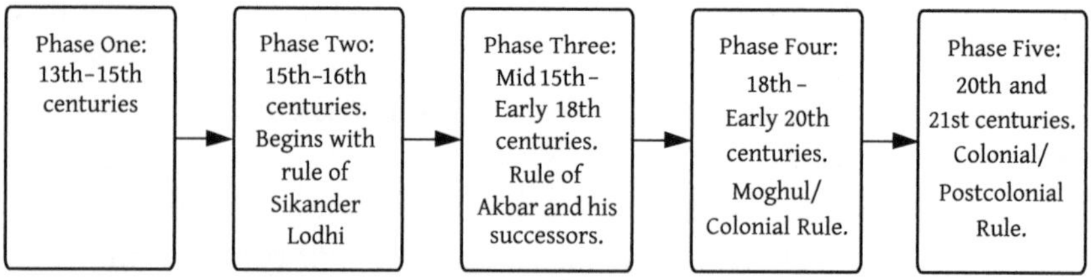

Periodization of education in India over time serves as a map of "Islamic education" compared to secular educational trends.

Islamic education. It serves as a capstone to a six-centuries-long tradition of an identifiably Muslim intellectual and scholarly tradition in India. It is representative of a hybrid Arabo-Islamic and Indo-Persian tradition of learning. As such, the Nizami curriculum is the most successful and durable version of that long-established knowledge tradition. Some texts used in this curriculum had already been introduced to the community of scholars in India as far back as the fourteenth century.

Nizamuddin's pedagogical method was to stress the rational core of the Muslim intellectual tradition; he selected specific texts for each subject area. He and other Muslim thinkers, like Shah Waliyullah, were of the same mind on the question of rationality. Waliyullah explicitly mentioned that divine inspiration instructed him to present Islam's teachings in "loose fitting garments with an abundance of demonstrative proof (*burhan*)."[5] Informed speculation, an approach encouraged by Ibn Khaldun, suggests that this feature of thought might resonate with both indigenous Islamic rational traditions and world trends at the time favoring rationality, especially with the rise of the West. Nizamuddin's intent was clear: to resuscitate the Muslim rational tradition was the best defense against perceived cultural and political threats from India's new political masters. As a mainstay the Nizami curriculum thus enjoyed a status akin to that of a canon in the madrasa tradition.

CANONIZING THE NIZAMI CURRICULUM

In an age of handheld technologies such as Kindles, iPads, mobile phones, cloud storage facilities, and technologies of presence, we have instant access to books, articles, and texts, if not entire libraries, via portable electronic gadgets. We feel empowered to have such an enormous amount of information at our fingertips. The biggest challenge to information users in the cyber age is to find the right filters to separate the gems of knowledge from the piles of useless information.

In the past, of course, people did not have instant access to limitless information. How did they process information and knowledge? In both the East and the West, scholars created portable digests of information. In the Latin West they called such portable texts and manuals by the name *vade mecum*. These were "texts to go" that a student carried wherever he or she went.

PRIMERS AND TEXTS

In the Islamic tradition, such "texts to go" were called *mutun*—pronounced *mu-toon*. *Mutun* is the plural of *matn*, pronounced *mutt-ne*, meaning "the surface of something" or "the visible or hard part of something," or it is another term for primers or core texts. Often core texts are short pieces of prose or rhymed verse. For the beginner, these primers sequence the foundational knowledge and subdivisions of each discipline.

In the madrasa, a subject or discipline is taught via assigned texts as a student advances from primers to advanced texts in each successive academic year. Sometimes texts are single-author primers. Some texts are designed and written by authors or coauthors for advanced students. On other occasions, an advanced text is a single-author commentary on a primer.

Commentaries are produced several decades or centuries after a text was composed. A key characteristic of a commentary is that it aims to remain authentic to the spirit of the original. Commentaries often resemble the original work in both method and style. The system is additive: the commentator adds his own understanding of the subject matter by providing illustrations. In this moral economy of knowledge, any new contribution is introduced by relying on the threads started by a previous author. But a commentator can also introduce material that was ignored by the original author.

Departing from a predecessor's style is a rare occurrence, something to be avoided. Often an author strives to design a commentary around a core text written by a predecessor in such a flawless and elegant manner that the reader hardly notices any authorial interruption, deviation, or time lag between the original and commentary. If it were not that the original text appears in parentheses, the reader will be surprised by the seamless representation.

Most texts or commentaries on texts have elaborate explanatory glosses in the margins to help the reader decipher the text. The marginalia elaborate or clarify an original author's terse remark or some unfathomable reference.

Innovation in knowledge does not mean that one challenges and critiques mainstream thinking; that is a very modern idea. Counterintuitively, one might ask the opposite question: why would people change their modes of thinking when the knowledge at hand serves their personal and societal needs?

Memory is the key instrument for acquiring and using text-based knowledge, but it is not a precondition. In the Indo-Persian scholastic tradition, students first study the primer—*matn*—in each subject matter. Attaining mastery of the primer, preferably by memorizing it, gives the student a solid foothold in the topics. All subsequent advancement in a subject matter is a grand elaboration of the original primer (*matn*). The substance of the primer material is invariably incorporated into the text of the commentaries and super commentaries.

ACADEMIC DISCIPLINES

Distinctive of the Nizami curriculum at its inception in the eighteenth century was the surfeit of rationalism. Students studied a total of seven texts on logic and three books on philosophy. The intellectual genealogy of Nizamuddin, the author of the curriculum, has much to do with it. Through his father, Qutbuddin, a line of teachers goes back six generations. It ends up in the sixteenth century with the rationalist and virtuoso scholar Mir Fathullah Shirazi (d. 1588), who cast his spell on a number of influential Indian scholars. Born and trained in Iran, Shirazi ended up in an influential position in the court of the emperor Akbar in Agra. One historian extols Shirazi's merits as "unsurpassed without an equal in the world," adding that if the entire archive of philosophical knowledge were destroyed, then Shirazi could singlehandedly reinvent it![6] This is high praise par excellence.

So it was Shirazi's influence that scalloped a robust Persian rationalist tradition into the Nizami curriculum. Indeed, the heavy presence of logic and philosophy in the early incarnations of the curriculum is a result of this Persian influence. At one point the curriculum listed five

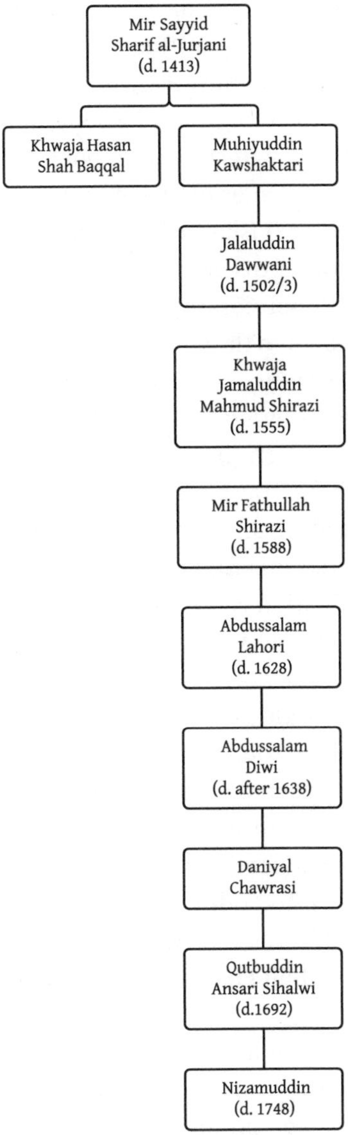

Significant Persian influence impacting the Nizami curriculum till the era of Shirazi.

texts on mathematics, with Euclid as a favorite. Paradoxically, during a subsequent mutation of the Nizami syllabus, beginning with the last decade of the nineteenth century, there was an inexplicable inflation of texts on subjects like logic, philosophy, and theology. I speculate that the increase in texts on rational discourses was designed to offset the rising growth in the teaching of hadith in the madrasas' curriculum.

At the inception of the twentieth century, the most dramatic change to the Nizami curriculum took place. The emphasis shifted to subjects like Qur'an exegesis, prophetic tradition, and Islamic law, while a parallel emphasis on the rational discourses, namely, logic, philosophy, and theology, was maintained. Today much of the material on rational discourses has been excised. A few texts remain in order to furnish students with explanations of keywords used in medieval Islamic logic and philosophical texts that might also be used in other disciplines.

With the curricular shift to the received opinion (*naql*) or Shariʿa-centered studies, the capstone year is dedicated to the study of prophetic traditions, hadith. Today the madrasa curriculum concentrates on the study of Arabic grammar, morphology, Arabic literature, Islamic law, theoretical jurisprudence or legal theory, premodern theology, Qur'an exegesis, and the interpretation of the prophetic traditions (hadith). Students are required to attend a yearlong reading and discussion session on sections of six major Sunni canonical books on prophetic reports (hadith). This effort then culminates in a graduation ceremony.

Shah Waliyullah originally proposed a shift toward the study of hadith in the eighteenth century. At the time, he also floated a hadith-focused curriculum; since the momentum was toward rational discourses, his proposal did not gain much support. It was only in the early twentieth century that the Nizami curriculum was amended and able to absorb a detailed hadith component. Prior to this change, most students studied only *The Niche of Lamps* (*Mishkat al-Masabih*), a compendium on hadith compiled by the fourteenth-century scholar Waliyuddin Muhammad b. Abdullah al-ʿIraqi (d. 1339), also known as al-Khatib al-Tabrizi. In other words, it took more than a century for Waliyullah's hadith-centered curricular proposal to gain traction.

The length of the madrasa academic program has gradually become shorter, from its previous eleven to nine years, to six or seven years, as a number of texts studied dealing with logic and philosophy were shed over time.

Attention to modern science remains peripheral. The study of English, computer literacy, and civics has become part of the curriculum of many madrasas. Yet these subjects do not enjoy serious attention as the other faith-related disciplines do. Interested students acquire writing and research skills in Urdu and Arabic by way of independent study with individual faculty members.

REFORMING THE CURRICULUM: ONGOING DEBATES

Today the efficiency of the Nizami Curriculum is widely debated. But many will claim that this debate had raged for most of the twentieth century. Its defenders aver the curriculum connects students to the canonical tradition, enhances their mastery of every discipline, and connects them to the knowledge of the faith and creatively equips scholars to solve new problems. But few have been able to rebut charges that the texts studied are redundant and at times impenetrable, save for a few scholars who have spent their lives mastering them.

Indeed, most texts are frustratingly terse, forcing teachers and students alike to scour commentaries and super commentaries for help. The multiple levels of calligraphic marginalia on each textbook page may look decorative, but they are taxing to the eyes and mind. For decades now, critics have petitioned for more lucid texts. But inertia has turned the texts and syllabus into inviolable monuments to the past, critics claim. The result is that students are poorly prepared and lack the confidence to critically engage the tradition in order to meet the needs of a changing world. Critics pointed out that students spent an excessive amount of time trying to master difficult classical texts without gaining any conceptual knowledge of the disciplines on which these texts were based.

Protagonists of the Nizami curriculum believe the canon of texts is infused with providential sanctity. They view any change to the curriculum as offensive and a step toward spiritual dereliction.[7] How? In the orthodox tradition there is a widely held belief that a favorable reception of a text or the good reputation of a scholar is a sign of divine approval. Many of these texts have been studied as classics over the ages, which gives the curriculum an aura of sanctity. In other words, the esteemed authors of the classroom texts also transmit their charisma and sanctity via their intellectual and spiritual formation to their readers, namely, the madrasa students. Hence, altering the canon—with its proven track record of success—is akin to rebuking God's favor.

Advocates of curriculum change list many reasons why the curriculum had become moribund. One chief reason was the protest mindset adopted by the ʿulama against British colonialism, which caused madrasas to avoid anything that was culturally related to the British. Hence, they avoided the study of the English language and Western disciplines. But the conditions of colonialism no longer exist, some counter. Now, the advocates of curriculum change argue that the study of not only English but also other modern subjects is indispensable to any serious educational endeavor. They urge madrasa administrators to revise their earlier position vis-à-vis cosmopolitan learning.

In fact, advocates of change invoke the authority of the staunchly anticolonial Muhammad Qasim Nanautvi, the cofounder of the Deoband school. He, they say, realized the importance of the English language back in the nineteenth century.[8] On returning from Mecca after pilgrimage by ship, Nanautvi was unable to communicate with the ship's captain except through a translator. Realizing the limits and frustrations of translation, he vowed to learn English and remedy his communication deficit. Unfortunately, he died shortly after his return from pilgrimage, and his vow went unfulfilled. Emboldened by Nanautvi's courageous vow, some madrasa figures claim that the Nizami curriculum is neither "as fragile as glass" that it should shatter at the mention of change nor so "sacralized" (*tabarruk*) that it would be polluted by alteration. Yet changes in both the curriculum and the mode of education in traditional madrasas still remain a vexed subject for countless reasons.

Differences in pedagogical philosophy among members of the madrasa community can be counted as another reason for a lack of consensus in order to embark on curricular reform. Some administrators refuse to relinquish the age-old system of education, where the mastery of texts is a sign of expertise in a subject. For others, more prone to change, texts are mere instruments to gain proficiency in a subject area and are thus negotiable; they prefer that a professor lecture to students with approved accessible textbooks written in a modern idiom.

So at the end of the day, the great strength of the Nizami curriculum turned out to be its greatest liability. Protagonists of the curriculum turned it into a monument. Ironically, for a pedagogy that once prized reason, it now yielded defenders who take refuge in a debilitating dogmatism. Many critics do raise the question as to whether the current madrasa system does not recycle intellectual mediocrity and portray it as piety.

TWEAKING THE NIZAMI CURRICULUM

Efforts to make systemic changes to the curriculum already began at end of the nineteenth century. Sir Sayyid Ahmad Khan (d. 1898) proposed curricular change as a proponent of modern knowledge. He established what later became the modern Aligarh Muslim University, which posed a challenge to Muslim orthodoxy in colonial India. Traditional scholars linked to the various madrasas became acutely aware of the knowledge gap between the modernizers on the one hand and the traditionalists on the other, but they were hamstrung to alter it. They were too committed to their ideologies; change would require a refashioning of who they were.

Sensing this growing gap between different classes of Muslims, a small group of traditional scholars established a reform movement known as the Council or Association of Scholars, better known by its Arabic title, Nadwatul ʿUlama. Its pioneer was Mawlana Muhammad Mongheri (d. 1918). A distinguished scholar and spiritual master, he grasped the challenges of his times. Troubled by internal sectarianism and a debilitating orthodoxy among rival Muslim groups in the face of daunting political and social challenges, Mawlana Mongheri led the reformists. Joined by prominent religious scholars in a founding meeting in the North Indian city of Kanpur in 1893, he started a new scholarly initiative.

Mongheri and his colleagues wished to train and educate Muslim religious scholars in the modern disciplines in order that they may be able to meet the enormous challenges of their time. Despite vocal opposition from conservatives, a new madrasa known as the Darul Uloom Nadwatul ʿUlama, shortened as Nadwa, was established in the city of Lucknow on the cusp of the twentieth century, in 1898. Armed with a reformed curriculum, Nadwa's founders believed, they would produce a differently skilled religious leadership that is capable of living up to its striking motto: "to combine the useful past with the beneficial modern."

The primary purpose of Nadwa was to remedy shortcomings in knowledge of science and the Arabic language. First, religious scholars needed to become familiar with the discourses of modern science with the aim to shape a new Islamic theology conversant with the scientific discourses of the modern world. Second, the absence of depth and fluency in the Arabic language hampered students' understanding of the classical tradition, so the Nadwa stressed the need to deepen the understanding of the Arabic language and the history of Islamicate culture. Such linguistic efficiency had the added benefit of facilitating transnational Islamic collaboration and furthering coherence within the global Muslim community.

Nadwa might not have entirely succeeded in its grandiose goals of making an impact on religious thought. It did, however, succeed in producing some very prolific authors who published in Arabic and local languages their contributions to historical studies in India. More modestly, it managed to trigger curricular debates among the Deobandi, Ahl-i Hadith, and, to a lesser extent, Barelvi madrasa networks, with mixed results. Some madrasas follow Nadwa's revised curriculum. More accessible and modern Arabic language texts are used in several disciplines, but the core texts of the Nizami curriculum in law, theology, and the study of the Qur'an remain unchanged. Throughout the twentieth century, very modest curricular reforms took place in madrasas based in India, Pakistan, and Bangladesh, even though reforms never became sufficiently far-reaching to meet the social and political needs of the reform-minded section of the traditionalists.

In the post-9/11 environment, pressure on madrasa communities to engage in curricular reform yielded few dividends. Madrasa authorities reject, with visceral contempt, the implied charge that terrorism and militancy are fomented in their institutions. International surveillance of madrasas and unsuccessful efforts by governments in India, Pakistan, and Bangladesh to take control of private madrasas through regulation have only contributed to heightened suspicion of foreign intentions and, in the process, have stymied much-needed curricular reform.

In several countries, the respective madrasa leadership cohorts continue to engage in extensive discussions about the reform of their institutions from curricular change to institutional revision. In the past decade alone, dozens of conferences and workshops were held in Pakistan, India, and Bangladesh to address a variety of issues.

This flurry of activity is suffused with varying shades of irony, ranging from disappointing to triumphal. It has rekindled the age-old question of the raison d'être of madrasas and their efficiency in a globalizing world. Unfortunately, little has been achieved in terms of tangible outcomes. At the same time, the madrasa leadership boasts that despite opposition from several quarters, the Nizami curriculum has remained viable and attractive, therefore promoting the growth instead of attrition of madrasas. Yet most institutions do recognize the shadows of constraints ranging from competition over financial resources to the need to respond to the challenges offered by a secularizing world rife with political instability.

INSIDER LESSONS

My own experiences in at least three madrasas of India offer me a unique vantage point to express a view on curricular developments. After several decades I have come to realize that the madrasa curriculum is really not designed to meet the needs of an undergraduate student. The texts are accessible only to students who have a strong grounding in Arabic and know something more than just the foundational debates in every discipline. To teach students Arabic side by side with these highly stylized and nuanced Arabic texts in the various disciplines is an exercise in frustration and results in a hollow form of certification for the majority of graduates.

Even though I did pretty well and worked hard on understanding the various subjects taught via the standardized classical texts during my madrasa years, the true beauty of the Nizami curriculum and its gems dawned on me only in my post-madrasa life. Once I was equipped with a great deal of history, modern philosophy, debates in religious studies, complex debates in modern theology, Islamic law, and moral philosophy—in short, as a graduate and postdoctoral student—only then could I begin to see the gems and value of the Nizami curriculum.

If I had it my way, I would propose that the study of the Nizami curriculum be assigned as a postgraduate program. Prior to that, students should undergo a foundational three- to four-year intensive program in which they are exposed to a wide array of Islamic and modern disciplines as prerequisites. In order to produce well-equipped undergraduate students, their exposure to disciplines such as Islamic law, legal theory, theology, Qur'an exegesis, hadith studies, Islamic history, and philosophy should be a prerequisite of their training. Students should be exposed to experienced professors who use a combination of accessible texts and effective pedagogical methods, including lectures and small group seminars. Language preparation, especially in Arabic and Persian, together with communication skills in Urdu and English will be indispensable. It is absolutely indispensable at this stage to give students exposure to the modern humanities and the social sciences so that they have the tools to grapple with the challenges of modern life. Graduates of this three- to four-year program will be sufficiently qualified to become mosque leaders, impart Islamic literacy to the young and old, communicate with a broader public, and serve a diverse religious sector from faith-based journalism, media, and publishing to staffing community-based organizations. The madrasa should retain its etiquette of self-formation and piety, which is its hallmark. This kind of training does indeed shape graduates to give guidance and serve as exemplars for a faith-based life.

Qualified students who wish to pursue serious academic training can study the Nizami curriculum at a graduate level, during which they will also specialize in various disciplines. This could be an exclusive concentration on the Nizami curriculum or one that is augmented by modern disciplines.

In the mid-twentieth century, a prominent scholar belonging to the Deoband school made a similar proposal to the one I offered above. Manazir Ahsan Gilani, the Deoband graduate whom we met earlier and who became a professor at the Osmania University in Hyderabad, not only authored the definitive biography of Deoband's founder Muhammad Qasim Nanautvi but also proposed reforms to the madrasa curriculum. Four madrasa texts, he proposed, should be translated into Urdu and be integrated into the high school and college curricula for Muslim students in postindependence India. Gilani's goal was to preserve Muslim identity in a multireligious and multicultural postindependence India with a Hindu majority via education. He recommended that Muslim students take college classes where subjects like the study of the Qurʾan, hadith, Islamic law, and theology are taught, in addition to the study of Arabic.

The more interesting part of Gilani's proposal got the least attention. He recommended that most of the existing madrasas be turned into the equivalent of functional middle and high schools. Only a select number of madrasas, he argued, should be preserved and dedicated to serious and advanced theological education. Gilani's proposal has, of course, fallen on deaf ears. Madrasa authorities are too wedded to the existing system with its trappings of Islamic authenticity. Clinging to tradition at times of crisis provides a certain solace.

Gilani's implied message about the Nizami curriculum coincides with mine. The Nizami curriculum requires a certain intellectual maturity to fully understand its purposes and goals. This can only be fruitfully mined at a graduate level, where it will deliver optimal dividends. In that way the curriculum will advance scholarship on Islam that will be of high quality as well as effective in terms of the needs of orthodox Muslim communities. But even the best proposals hardly received serious attention.

Yusuf Binnawri (d. 1977) was a larger-than-life figure in Pakistan's Deobandi circles. He was a man of demonstrable credentials in classical Islamic learning combined with a strong personality and fiery passions. Binnawri and Gilani were reputed students of Anwar Shah Kashmiri

(d. 1933), a major intellectual and scholar in the Deobandi firmament. While directing and leading his own influential madrasa in Karachi until his death, Binnawri too realized the need for curricular reform.[9] He petitioned for the inclusion of modern disciplines in the madrasa curriculum among his peers and aimed to improve the teaching of the Arabic language. Despite the radiance of his fame, even he could not effectively implement any substantive curricular change at his own institution, which he administered on a tight leash, apart from cosmetic changes. Inertia, resistance, and a lack of vision have cumulatively hobbled the intellectual project of madrasa education, where the piety aspect repeatedly outweighs the scholarly dimension. If only the advice of Ibn Khaldun was heeded and the madrasas taught, the history of Muslim disciplines, especially the biographies and histories of the texts and authors studied in the Nizami curriculum, then the beauty and complexity of this tradition of learning might be appreciated.

Adapted versions of the Nizami curriculum are now taught in all madrasas—irrespective of Deobandi and Barelvi franchises—in South Asia and their satellite institutions around the world. Madrasas in the United Kingdom, South Africa, and the United States connected to these franchises enjoy greater freedom to tinker with the curriculum and to substitute older texts with more modern ones.[10] But on the Indo-Pak subcontinent, rivalry between competing madrasa communities makes tampering with the curriculum a costly political exercise. At stake is the prestige of the franchise: curricular reform will affect the authenticity of the institution that goes through with reform. Madrasa administrators are impelled by many scruples to delay introducing curricular change.

Exempt from such misgivings are perhaps the Ahl-i Hadith madrasas and those affiliated to the Jamat-i Islami. This smaller subnetwork of madrasas feels no obligation to follow the Nizami curriculum, since they are firmly in the reformist camp of Islamic thought and often challenge the established Hanafi orthodoxies affiliated to the Deobandi and Barelvi schools. Indeed, many of institutions in the Ahl-i Hadith subnetwork have tried to internationalize their curricula in order to resemble developments in Islamic studies in the Arab Middle East.

So when the intellectual edge of the Nizami curriculum taught in the madrasas is underplayed, in my view, a new predisposition replaces the emphasis on scholarship. I call this hyperemphasis on piety at the cost of robust intellectual thought the emergence of a Republic of Piety that replaces the Republic of Letters.

REPUBLIC OF PIETY

Changes to the Nizami curriculum have coincided with the gradual alteration of the function and, by implication, the raison d'être of the madrasa in modern South Asia. It has morphed from being an academic cum religious institution into an exclusively religious institution. A renewed focus on prophetic traditions, Islamic law, and traditional theology displaces philosophy and critical and complex mystical traditions, and ignores modern disciplines. The madrasa now plays a new role: it promotes piety, a lowest common denominator. The accent is on cultural preservation and to entrench Muslim identity through a stripped-down version of traditional learning.

The contemporary madrasa, for example, retains only a fraction of the classical humanistic tradition of Islamic learning. In fact, many madrasa authorities now explicitly say that the raison d'être of the madrasa is not to produce intellectual giants but to cultivate men and women of pious predisposition. Most madrasa graduates are deeply enmeshed in pious religious endeavors such as preaching, evangelical work, publication, promoting mosque activities, media activity, and teaching. The majority of graduates are everyday practitioners, not armchair philosophers or reflective citizens. Any chance of reinvigorating a robust discursive tradition that meshes with the rhythms of modern life for now remains moot.

When madrasa graduates and madrasa authorities defend Islam from external challenges, they do so by preaching religious tradition with a religious truth, not a vibrant discursive truth. Madrasas now view it as their purpose to defend the traditional intellectual tradition from the secular knowledge spheres supported by the nation-state. But many madrasa authorities are questioning whether their graduates are sufficiently equipped to combat such challenges without the requisite knowledge skills. This has plunged the contemporary madrasas of South Asia into a deep crisis of relevance, even though most soldier forth, ostrich-like, without any adequate resolution of the challenges. Finding scapegoats—the West, secularists, modernizing Muslim elites—is a convenient excuse to deflect the problem.

CONCLUSION

The study of classical texts was once the pride of an intellectually robust madrasa tradition. Today, the relevance of these texts has come under intense scrutiny, both from those within madrasa communities and from those outside them. This is the case even as madrasa graduates are expected to become the learned in matters of religion and to command a broader competence in the relevance and uses of these texts. Have the classical texts that are still taught in the madrasa become talismans of authenticity? While these texts serve as an archive of Muslim memory, history, and practice, there remain questions as to whether the madrasa curriculum can produce competent graduates who can really serve the public good in the twenty-first century. Debates about the viability and efficiency of madrasa curricula have raged for decades without adequate resolution, since the madrasa-based jury itself is divided.

Few will challenge the claim that the madrasa curriculum succeeded in producing an antique form of normativity, what we would otherwise call an Islamic orthodoxy. Some sections of the madrasa community are themselves agnostic as to whether the educational model they offer will be sufficient for a renewed and revitalized normative tradition that claims to be authentic and orthodox and yet relevant to the world.

Growing literacy, the ongoing information and digital revolutions, and a rapidly altering public sphere, many observe, have all expanded the much-vaunted Muslim Republic of Letters beyond the medium of books and teachers. An entire citizenry of cyber-connected Muslims live outside the madrasas. They debate and discuss in myriads of media and formats how to advance the public good in different languages and moral registers. Within and outside the madrasas, people are questioning, with an air of pessimism, whether the madrasa—its curriculum and graduates—are equipped with the skills, talents, and vocabularies needed to participate in this emerging global public sphere.

Yet many madrasa authorities are actively striving to make themselves relevant to the needs of the current epoch. The reflexive response on the part of some is to be defensive against criticism and to exhibit triumphalism about success with their audiences despite meager resources. But some among the madrasa communities do admit that they are indeed participants in the public sphere and claim to do so on their terms and values, and are bound to adopt more realist positions on a range of issues. Since madrasas do not fit well into a nation-state's "vertebral globalization" strategy, might there be an opportunity for them to become participants in "cellular globalization?"[11] These transnational madrasa networks can effectively replicate themselves without central messaging and espouse an international civil society with humanist goals.

So the question remains: will the public sphere, with its hegemonic discourses, be open to multiple languages and a plurality of forms of the "good," including the "good" as articulated by the madrasa communities? Will madrasas take advantage of cellular globalization by adopting an alternative polity on a vast scale, or will we witness a turn in the opposite direction where more traditional forms of globalization will become manifest with its parallel public spheres? Are we heading for a new tower of Babel with increasing levels of incommensurability among communities and an epic clash of values?

PART THREE

Politics of Knowledge

Hadith studies are at the heart of the contemporary South Asian madrasa. Hadith is the source of the Sunna, the model and normative practice of the Prophet Muhammad that all pious Muslims aspire to imitate. The Indo-Pak subcontinent has long taken pride in advancing the study of hadith. Madrasa life culminates in the study of hadith as both a pious and scholarly practice at once.

CHAPTER SEVEN

Preserving the Prophet's Legacy

LANDSCAPES OF PIETY

Mufti Muhammad Taqi ʿUsmani is a distinguished traditional Pakistani scholar affiliated to the Deoband school in Pakistan. Like his equally renowned father, Mufti Muhammad Shafiʿ, Taqi ʿUsmani is a mufti, an expert authorized to issue scholarly opinions (fatwas) on matters related to Islamic legal and ethical teachings. For some years he served as a judge on Pakistan's Shariat Appeal Court. Nowadays he serves on several influential advisory boards of internationally renowned Islamic banking and finance institutions. His innovative views on Islamic banking and more sober views on politics have earned him some notoriety among sections of Pakistan's clergy. Many have unleashed their fusillades of angry denunciations of ʿUsmani's views on Islamic banking in print.[1]

Taqi ʿUsmani prides himself as being a conservative traditionalist. His reflections after a visit to a well-established and prosperous madrasa in the Indonesian capital, Jakarta, some years ago are quite revealing. "I requested to see the classrooms of the madrasa," ʿUsmani writes, "and so the principal guided me there."[2]

Keeping in mind the extraordinary deference for the study of hadith in orthodox South Asian madrasa circles, Taqi ʿUsmani's curiosity to know how this subject was taught in Jakarta is not surprising. But his reaction, recorded in theatrical detail, shows the polarized and highly differentiated perspectives among Muslims, especially on matters of gender. Let's hear ʿUsmani in his own words: "When I reached the *dar al-hadith*, the auditorium where prophetic traditions are taught, I saw to my growing incomprehension, dismay, and sadness, a mixed gathering of men and women auditioning a class on prophetic traditions (*hadith*). I asked the principal in total disbelief: 'You even have gender-mixing during the study of *hadith*?' The principal took a small sigh, and replied: 'Yes, this is our Indonesian Islam and we provide a robust version of this education here.' "[3]

Gender mixing causes emotional turmoil to the maudlin ʿUsmani. Here is a case of differences in Muslim moral temperament. A version of Indonesian orthodoxy allows gender mixing in religious education like the madrasa that ʿUsmani visited. This very same practice of gender mixing is not only an anathema but is also unthinkable to South Asian madrasa orthodoxy. ʿUsmani soon displaced this unpleasant experience in Jakarta with the fond memories of the founders of the Deoband madrasa to which he is affiliated. "At that moment [in Indonesia]," ʿUsmani writes, as he exults in his pious South Asian scholarly ancestry, "I appreciated those scholars (ʿulama) who inhabit the coarse mats of the unsightly madrasas [of South Asia] but who surely emulate the exemplary norm of the Prophet in their institutions."[4] His statement records not only the physical distance in miles between Deoband and Jakarta but also the distance in religious temperament and sensibility between different brands of Islam and orientations among Muslims as the variation between South Asian and Indonesian orthodoxies in this instance reveals.

In order to understand ʿUsmani's reaction, it is necessary to grasp the reverential status the study of hadith enjoys in South Asian madrasas. Hadith literature provides the details for a life of practice that leads to salvation. Madrasa education is dedicated to this goal. For Muslim orthodoxy, the *Sunna* enjoys the same authority as the Qurʾan. Therefore, the ʿulama and the madrasa-based orthodoxy often severely criticize modernist interpretations of Islam that either neglect or skeptically dismiss the authority of the hadith/*Sunna*.

Why do scholars in the madrasas attach such a high premium to the teachings of the Prophet Muhammad? Muslim orthodoxy hopes to instill

Canon of Sunni Hadith Books

In madrasas, the capstone year consists of a review of at least major collections of hadith books, known as the six authentic books in the Sunni canon. The books of Bukhari and Muslim are studied with great care, while selected sections of the other books are studied during that year. Some madrasas may add few other books from which some chapters are read.

Sahih (Authentic Book) of al-Bukhari (d. 870)
Sahih (Authentic Book) of al-Muslim (d. 874)
Jamiʿ (Collection) of Tirmidhi (d. 892)
Sunan (Traditions) of Abu Dawud (d. 888)
Sunan (Traditions) of Nisa'i (d. *c.* 914–15)
Sunan (Traditions) of Ibn Maja (d. 886)

Additional books that are read:

Shama'il (Character Portrait) of Tirmidhi (d. 892)
Muwatta (The Trodden Path) of Malik (d. 795)

in believers a reverence for the charisma of the Prophet Muhammad, so that they almost spontaneously live according to prophetic norms, *Sunna*, in their daily lives. Orthodox versions of the global Islamic revival, like the Tabligh movement, are especially nourished by South Asia's Deobandi madrasas. The Tabligh registers phenomenal success in popularizing the practice of the *Sunna* among devout practitioners. But they are not alone. Other brands of Muslim orthodoxy, such as the Barelvi school and the Salafis, also embrace the *Sunna*. A telltale sign of the embodied *Sunna* is Muslim men sporting fist-length beards and long shirts, covering their knees, with their pants raised above their ankles, while conscientious women completely cover their faces. Critics of madrasa orthodoxy, of course, say that the *Sunna* is more than paraphernalia. Orthodoxy, critics claim, often ignores the substantive moral teachings of the Prophet by obsessing with the cultural expressions of Arabian Islam.

Yet, for madrasa orthodoxy, norms exemplified by the Prophet Muhammad evoke pious memories. Therefore, every time the Prophet Muhammad's name is spoken in class, the professor and students pray for blessings and salutations on the Prophet, by repeating the invocation in Arabic *sallallahuʿalayhi wa sallam*, meaning, "God's prayers and peace be upon him." But most Muslims too repeat the invocation on the mention of the Prophet, so it is not a unique practice to orthodoxy. The professor who teaches hadith is known as the "master of hadith studies"—*shaykh al-hadith*—and occupies the highest academic honor, a position more prominent than the professor who teaches Qurʾan commentary.

EMBODYING THE PROPHET IN SCHOLARSHIP

Preserving the memory of the Prophet as a model worthy of emulation and remembering his Companions as pious role models is the desideratum of those who self-identify with madrasa orthodoxy, whose perspective on the *Sunna* is explained below. The Qurʾan addresses the Prophet Muhammad and asks him to announce, "Say [O Muhammad]: 'If you love God, then surely follow me' "; in other words, follow the Prophet's teachings. If you do so, then the verse promises "God will love you and forgive your sins: for God is often forgiving, most merciful" (Q 3:30).

Observing this Qurʾanic commandment, male and female figures in seventh-century Arabia meticulously witnessed the Prophet Muhammad's practices, utterances, and endorsements of the actions of others. Then they recorded these narratives for posterity, first in oral reports and in later generations through writing. Portraits of the Companions of the Prophet and how, as members of his community, they understood his teachings were also recorded. Hence, what came to be known as the "path" (*Sunna*) is, in reality, a repository of moral norms and values, which are—here is the crucial part—experienced in a lived community. Of course, the *Sunna* is documented in reports, which follow complex protocols of interpretation.

Scholars painstakingly collect, verify, vet, and interpret these reports dating from antiquity to modernity. The task of interpreting huge quantities of prophetic reports is associated with scholarly prestige and competition, which in turn generate their own controversies. Reports are plagued by variants and inaccuracies and are, at times, subject to outright forgeries. And task forces of dedicated scholars do vigilantly expunge unreliable material over time.

A life based on the *Sunna* is how a devout Muslim gains proximity to the Prophet Muhammad. But reports constitute only one source of authority that mediates the Prophet Muhammad to believers over time. Belonging to a lived community of practitioners, in whose daily rhythms the prophetic practices unfold, is an equally indispensable source. Therefore, imitating the Prophet Muhammad is a cardinal part of Islam's teachings. How exactly Muslims should emulate the Prophet is, of course, a topic eagerly debated in scholarly and lay circles around the world today. Disagreements account for the diversity of practices among Muslims. For some, only the moral teachings taught by the Prophet constitute the *Sunna*. For others, even his routine actions, such as eating and drinking, are equally worthy of emulation.

South Asia's madrasas, in all their diversity, are proud to be the last bastions that take seriously the study and a life of practice based on the prophetic norms. They view the preservation, dissemination, and advancement of the teachings of the Prophet Muhammad as the highest service a scholar can render to the faith and regard it as a mark of loyalty and devotion to the Prophet.

The *Sunna* and the Qur'an, the revelation vouchsafed to the Prophet Muhammad through direct inspiration, are the two treasured sources of Muslim teachings. The documents of the *Sunna* are skillfully studied by generations of madrasa-based scholars. Scholars in the madrasas thrive on their authority and skill to interpret the hadith in a reliable manner, whereas some skeptical Western scholars dismiss large portions of this corpus as inauthentic.

DOCUMENTING THE PROPHET MUHAMMAD IN INDIA

South Asia as a region has been connected to hadith scholarship dating back to the eighth century. During Abbasid rule, small Arab expeditions from far-off Baghdad reached the port city of Bharuch on the banks of the Narmada River in the state of Gujarat in today's India. Among the newcomer scholars who landed in Sindh first and possibly later in Gujarat was one Abu Bakr al-Basri (d. c. 776).[5] In the annals of Islam, he competed with other scholars for the distinction of being among the first to have compiled a book on hadith.[6] The fact that Basri was buried somewhere around 776 C.E. on the eastern shore of the Gulf of Khambhat, perhaps near the town of Bhadbut, remains a source of great pride and honor for Muslims living in the state of Gujarat specifically and for the people of South Asia generally.

Other Arab Muslim explorers, scholars, and travelers also ended up in Gujarat. Several wrote valuable commentaries on the most revered of Sunni canonical hadith collections, namely, the *Authentic Book of*

Bukhari.[7] Figures like Sayyid ʿAbd al-Awwal al-Husayni produced one such precious hadith commentary, sources say, when he reached Gujarat. In other words, the bridge between premodern India and the Middle East was mediated by crucial scholarship on Islam as a faith tradition. At the time, scholarship dedicated to Islam's teachings emanating from India boosted the reputation of this region and ended its status as a backwater. By the mid-eleventh century, the imprint of Islam was so strong that the city of Bharuch in Gujarat boasted a madrasa and a cathedral mosque. Muslim institutional presence flourished long before Muslims took political power in that part of the subcontinent. Religious diversity, made possible by tolerant Hindu rule, advanced religious pluralism in that early period.

Muslims in South Asia take particular pride in showcasing their contribution to memorializing the Prophet Muhammad. Internationally renowned scholarship on hadith flowers in South Asia—India and Pakistan—a tradition that continues to this very day. Through print and other means of communication, these scholarly labors were shared with other centers of the Muslim world. Highly reputed teachers and institutions drew students to study in Gujarat in the thirteenth century onward. Today, many madrasas in Gujarat flourish thanks to the largesse of Gujarati expatriates around the world.

AUDITING CLASSES

After an absence of more than two decades from the madrasa world, I audited a few classes in Gujarat, the Indian state in which I had begun my own madrasa career. I sat in on classes on Islamic law and hadith. And on occasion, when a teacher did not show up, I sat around with dozens of students whom I quizzed and who asked me a range of questions about scholarship in the West and, most importantly for them, the reception of Islam in the West in a post-9/11 world.

Returning to the madrasa classroom brought back a flood of memories, feelings, and emotions of my past. I distinctly recall the way I was made to understand the close connections between learning and piety, especially the sacrality of knowledge. As a learner, tradition taught, one is on par with a warrior defending God's just cause (jihad), a deeply held value and aspiration. Not only was the ink of the scholar greater than the blood of martyrs, but the mere sensation that one is entering an extremely noble and cherished cause of learning that holds out consequences for one's salvation was an overwhelming feeling and an emotion difficult to cast off. An unnerving thought is also engraved on the psyche of the novice: to betray the responsibility of knowledge vouchsafed is to court damnation.

AUDITING AN ISLAMIC LAW (*FIQH*) CLASS

Some ten miles (16 km) from the bustling city of Bharuch is the town of Kantharia, with a population of about 20,000. Three decades ago it was a large village, but today it has the infrastructure of a vibrant rural town. In part, this has resulted from the presence of Darul Uloom Kantharia, one of at least a half dozen medium-sized and fairly well-heeled madrasas in the Bharuch district of Gujarat. Most of the madrasas in this region follow the theological line of the Deoband school, while a smaller number are affiliated to the Barelvi school. The students at the madrasa come from nearby villages, but some are from other parts of India with a smattering of international students.

About a thousand students enroll in the two- to three-year program to memorize the entire Qur'an at the Kantharia madrasa. Each person who completes this pious feat is known as a *hafiz*, plural *huffaz* (pronounced *haa-fizz*). Literally, the word *hafiz* means "protector" or "preserver." In other words, those who memorize the Qur'an also protect it. For the majority of this cohort, Qur'an memorization with some elementary theology is a terminal qualification. Most graduates of this program will pursue other careers. But communities honor them for carrying the Qur'an in their hearts. Some will become prayer leaders at mosques, especially during the month of Ramadan when the entire Qur'an is recited in nightly vigils. A handful will hone their vocal skills to become "reciters" (*qari*, pl. *qurra'*), specialists who recite the Qur'an in various melodious styles and will perform at special events in mosques, public events, and religious ceremonies.

Yet a smaller cohort will enroll in advanced theological studies, to be qualified as religious scholars ('ulama). Some 500 students enroll in this nine-year program at Kantharia, and about 40 students graduate annually after completing the Nizami curriculum of Arabic texts.

At Kantharia I audited a class taught by a senior faculty member. The subject matter was prophetic traditions, hadith. It was Christmas, but in madrasas on the Indo-Pakistan subcontinent it was just another regular school day. Mufti Isma'il Sarodi was from Sarod, a town at some distance

Mufti and Fatwa

A mufti is a jurist qualified to issue academic opinions on matters of Islamic law, that is, a specialist in *fiqh* and Shariʿa matters. Through training, apprenticeship, experience, and peer recognition, a jurist becomes a mufti. In the early period, jurists hardly ever used this epithet to indicate their status. It has become popular in the modern period. Various Muslim empires had muftis who gave rulings representing the juridical tradition on matters of public and private concern. Modern nation-states now appoint muftis who are in the employ of the state and represent the juridical tradition via the modern state.

The decisions issued by muftis, preceded by a specific query, are called fatwa(s). Fatwas are not edicts but rather scholarly opinions based on research done by the muftis who navigate the canons of their juridical tradition. In the West, the word "fatwa" gained some notoriety when Ayatollah Khomeini of Iran pronounced that the Indian-born British novelist Salman Rushdie should be executed for insulting the Prophet Muhammad in his novel *The Satanic Verses*. In popular Western media, the term has incorrectly earned the emblem of an edict. Colloquially, in the West, "fatwa" means "death sentence," an understanding that is far removed from Islamic law. Mufti is a common title among Sunnis, while the title *mujtahid* or *marjaʿ* is used among Shiʿas. Historically fatwas carried only the force of tradition, not that of state power. However, in several modern nation-states, the invention of an official state mufti changes the equation. In these cases, the mufti is armed with state authority; therefore, his view carries some amount of coercive power when it enters into the country's court system.

from Kantharia. He was an ethnic Gujarati. And as his title, mufti, suggests he was qualified to issue nonbinding opinions on Muslim law.

ELUCIDATING THE TEXT: CAT SALIVA AND RITUAL PURIFICATION

On the day I audited, Mufti Sarodi was teaching a graduating class a capstone text authored by a tenth-century scholar, Abu Jaʿfar al-Tahawi

(d. 933), from Upper Egypt. Tahawi's text gave readers an up-close view of how the techniques of interpretation (forensics) are applied in Islamic law. Islamic law is popularly called *fiqh* or Shariʿa interchangeably, although there are technical differences between the two. The day's lesson showed how different reports and Qurʾanic verses and juristic interpretations were stitched together to constitute an argument. The interpretive process is called hermeneutics, and several technical terms capture the nuances.

An interpreter can "elucidate" a text of the Qurʾan or a hadith report by connecting it to other passages of the scripture or any other authoritative source. A linguistic clarification of a word or a concept can also amplify or narrow the clarification, which is generically called "exegesis" (*tafsir*). When the literal meaning of the text is dovetailed to other materials or sources of information, then it results in an "expansive interpretation" (*taʾwil*). Sometimes a reader might steer a set of passages in one of many possible directions in order for the material to make sense. Such an interpretation is called an "actively guided" or "steered interpretation" (*tawjih*). Sometimes a text merely needs "surface/superficial explanation" or commonsense "gloss" (*sharh)* for it to be comprehensible.

So why is Tahawi's text so cherished in the syllabus? The virtue of his text is that he combines two fields of expertise. He is a specialist who evaluates and authenticates reports (hadith) attributed to the Prophet Muhammad. And as a jurist (*faqih*), he offers skillful interpretations of the law. Hence, the title of his book: *Commentary on the Meaning of Prophetic Traditions* (*Sharh Maʿani al-Athar*).

Tahawi's text enjoys favorite status thanks to its antiquity. First, this is a thousand-year-old text. Second, a twist in Tahawi's biography altered his career, making him attractive to readers on the subcontinent. Here is why: the majority of South Asian Muslims identify with the Hanafi school founded in eighth-century Iraq.

As an Egyptian, Tahawi at first studied with a foremost jurist called al-Muzani, a distinguished student of Shafiʿi, the founder of a rival law school to the Hanafis. Tahawi was also a blood relative of Muzani; the latter was his maternal uncle, who was affiliated with the Shafiʿi school. Tahawi apparently famously revealed that his uncle, Muzani, clandestinely, but admiringly, studied the writings of Abu Hanifa, the founder of the Hanafi school, and his uncle's stealth admiration convinced him to switch sides to the superior Hanafi school! Where are such interschool

Students interacting with faculty at Jamiʿa Naeemia, Lahore, Pakistan. (Picture: Amjad Pervez)

rivalries still appreciated today? Actually, in South Asian madrasas, the Hanafis insist on enforcing their bragging rights.

Some fifty graduating students sit in horseshoe formation around Mufti Sarodi to learn more about Tahawi's intellectual genius. Mufti Sarodi is seated on a cushioned wooden platform while students squat on durable carpets, with their large quarto-sized textbooks resting on small benches. As soon he is ready, one student audibly reads the medieval text in fluent classical Arabic. Students spend a good deal of time in preparing the Arabic text before class, in order not to suffer correction from the professor. This day Tahawi's text is read flawlessly, and at some point Mufti Sarodi asks the reader to stop in order to start with his explanation.

The texts the students study are in Arabic, but the language of instruction is Urdu. Mufti Sarodi's mother tongue is Gujarati, but Urdu has become the dominant language of instruction in madrasas. In multilingual India and Pakistan, the Urdu language enjoys the rank of a second Islamic language, since it is widely used in sermons, Islamic education, and a large publishing industry. Once upon a time, Persian enjoyed a privileged position as a teaching language, but it has since been replaced by Urdu. Bengali vernacular instruction is used in the madrasas of West Bengal and Bangladesh. Other regional languages are used in the southern states of India. Publications and media in these languages also abound. In other words, the languages of Islam are many.

The lesson is from Tahawi's *Book of Purity*. Discussions of ceremonial and ritual purity are the first chapters in any classical textbook on Islamic law. What items defile a body, which foods are edible, and how purity is restored through ritual acts of purity all point to a larger symbolic system of a faith community.[8] Most of Mufti Sarodi's students are already familiar with the basic questions on matters of rituals and practices. Now they will try to figure out why the Hanafi school accepts some prophetic reports on the topic of ritual purification and why they ignore others or give them different interpretations.

All Muslim rituals are performed in a state of purity; therefore, ritual cleansing is a prerequisite for all religious acts. There are two states of ritual impurity: major and minor states of pollution. Both men and women after coitus and women after childbirth and at the end of a menstrual cycle take a full body bath or a shower in order to exit a state of major pollution.

Bowel movements of any kind, flatulence, vomiting, and blood oozing from a wound are all minor polluting acts in the opinion of some; some schools disagree, for instance, and do not deem oozing blood as a polluting act. Purity is restored with a ritual washing of certain limbs in a particular fashion called *wudu* (pronounced *who-dhu*). *Wudu* is done with water and performed before the five daily prayers or is a preferred state before touching the Qurʾan to read it—or prior to any pious act, for that matter.

Mufti Sarodi's speech is low and measured; his manner is assured as he deciphers the text and provides his gloss on words. At times he vaults between the text under discussion and other anteceding texts in the same book, or points to materials in other sources. The lesson is a combination of translation, commentary, and the threading of concepts with which the students are somewhat familiar.

Before Tahawi provides the reader with the words of the Prophet Muhammad, he first lists the names of the narrators for each report he has included in his book. If necessary, Mufti Sarodi points to flaws in the transmitters listed in one of the six links in every narrative. Flaws identified in a narrator can downgrade the authority of a report, making it vulnerable to counterarguments. Scholars with expertise in hadith studies command knowledge of the biographies and scholarly lineages of thousands of narrators and authorities.

The topic of discussion today is the status of water after a cat drank from it. In other words, if cat saliva mixes with water, is that water usable for the purpose of ritual purification? Is cat saliva a ritual pollutant? Well, the short answer is that it depends on how you interpret the various reports that were handed down over the centuries and reported from the Prophet. It is all about interpretation or hermeneutics. In Muslim practice, any remaining food or drink consumed by an animal is subject to certain rules, depending on the type of animal involved. Here is Tahawi's detailed answer to the question on the status of cat saliva.

Tahawi first examines a cluster of prophetic reports on this topic. Why would prophetic reports be an important source for him? If you recall, he wants to demonstrate that the view of his school, the Hanafi school, is consistent with a premier source of authority, namely, the traditions stemming from the Prophet.

The inquiry on the status of cat saliva centers on one report among many others that goes like this:

> Kabsha, the daughter of Kaʿb, the son of Malik, who was married to the son of Abu Qatada, reports that Abu Qatada [her father in-law] visited her and she poured him some water for purificatory rituals. A cat lapped at his water, and so he held out the water for the cat to drink until it was sated. "He [Abu Qatada] noticed my body-language," Kabsha said, "as I observed him, so he preemptively responded: 'Are you surprised, oh daughter of my brother, at what you had just witnessed?' " She said: "I replied: 'Yes.' He [Abu Qatada] replied: 'Indeed, the Messenger of God, on whom be peace and blessings, said: "A cat is not impure. Her [ritual] status is like that of one of your male and female domestic servants."' "[9]

Tahawi first bulks up the evidence to support his claim that cat saliva does not pollute water for ritual purposes. For further support, he cites a slightly variant report, drawing on the Prophet Muhammad's personal practice and domestic life. ʿA'isha, one of the Prophet Muhammad's most knowledgeable wives, said, "I and the Messenger of God used to bathe from a vessel of water from which a cat had taken a drink."[10] From these cumulative reports, Tahawi informs us, the meaning of the report is that water mixed with cat saliva is ritual-friendly and not polluted because the Prophet authorized it. That is the plain meaning of the rule Mufti Sarodi elaborates, an interpretation that is also held by two of the most famous disciples of the famous jurist Abu Hanifa, namely, Muhammad al-Shaybani (d. 805) and Qadi Abu Yusuf (d. 798).

Yet Tahawi's patient reader soon finds another meaning winking at him or her that is derived from the same statement of the Prophet. The reader resorts to a rule of interpretation called in Western hermeneutics as the "mischief rule," whereby one tries to construe the intent of the legislator. What the Prophet actually *intended* is the "mischief rule" in the fragment "A cat is not impure. Her [ritual] status is like that of your male and female domestic servants."[11]

So how does Tahawi give this fragment of text a different interpretive spin in the light of the report of Kabsha saying cat saliva is okay? In order to push back against the plain meaning of the fragment, he resorts to creating a new frame. The fragment of the report, he explains, is addressed to people who *already knew* that cat saliva was prohibited! For this audience the fragment "a cat is not impure" is not a response to a question about the ritual status of cat saliva but rather something else. The fragment explains that when household animals with *impure* saliva, like cats, brush against your clothes, then they do not pollute your clothes. In other words, the coats of cats are not impure, but cat saliva might be impure for ritual purposes.

Tahawi is not deterred by the rhetorical force implicit in the analogy of the Prophet's statement: cats are, ritually speaking, just as nonpolluting as domestic servants. To his mind the analogy is not about the saliva of domestic servants; rather, it is about "touching" or "brushing" domestic servants whose bodies and clothes might have been polluted as a result of their work. He clarifies: the touch of household pets is as ritually harmless or nonpolluting as is physical contact with domestic servants. (This does raise the question whether touching domestic servants might have been viewed as polluting at some stage if their bodies were contaminated with impurities as a result of their work.)

In providing this new interpretive frame, Tahawi distinguishes between two sets of prophetic reports. One set of reports talks about the bodies of cats being nonpollutants if one touched them or brushed one's clothes against their coats. Another set of reports discusses the status of anything polluted by cat saliva.

By explaining away the various variant reports, Tahawi can unambiguously rely on one report that he purports gives the definitive view.

Five Moral Categories/Values of Islamic Law

In terms of Islamic law, all human acts fall into five categories. Obligatory (*wajib/fard*) means that you must comply or never omit to follow a rule. Forbidden (*haram*) means never do or commit an action or else face sanctions attached to the omission or commission of certain acts. When the evidence does not make an act either obligatory or prohibited, then it falls into a twilight zone of either encouraged (*mustahabb/mandub*) or discouraged or reprehensible (*makruh*) acts. The default mode for all human acts is permissible (*mubah*). It is evidence that makes an act fall into one of the previous four categories.

"Anything touched by cat saliva," the Prophet said, "is to be tossed away and the utensil should be washed once or twice."[12] After sifting through all the variant and seemingly contradictory reports, Tahawi is now confident to pose a counter-opinion. After comparing two different constructions of the reports he reviewed, he leans in favor of the second reading. Cat saliva, he announces a view of the Hanafi school, on a scale ranging from permissible to impermissible falls in the category of "strongly discouraged" (*makruh*) pollutants on the grounds of an overwhelming burden of evidence.

Mufti Sarodi explains that Tahawi's preferred view squares with Abu Hanifa's opinion. Tahawi is now confident to further declare a general rule: the saliva of animals whose meat Muslims were allowed to consume were also ritually clean animals. What kind of animal saliva is ritually polluting for Muslims? Since Muslims are forbidden to consume cats and dogs, their saliva falls in the prohibited/abominable zone depending on how one evaluates the strength of the evidence.

Now before word gets out that Islam views cats with repugnance, readers should be aware of a spectrum of views within Islamic law that assigns different values to *cat saliva*, not an outright abhorrence for cats. To the contrary, many anecdotes reveal the Prophet Muhammad being so fond of cats that he was loath to disturb a sleeping cat lying on his garment. If the Hanafi school views cat saliva as ritually classified as "abominable" but not categorically impure, then the Shafiʿi school unanimously views the saliva of most household animals, apart from dogs, to be ritually pure.

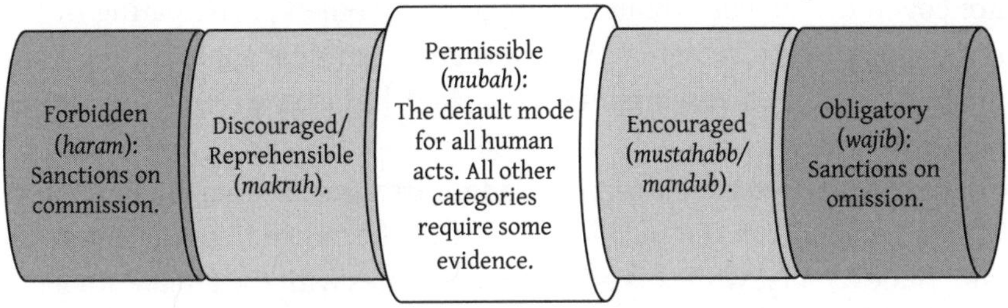

A visual schematization of Islamic moral values.

What should be obvious from this discussion is that the tens of thousands of prophetic reports are not only subjected to verification for authenticity but also subject to interpretation. Interpreters too take different approaches and would therefore generate different narratives and accounts of the material they had studied, as the above example on cat saliva proved. These kinds of refined debates possibly occur in the adjudication of thousands of topics in Islamic law and the study of hadith.

Today men play a prominent role in the interpretation of prophetic reports. In the past, women played a significant role in transmitting prophetic narrations. With the growth in women's madrasas one could in the foreseeable future see a greater number women also engage in the study and interpretation of hadith.

GENDER AND PIETY: WOMEN'S MADRASAS

Muslim orthodoxy definitely believes in the adage where "the hand that rocks the cradle rules the world." Educating young women at female-only madrasas is a growing trend throughout the subcontinent. A number of women's madrasas have been established in the Indian state of Gujarat in particular but also in other regions of India, Pakistan, and Bangladesh. It was impossible for me as a male researcher to get access to the administrative offices of any women's madrasa unless I had a close relative studying there. Meeting female students and faculty for interviews was out of the question.

Based on their reading of Islamic teachings, almost all South Asian madrasa authorities advocate a strict segregation between men and women in public life, as illustrated by Mufti Taqi ʿUsmani's pained comments on the gender-mixing he observed in Jakarta. Women are rarely seen on male campuses except in strictly veiled dress where their faces are covered. The very thought of men and women participating in the same class is an anathema. A few excellent ethnographic studies conducted by women researchers have shed light on diverse aspects of women's madrasas.[13]

Often a married couple serves as administrators of women's madrasas. The male conducts the public business of the institution and interacts with male faculty, while his wife communicates with the female students and female faculty. Faculty and female students associated with the women's madrasas are allowed to venture into public only on the condition that they wear the face veil, called *purda*. Wearing the *hijab*, a head covering that allows the face to be visible, is for most orthodox madrasa authorities a scandalous violation of Islamic tenets but still a preferred mode of dress compared to no hair covering.

Lahore, Pakistan: Madrasa ʿAʾisha

Lahore is a historic, sprawling Pakistani city that serves as the capital of the state of Punjab. Home to many male madrasas, it also houses several women's madrasas. Since I could not audit classes at a female madrasa, my key informant about female madrasas is a Duke University graduate student from Pakistan, Mashal Saif. Educated at the Convent of Jesus and Mary in Lahore, she followed that with a liberal arts college education in the United States, and then pursued a graduate degree in religious studies at Duke University. During her research in Pakistan, Mashal audited classes at Jamiʿa ʿAʾisha, a madrasa near Lahore's famous Defense Colony, for several weeks. Her report about student life in a women's madrasa provides a sense of the rhythms and practices within this institution.

Jamiʿa ʿAʾisha has been in existence for nearly a decade. It was founded by Mufti Matlub, who, for some time, was an imam at a mosque near Defense Colony, hence his familiarity with Mashal's father, who also serves in the Pakistani army. This connection smoothed the way for Mashal to attend the madrasa even though she was not pursuing a full-time madrasa career. Mashal was primarily attending the madrasa for personal enrichment and to deepen her knowledge of traditional Islamic teachings and observe women's madrasas for the purposes of her scholarship on Muslim practices in Pakistan.

In order to participate in madrasa life, Mashal had to conform to the institutional requirements of wearing a burqa, a loosely draped piece of outer clothing that covered her entire body and face. Once in class, all the students would remove their burqas since they were now in an all-female environment, away from the prying gaze of men whom these women were not permitted to see. Women are not permitted to see and interact with men whom they could potentially marry. Most of the female students wear a standard white *shalwar-kameez* outfit, baggy pants and knee-length shirts with large maroon shawls covering their hair. Among themselves, different female students vary in the way they cover their hair. While some are strict and cover their ears and every strand of their hair, others will let their rectangular scarves (*dupattas*) slip off their heads. Of course, women are not required to cover their hair in an all-female segregated space. But for some female students, covering their hair even among women demonstrates their personal discipline of piety and that decorum is most obviously a sign of respect when reading religious texts.

Frequently, teachers did not show up for class, a fact that surprised Mashal, given the punctuality she experienced at the Convent of Mary and Jesus. During such free time, students would resort to painting their hands with henna. These were periods with a festive air of laughter, banter, and fun. In those playful moments, Mashal reports, this gathering of fourteen- to twenty-year-old girls from lower economic backgrounds would talk about their personal lives. Some would curiously ask Mashal, who comes from a middle-class (meaning elite) background, what kinds of clothes she wore when she was outside the madrasa environment. So conversations about clothes and fashions, colors, and designers were frequent. Mashal, in turn, was surprised that many of the girls disclosed that their fathers or brothers purchased their clothes. Yet these young women would also talk excitedly about what they wore to a recent wedding feast, for in such segregated spaces they could display their finery to other women.

Since arranged marriages are customary in certain sectors of Pakistani society, conversations about potential spouses are equally frequent. One student told Mashal of her engagement to a boy, whom she had not seen. Only her family had seen the prospective groom. The only information her family shared with her, Mashal told me, was that her future husband was "very good looking," a fact that, to Mashal's ears, implied that she was "marrying up."

Some of the girls did have secular schooling and possibly did do some math and science at grade four or five of their schooling. A few joined the madrasa at the age of fifteen or sixteen, after completing the twelfth grade of their secular education, but most of the girls studying in the madrasa did not complete high school.

The girls spoke passionately about their faith and its importance in their lives, Mashal said. Advancing the cause of Islam in one form or another was their highest goal. Some fostered the wish to marry men who were in the Tablighi Jamaʿat, a group committed to *daʿwa*, evangelizing fellow Muslims to be more observant of their faith. At the same time, many girls were apprehensive of being married off to men, who in their words were "illiterate" spouses whom they feared would not be their intellectual equals.

The segregation of female students from male teachers is strictly enforced. During lectures, the male teacher sits behind a walled partition with a curtained window, which allows his voice to reach his audience. During daily roll call for attendance, only a student number is called out, not the name of the female student. The strict enforcement of *purda* requires anonymity. The association of a name with a female voice is taboo. Even during a class, the sequestered male teachers are oblivious to what the female students do in their cloistered space. One student, Mashal said, was babysitting a niece in class without the knowledge of the teacher on the other side of the divide.

In madrasa orthodoxy, a female's voice is part of her identity that has to be guarded as part of her "privacy" (*ʿawra*). Strict segregation rules are designed to create a firewall against potential temptation between the females and the few male teachers who could be ensnared into forbidden relationships. Even the architecture of some female madrasas, as an ethnography of a school in Delhi reveals, is shrouded "in purdah or 'veiled,'" in order to protect its inhabitants from the outsiders' gaze.[14] Despite this strict enforcement, there have been reports from women's madrasas in different parts of the world where these strict protocols were breached amid great scandal.

The curriculum designed for women is a reduced version of the Nizami curriculum. The period of study varies, depending on what kind of preparation entrants receive prior to studying for the *ʿalimiyya* or *fazilat* degrees. In places like the Madrasatul Niswan, in Delhi, the program is condensed into a five-year curriculum, and at the Madrasa ʿAʾisha in Lahore, it is reduced to four years. Most of the texts women are taught focus on Islamic law and the rules of piety. They study Arabic grammar, some

Arabic literature, Urdu grammar, and prose, as well as advanced texts on Qur'an exegesis and the major books of hadith in addition to courses on English and civics.

Many of the philosophy, logic, and advanced Arabic literary texts are not taught in the women's madrasas. However, women do study selections from the classical books on Hanafi law, from legal theory to the applied law books such as the *Hidaya* and selections from the main books of hadith, such as Bukhari, Muslim, and the other Sunni canonical books. Mashal did, however, observe that the female students were very enthusiastic learners. They would take copious notes when the teachers did show up for class. And the most important feature of student-teacher interaction, even in the gender-segregated environment, was the analysis of the Arabic texts. Students earnestly worked with their teachers to decipher the meanings of the texts they studied.

While knowledge of the tradition is a highly valued trait in male and female madrasas, excellence in knowledge is always secondary to moral formation. The goal of a madrasa education is moral and ethical excellence. Scholarly excellence, while equally praiseworthy, is not an end in itself.

In both the Lahore and Delhi madrasas, female teachers serve as both instructors and mentors to the girls. At Madrasa ʿA'isha, female teachers like Baji Amina, "Elder Sister Amina," who is a graduate of the Lahore madrasa, are closely associated with the family of the founder and play a major role in the institution. Male teachers defer to female teachers to handle topics related to Islamic ritual purity specific to women's physiology like menstruation, childbirth, and postcoital rituals. Baji Amina teaches those themes in keeping with modesty and decorum.

MEN'S MADRASAS

Lahore, Pakistan: Madrasa Ashrafiyya

Mawlana Akram Kashmiri is in his late forties and is the equivalent of a provost at one of the foremost Deobandi madrasas in Pakistan, the famous Madrasa Ashrafiyya, in a busy part of Lahore. From the region of Kashmir, as his name indicates, he is energetic. He stands just over five feet tall and sports a graying beard and close-cropped hair. He is knowledgeable about how the media work and is vigilant against any association of the madrasas with terrorism. He speaks slowly and clearly during our wide-ranging interview. I probed him on the links between the madrasas and the ongoing terrorist activities in Pakistan, especially the links between the Pakistani Taliban and the Afghan Taliban.

Kashmiri categorically denied any links between the madrasas and terrorism. While he decried suicide bombings inside Pakistan, he did, however, deem suicide bombing to be a legitimate means of warfare in other theaters of conflict as diverse as Palestine, Kashmir, and Afghanistan. Like scores of others in the madrasa community, he felt it totally justifiable to oppose America's occupation of Afghanistan. He was severely critical of Pakistan's military-run government for its slavish adherence to directives from Washington.

Religious scholars, namely, the ʿulama like him, are the "door keepers" of the correct interpretation of Islam, Kashmiri proudly proclaimed. Yet he was equally enthusiastic to reform the madrasa curriculum in order to make it more relevant to the needs of the time. Kashmiri was willing to concede to the use of modern knowledge on the condition that it did not conflict with Islam's foundational theological strictures. He admitted that ethical solutions to modern practices can be found if scholars resort to new interpretations of law (*ijtihad*), as long as such remedies were consistent with the inherited framework of knowledge. Conceptually, his frame of knowledge only partially engages a modern worldview.

I attended Kashmiri's class on hadith where he taught an early collection of hadith compiled by the hadith scholar and jurist of Medina, Malik bin Anas, called *The Trodden Path* (*Muwatta*). On this day the class was about postcoital purity rituals. After sex, both men and women are required to have a full bath, which includes the washing of the hair. But what if one is not in a position to take a shower but wishes to continue to sleep or do any other mundane activities besides religious rituals before taking a shower? Well, in that case it is preferable, but not obligatory, to take a minor ablution, the ritual of *wudu*.

Throughout his lecture discussing multiple hadith reports and their variants, Kashmiri showed great interest in stressing the underlying wisdom of the *Sunna*. Since different schools of interpretation center around specific clusters of reports, Kashmiri pointed out, providence makes it possible for the prophetic *Sunna* to remain alive in the practices of people in all its diversity. He cited a famous saying of the Prophet Muhammad: "Difference among my community (umma) is a blessing." This is how Islam accommodates multiple interpretive traditions, Kash-

Mawlana Anzar Shah Kashmiri, professor of hadith studies at the Darul Uloom Deoband (Waqf), son of the famous Anwar Shah Kashmiri, and a champion of curriculum reform. (Picture: Rodrigo Dorfman)

miri rejoiced, allowing esoteric Sufi interpretations to jostle alongside the views advanced by theologians and jurists, each with their characteristic emphasis. Madrasa communities also have to deal with sharp theological disagreements.

Remember the Deoband-versus-Barelvi divide that I discussed earlier? After visiting the Deobandi Ashrafiyya madrasa, I crossed the city of Lahore and, with it, that ideological schism, to visit a Barelvi madrasa in another part of that ancient city.

Lahore, Pakistan: Jamiʿa Naeemia

The famous Barelvi madrasa, Jamiʿa [Naʿimiyya] Naeemia, also sits in a bustling part of Lahore. I was unable to meet the president of the madrasa, an important countervoice to the Deobandi interpretation. Why? Pakistan's then military dictator, General Parvez Musharraf, imprisoned Mawlana Dr. Sarfaraz Naeemi, the president of Jamiʿa Naeemia.

Naeemi led the public protests against the Danish cartoons that were deemed to dishonor the Prophet Muhammad and outraged Muslim sentiment globally. He also petitioned the government of Pakistan to pioneer an effort at the United Nations in order to create an international protocol that would protect prophets and sacred figures of all religions from blasphemous and denigrating representations. Public disturbances associated with Naeemi's protests and petition resulted in his arrest.

After his release from prison, Mawlana Sarfaraz Naeemi condemned the suicide bombings that engulfed Pakistan. He denounced the bloodletting favored by the Pakistani Taliban whose conduct, in his view, was the antithesis of Islamic teachings. Militants in Pakistan started to target critics. In June 2009 a suicide bomber killed Mawlana Sarfaraz after the weekly Friday prayer at an office in his mosque-madrasa complex in Lahore, along with at least two others. In 2010 the Taliban killed a prominent physician and religious activist, Dr. Farooq Khan, who was active in the Swat Valley. In the same year militants killed at least six intellectuals.[15] On the chessboard of the killing fields that is Pakistan and Afghanistan, the Taliban often get credit for spectacles of violence, but they might not be the only ones fomenting it.

Sarfaraz's brother, Mawlana ʿArif Naeemi, who spoke to me at length, was highly critical of Pakistan's military dictatorship at the time and viewed this group as a major source of Pakistan's ills. Already in 2005 several dozen people had been killed, including a group of clerics aligned to the Barelvi school when a suicide bomber detonated explosives at a religious celebration commemorating the birthday of the Prophet Muhammad at Nishtar Park in Karachi. In ʿArif Naeemi's view, a clandestine, dirty-tricks unit of Pakistan's byzantine military establishment was most likely behind the Karachi atrocity. All visitors to Jamiʿa Naeemia when I visited were reminded of this terrorist atrocity by a large, wall-sized graffiti in Urdu: "There should be accountability for the bloodshed at Nishtar Park."

Even though the Deobandi school opposes, on theological grounds, the birthday ceremonies in honor of the Prophet Muhammad, a practice condoned by the Barelvis, ʿArif Naeemi categorically ruled out that the Deobandi-Barelvi rivalry could result in this level of heinous bloodshed. Such spectacles of violence, in his view, only served the military dictatorship in order for the latter to show that only their iron grip could govern Pakistan. But then conspiracy theories are rife in Pakistan, and it will be long before the truth is known as to who were actually behind these horrific killings and many others.

While Lahore is an important intellectual center for all major madrasas on the subcontinent, the Barelvi school and its madrasas are equally influential and visible in North India.

Entrance to the Jamiʿa Naeemia madrasa in Lahore with antiterrorism security precautions following a fatal suicide attack on Dr. Mawlana Sarfaraz Naeemi. (Picture: Amjad Pervez)

Tomb inside the madrasa of Jami'a Naeemia where its founder, Mufti Muhammad Husayn Naeemi Ashrafi (left), and his son, Dr. Mawlana Sarfaraz Naeemi, were laid to rest. (Picture: Amjad Pervez)

North India's Madrasa Hinterland

What Mark Twain said about Varanasi, previously known as Benares, as "older than history, older than tradition, older even than legend" is equally true about the hinterland adjacent to that ancient Hindu city. In the cultural ecology of the region, Hinduism's history is legible, dating back millennia. Hinduism, the tapestry on which Islam layered itself a thousand years ago, is less visible, yet elements of it are elaborately woven into the rhythms of many medium-sized cities, small towns, and villages of Uttar Pradesh, one of the largest states of India today.

Dotting the region are mosques, Sufi shrines, spiritual lodges, orphanages, secular Muslim schools, and colleges apart from an assortment of madrasa franchises. It is an elaborate history that predates the partition of the subcontinent into first two modern nation-states, India and Pakistan, and then a third, Bangladesh, when East Pakistan gained independence from its western half. These radii spread their Islamic influence out to other parts of the subcontinent. These centers in Uttar Pradesh give northern India its distinction as a focal point of Islam on the subcontinent.

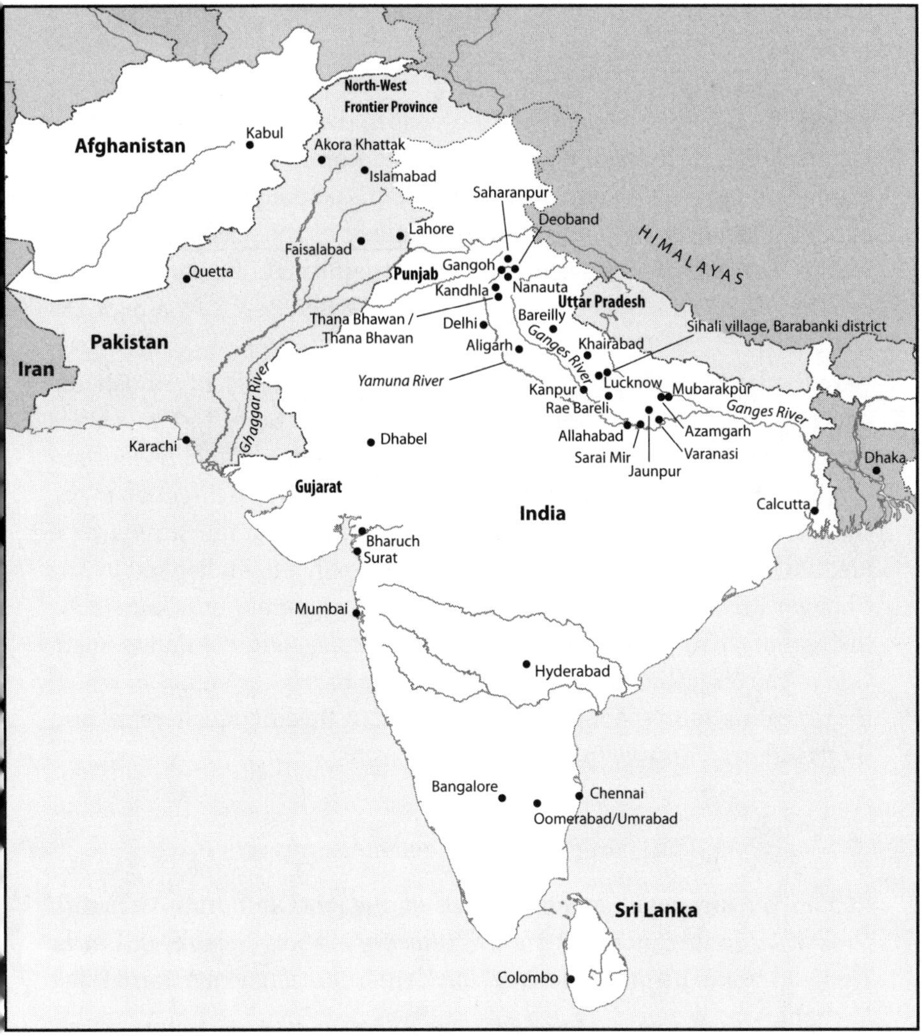

Geographical distribution of the main centers of traditional learning in South Asia.

In this North Indian region everything eastward of the city of Kanpur, in what is today known as the state of Bihar, was in Mughal times known as Purap. Back then it was an intellectual heartland for scholars and learners; towns and cities housed experts in different disciplines of Muslim religious thought. Jaunpur, for instance, was renowned for scholars whose mastery of Arabic literature, logic, and philosophy was unrivaled. Novices in mysticism retreated to Rae Bareli and its environs, where spiritual masters would show aspiring "physicians of the soul," another way to describe mystics, how to succeed in their pious aspirations.

In the vicinity of Azamgarh, several madrasas flourish thanks to the efforts of people who trace their descent to distinguished forebears of Islam's first generations, known as the Siddiqis and the Faruqis. They trace their descent to Islam's first caliph, Abu Bakr al-Siddiq, and to ʿUmar al-Faruq, respectively. Other families known as the Ansaris find their link to Abu Ayyub al-Ansari, another distinguished Companion of the Prophet Muhammad whose descendants reached South Asia over the centuries.

In the late nineteenth and early twentieth centuries, several Islamic educational institutions were seeded in this region. Some forty-six miles (74 km) from Varanasi is a small town, with a population of fewer than 100,000, called Mubarakpur. A traveler coming from the direction of the Ganges River first drives through Azamgarh, by Indian standards a medium-sized city, before reaching Mubarakpur, a town flanked by the Ghaggar River, its main agricultural lifeline. Mubarakpur is known for the manufacture of saris, unique dresses worn by South Asian women. One of the largest madrasas affiliated to the Barelvi orientation, which is also called Jamiʿa Ashrafiyya, is located in this town, where several thousand students live in residence.

Mubarakpur, India: Jamiʿa Ashrafiyya

At Jamiʿa Ashrafiyya I audited a class on the most authoritative hadith book in the Sunni canon, *The Authentic Book of Bukhari* (*Sahih al-Bukhari*). The professor of hadith, called the *shaykh al-hadith*, Shaykh Asrarul Haqq Misbahi, was wizened by age and showed deep marks of piety on his face: a long beard and a black mark on his forehead signaling lifelong prostrations in daily prayers. Like all teachers in the madrasa who wear some kind of head covering, he wore a pitched ship-shaped cap on his head.

The compiler of *The Authentic Book of Bukhari*, Muhammad bin Ismaʿil al-Bukhari (d. 870), is from Bukhara, a city located in present-day Uzbekistan, as his name indicates. Sunni Muslims immortalize his intellectual labor. He compiled a collection of authentic hadith, earning his collection the honorific as being "the most authentic book, after the book of God," meaning second only to the authenticity of the Qurʾan.

More specifically the lesson was on the military expeditions of the Prophet Muhammad, in particular several events related to the Battle of Uhud in 625 C.E. Muslims over the ages know of this historic battle, when the nascent Muslim community in Medina was almost annihilated by its Meccan foes.

Many of the reports in this section of the Bukhari text are counter-intuitive. It is a mixture of reports ranging from accounts of defeat, heroism, and martyrdom of the Prophet Muhammad's Companions to marriage-related stories and elucidations of Qurʾanic passages, among other things.

Shaykh Asrarul Haqq discussed a report dealing with the marriage of a Companion, called Jabir. How does marriage feature in this section? Jabir's father was martyred during the Battle of Uhud. As Jabir is a son of a martyred hero, aspects of his domestic life slip into this section on military expeditions.

Here is how the narrative goes:

> The Messenger of God, on whom be peace and prayers, asked me: "Are you married, Jabir?" I replied: "Yes." He asked: "To a virgin or a matron?" I replied: "To a matron." To which he replied: "Why not a young wife who would indulge you?" I replied: "Oh Messenger of God. My father was killed on the day of Uhud and left me with six daughters, all of whom were my sisters. So I was reluctant to add another inexperienced girl to that gaggle of women. I preferred a woman who could groom them (lit. 'comb their hair') and take charge of them." To which the Prophet replied: "Perfect! You did the right thing."[16]

First, the report shows the Prophet Muhammad cared for the family of the fallen heroes, those martyrs who gave their lives in the cause of faith, like Jabir's father, that is one moral of the story, Shaykh Asrarul Haqq explains. Second, Jabir's maturity is lauded for his choice of a spouse who would be a caregiver to his dependent sisters. A man who takes responsibility for his dependent siblings in the absence of a father deserves to be admired is the other moral. In acting morally Jabir shares in the honor his father attained as a martyr by carrying out his father's responsibilities.

An exegesis of a verse of the Qurʾan is addressed by another report. The verse in question talks about the psychological anguish some of the

Muslim warriors experienced during the Battle of Uhud but is partly ambiguous. It reads, "When two of your groups were on the edge of losing heart, although God was their protector. So let the believers trust in God" (Q 3:122).

Who are the two groups, and why were they losing heart? The Qur'an does not clarify these inferences. Only the study of hadith can shed light for Qur'an commentators to decipher the identity of the unnamed "two groups." Two tribes allied to the Muslims, the Banu Salima and the Banu Haritha, wavered when defeat stared them in the face and were on the verge of defecting to the side of the Meccan enemy. Hadith reports explain how their semipublicized defection affected the morale of the other Muslim fighters, but at the last minute, the two tribes reversed their decision. Without this backstory found in the hadith literature, the Qur'anic verse counseling the believers to place their faith in God and not allow themselves to be swayed by the material outcome of any battlefield victory or defeat would not make complete sense. But once the hadith provides the contextual backstory, the meaning and significance of the Qur'anic verse is amplified.

Class discussion then shifted to another hadith extolling the bravery of a Companion, called Talha, during the Battle of Uhud. While shielding a wounded Prophet Muhammad, Talha was injured as a result and became paralyzed in one hand. Talha's sacrifice was an index of his faith, Shaykh Asrarul Haqq explains, and more so he demonstrated his selfless love for the Prophet Muhammad.

Recall that all Muslims are required to love the Prophet Muhammad above all others as an expression of faith. Among the orthodox madrasa franchises, the Barelvi school has made love of the Prophet its signature credo. Mawlana Ahmad Raza Khan, the spirit behind the Barelvi movement, called himself the "servant of Mustafa"; Mustafa means the *Purified One*, and it is one of the honorifics of the Prophet Muhammad. Shaykh Asrarul Haqq identifies with the Barelvi tradition and therefore his expansive elaboration on how the Companions demonstrated their love for the Prophet fits that school's signature narrative on this topic.

Continuous exposure to stories in which the Companions showed their love for the Prophet in the hadith literature is meant to inculcate similar sentiments for Islam's messenger in the students. Given this foundational teaching of love for the Prophet, it should be apparent why Muslims around the world react with indignation, horror, and passion when the Prophet Muhammad is defamed or his honor, reputation, and dignity are assailed. In these matters too, especially in Pakistan, the Barelvi school mobilizes the public in highly impassioned tones.

One report describes how the Prophet's wives and other females were providing first aid during the Battle of Uhud. Bukhari's reports give graphic accounts of women scurrying with exposed shins and calves while performing triaging duties. Bukhari also reports how women provided water to the fighters and nursed the injured.

After listening to these reports, I was again surprised by the activist role women played in early Islam, in contrast to the highly segregated environment I was witnessing in the madrasas and among orthodox constituencies. I am sure madrasa students are equally puzzled. Why, students might wonder, does present-day madrasa culture strictly segregate the sexes when reports provide visual accounts of female nurses and activists on the battlefield during the Prophet's time? Some might provide an apologetic that the necessity of war required their participation after which they should be cloistered. The authors of the hadith compilations, it appears, had no compunctions in providing detailed descriptions of the women in the Prophet's time. If the students at Jamiʿa Ashrafiyya in Mubarakpur had any questions about these reports, they did not ask them of their professor on the day I audited the class.

Shaykh Asrarul Haqq quickly glosses over these events. These activities of women, he explains, were only permissible before the enforcement of the rules of *purda,* when the strict covering of women's bodies and the enforced segregation between the sexes became requirements. It became clear that Shaykh Asrarul Haqq found these accounts of Bukhari slightly troubling to his own predisposition and quickly moved on to other topics. But in another madrasa the interpretation of this very same event was explained differently.

Lucknow, India: Nadwatul ʿUlama

A few days later I found myself in the city of Lucknow at the Nadwatul ʿUlama, my alma mater. With fifty other students I attended the class of Mawlana Sayyid Salman Husayni Nadvi, my teacher several decades ago. He was now a senior figure in the Nadwa hierarchy and enjoyed growing national and international visibility and recognition for his scholarship but especially for his sometimes strident public advocacy. By sheer coincidence, the day I audited his class, the lesson in the *Authentic Book of Bukhari* was indeed the same topic that I had audited a few days earlier in Mubarakpur: the events surrounding the Battle of Uhud. But this is Nadwa, where the institutional credo is to give the message of Islam some relevance to life in the modern world. So here, in Mawlana Salman's class, some aspects of the hadith received different interpretations.

Mawlana Salman proudly lauded the role women enjoyed in the history of Islam and extolled their battlefield service as recorded by Bukhari. Emphasizing Islam's egalitarianism, he energetically pointed out that the Prophet's wife, ʿA'isha, as the wife of the commander-in-chief, was herself involved in nursing and support duties during the Battle of Uhud. No one was exempt from making a sacrifice, he made sure to point out. While the rule of gender segregation, *purda*, only came into effect after the Battle of Uhud, Mawlana Salman unapologetically stressed that it was eminently permissible for women to serve in the battlefield during wars.

He scoffed at "narcissistic clerics" who, in his words, objected to such female roles without any foundation. Why was he so critical of antifemale clerics? In his view, such clerics lacked any argument or understanding of the social realities Muslims confront today. His point was to show that Islam advances what could be termed progressive values, though he never used the word "progressive." Having Shaykh Asrarul Haqq and Mawlana Salman debate the interpretation of this hadith of Bukhari would indeed be illuminating. While such a scenario is unlikely to occur, what this shows is that madrasas are not monolithic and internal differences, albeit few, still exist.

Parenthetically but in firm tones, Mawlana Salman also pointed out that in terms of Muslim ethics, first aid and health workers enjoyed immunity during wars. And, as a counterpoint, he referred to the U.S. wars in Iraq and Afghanistan, where even hospitals were not immune to military attacks. Mawlana Salman is extremely critical of American and European designs in planning wars and invading parts of the Muslim world, and based on the way he airs those views, some might even call him a firebrand.

CONCLUSION

South Asia's orthodoxy views service to hadith scholarship over the centuries to be the single most important contribution the region made to global scholarship on Islam. With hadith comes the revival of the *Sunna*, the norms and values advocated by the Prophet Muhammad, which is a core value of orthodox Islam. A *Sunna*-centered orientation also had the advantage of energizing Islamic law and theology with its claim to once again authentically dip into the prophetic spirit of renewal. In many ways reason-centered religious discourses always had to contend with challenges arising from *Sunna*-centered tradition-based authority. For more than a century now, the latter trend has been hegemonic. Yet the rationalist tradition in contemporary madrasas dabbles in an outdated rationalism and philosophy where rhetorical soundings surpass efficiency.

The absence of an updated and robust rationalist dialectic blended with a *Sunna*-centered approach to religious knowledge has only fomented an exclusionary faith-centered or hidebound received tradition-centered mindset. This mindset generates extraordinary hurdles and roadblocks for religious discourse to engage with the challenges of the time. Institutional reforms, without substantive intellectual reformation, tend to yield fewer discursive dividends but a surfeit of apologetics.

Ethical registers and narratives supported by centuries-old Islamic learned traditions are the stock-in-trade in madrasa classrooms all over the subcontinent. Narrations about hadith, Islamic law, Qur'anic exegesis, and theology occupy a central place. Students do not study politics, health care, or economics in the language and idioms that secular educated people are exposed to. Yet what is unique about madrasa education is that at opportune moments some professors will connect classroom themes to real-life issues.

A good example is when some professors talk about the ethics of humanitarian care during warfare. Of course, the frame of reference, experiences, and background knowledge of the professors play a decisive role in their interpretations. For this reason, it is no surprise that their points of reference and the authorities they cite in discussions of, say, global politics will not be identical to the authorities and language that professors at a modern and globalized university would invoke. But differences in perspectives are realities that an increasingly globalizing world will be forced to come to grips with. If globalized elites fail to register the perspectives formulated among subaltern communities, like madrasas, then the failing is theirs and to their peril. Of course, the madrasa communities too would be missing out on perspectives that others hold with serious consequences for intercultural dialogue.

Leading a good life and attaining salvation in the hereafter are the main purposes of learning in the madrasa-sphere. Theoretically, knowledge is both worldly and otherworldly. Some sectors of the madrasa world emphasize salvation almost to the exclusion of knowledge for right living and worldliness. The rise of the secular nation-state forces madrasa communities to encounter the secular-religious divide and challenges their traditions with the modernist nature-versus-culture divide. Mainstream madrasa advocates rhetorically give priority to cosmographic fragments of knowledge, while a minority of scholars petition for a balanced emphasis on knowledge of the world. But all agree that learning is integral to right living.

CHAPTER EIGHT

Believe, Learn, Know

"Come in; sit down. It has been a long time." Mawlana ʿAbdul Khaliq Madrasi welcomes me with a broad smile after I briefly introduce myself and jog his memory with names of my cohort.[1] I came unannounced to Deoband, where he is now a deputy vice-chancellor at the world-renowned seminary. He squints his eyes while scrutinizing me, trying to recall our connection decades ago. He has aged well and has not lost any of his good looks and charm that were characteristic three decades ago. I find Mawlana Madrasi nursing a water pipe in his spacious campus room, where several other faculty members joined him for a smoke and a cup of tea, *chai*, in the mornings and evenings.

He and I go back several decades, when I was a mere beginner student at Deoband and he, at the time, a newly minted professor of Arabic literature from the city of Madras, hence the distinct affiliation of his name, Madrasi, a reference to the southern coastal city now renamed as Chennai. He is a rarity in Deoband among a largely North Indian faculty. Humorous and eloquent, he would often challenge us in our pietisms with skeptical questions. Frequently, he made students aware that the madrasas were failing in their mission to equip graduates for the challenges of the real world. He favored a more vibrant and socially relevant intellectual environment and was prepared to trade in the old curriculum for a new, radically revised one. But his bruising criticism was reserved for the poor Arabic teaching in the madrasas, which disadvantaged students.

Decades later, it seems that his youthful vigor has given way to a more pragmatic disposition. Mawlana Madrasi might have lost the battle to transform the intellectual terrain of the Deoband madrasa, but he is now building something else: madrasa infrastructure. Under his watch and as his legacy, the Deoband campus now boasts an elegant marble mosque, a new library, and vastly improved dormitory facilities for students.

So the madrasa continues in its vintage learning mission and aging curriculum, albeit with upgraded facilities. So what sets the madrasa apart from other forums of learning and scholarship within Islam? Its tenacious ability to link knowledge to belief makes it a template for the formation of a self that is ultimately aimed at the attainment of salvation. Earlier incarnations of the madrasa over time had similar objectives of furnishing students with the knowledge of faith.

In earlier days, however, it appears that the curriculum was more tightly tethered to the social reality surrounding the madrasa. Centuries ago madrasas possibly had more intellectual synergies and demonstrated a greater intellectual investment in the "secular" reality of their surroundings. The contemporary madrasa focuses largely on salvation matters and restricts its intellectual ties to its immediate social reality. One reason for this state of affairs is because madrasa communities adopt a narrow account of the meaning and end of knowledge while ignoring an inclusive account of what knowledge is.

IMAGINING KNOWLEDGE: WHAT IS KNOWLEDGE?

All the major madrasa franchises, irrespective of their internal differences, converge in their common understanding that only knowledge of salvation deserves the epithet of *knowledge*. Only the brave challenge that view, like Mawlana Madrasi and a few others. The minority argue that knowledge is more inclusive than merely knowledge of faith and salvation that are tied to a cosmographic narrative. Other forms of knowledge are equally necessary, they reason, in order to establish a worldly or secular order but also for Muslims to inhabit and flourish in the world, living according to the principles of their faith tradition. And that makes all the difference, insider critics of the mainstream madrasa knowledge project say, as to how knowledge of salvation ought to be adapted to a changing world.

But the hegemonic paradigm of knowledge prevalent in madrasas carries the imprint and legacy of Muslim theology, called dialectical theology (*ʿilm al-kalam*). How? If Greek logic and philosophy were both pressed into the service of theology, then "the queen of the sciences" has also left a strong theocentric imprint on the way knowledge itself is conceived in Muslim philosophy. Readers should not be surprised to find that past Muslim theologians showed a robust interest in reason and cared a great deal about ethical outcomes in human living. Yet if you pushed a serious theologian to decide between two highly desirable outcomes, say, to choose between attaining excellence in ethical practice on the one hand and gaining excellence in knowledge on the other, you might be surprised by the counterintuitive reply you will get.

The view most folks in the madrasas take is the one outlined by the polymath and virtuoso scholar al-Sayyid al-Sharif al-Jurjani (d. 1413), whose many texts are widely read in the curriculum and who unhesitatingly declares, "Perfections in learning are superior and more valuable."[2] So why does he rank excellence and perfection in knowledge to be higher than ethical practice? "Because there is no greater perfection," Jurjani claims, "than knowing God, the Sublime."[3] Therefore, *knowing* things is ranked to be higher than *doing* things, for a simple reason: knowing God opens the path to salvation, and one always has to act on the basis of knowledge.

So what qualifies as knowledge in traditional Muslim thinking? It is common to hear Muslims say that the Prophet Muhammad commanded them to "seek knowledge from the cradle to the grave." In another tradition, the Prophet was said to counsel, "Seek knowledge, even unto China"—a very distant destination indeed in seventh-century Arabia, one that conjured for Arabs a totally foreign civilization. To acquire knowledge thus became an essential obligation on every Muslim, male and female.

And specialization in learning not only is desirable but unleashes unspecified human potential. Human potential, the nineteenth-century Indian scholar Shah Muhammad Ismaʿil explained, is deployed in mundane, everyday activities as well as in imaginative and sensory pursuits.[4] Deepening one's knowledge in order to reach excellence in a specific area of learning like philosophy or an artistic skill like poetry or a physical skill enhances the practitioner to reach new heights and feats of accomplishment. The abundance of potential is evident when comparing "how different the knowledge of amateur laypersons appears when compared to the knowledge of refined philosophers," he writes.

The Arabic word for knowledge is *ʿilm*, a word used in its Arabized form in multiple languages. From the *ʿi-l-m* root, one derives the word *ʿalim* (pronounced *aa-lim* like the *im* in "h*im*") and its plural *ʿulama* (pronounced *oe-la-maa*), meaning the learned or the scholars. These days the term is often used to describe members of the Muslim clerical establishment.

So how did the command to acquire knowledge turn into a command to acquire only religious knowledge? The Qurʾan, in an oft-cited passage, invites people to observe nature, look at the skies, admire the mountains, and adore the diversity of the surround of flora and fauna. One underlying purpose of this invitation is to stress the deep connection that knowledge makes between self-awareness and faith in God. So this passage concludes, "Those in awe of God from among His servants are the ones who are *truly knowledgeable*" (Q 35:28).

So who qualifies as the knowledgeable and learned (ʿulama) persons mentioned in the Qurʾan? Do the carriers of all kinds of knowledge and wisdom qualify as the *knowledgeable* persons designated in the Qurʾan? Or is this epithet, "knowledgeable," only restricted to those who specialize in knowledge of salvation, namely, knowledge of the faith tradition? What kind of knowledge creates awe and reverence for God? Does science not enable us to behold the layers of complexity in an atom or in the cosmos? Or does knowledge provided by the prophets alone enable one to think about the meaning of the good life, its purpose and end? Does only prophetic knowledge inspire us to be in awe of God? Should carriers of both kinds of knowledge not ideally qualify as the knowledgeable and the learned ones? Debates on these themes have raged for centuries.

The very first revelation to the Prophet Muhammad in seventh-century Arabia was a command to recite. To recite what had been revealed was also implicitly a command to acquire knowledge. If the first verse was "Recite!" then the earliest thumbnail message in the Qurʾanic revelations emphasized five themes: reciting/reading, God, creation, learning, and writing.

Read, in the name of your Lord, who created:
Created humans of clotted blood.
Read, for your Lord is most generous

Qur᾽an

The word "Qur᾽an" means either "recitation" or something "held together." It consists of 114 chapters and roughly 6,000 verses. Liturgically, the Qur᾽an is divided into 30 portions, *juz᾽* or *ajza᾽*, in order to facilitate its daily reading. In norms of Muslim piety, it is a highly desirable goal to recite one portion of the Arabic scripture daily in order to complete the entire Qur᾽an during a calendar month, a feat many people accomplish during the month of Ramadan, the month of fasting from daybreak to sunset.

The one who taught the use of the pen,
Taught the human being what he/she did not know. (Q 96:1–4)

Modern readers of the Qur᾽an take some liberties in translating the Arabic command "*iqra᾽!*" to mean, "Read!" It is important to remember that in an oral culture that word meant simply to "recite"—from memory. Since the advent of writing and the later dominance of print culture, however, most people understand that command to be an invitation to *read* the Qur᾽an from a written source instead of *reciting*. This is a stunning example of how the meanings of the past change in accordance with how subtly our social imaginary is altered. Most people today find "read" to be appealing and regard "recite" as an odd meaning for *iqra᾽*. If anything, it demonstrates how words and meanings shift in their use and signification.

Regardless, the tradition of *reciting* the Qur᾽an from memory continues. Hundreds of thousands of men and women all over the world do memorize the entire Qur᾽an: both to embody the sacred word and to recite revelation.

Furthermore, the mention of the pen in the Qur᾽an is an allusion to a cosmic connection that requires every human being to secure knowledge. The pen, after all, is an instrument that affects human destiny; the reference, in a vital early chapter (*sura*), "The Pen," is suggestive of a maturing humanity connected to a transcendent Creator. The plain exegesis of this chapter of the Qur᾽an implies that once the majesty of God is recognized, a Muslim life should in reality center on reading, learning, and writing! In short, an ideal Islamic life is centered on inquiry.

Viewed along with other passages of the Qur'an, "The Pen" implies that a Muslim community should live, and must live, on a diet of wisdom based on inquiry. Muslims from very early on recognized that the pursuit of knowledge of God, inquiries about the universe, human beings, and about all creatures must also lead to a deeper understanding of the human condition. Knowledge deepens the requirements of faith and opens the doors to wisdom (philosophy) in order to unveil the complexity of human existence.

THE MANY FACES OF KNOWLEDGE

Folks in the madrasa-sphere are very comfortable talking about knowledge that is embedded in practices and applied to their bodies and lived environments. Modern-minded folk often deride embedded knowledge as subjective. This is partly explained by the fact that some philosophical elements associated with Western modernity have made a fateful and hard divide between subjective experiences and objective ones: the former is bad, the latter is good. If madrasa-based knowledge is deemed subjective, then it is only true from such a modern perspective. However, even this modern perspective is now increasingly being questioned.

Knowledge taught in the madrasas does not neatly distinguish between, say, a subjective experience and an objective one, or where concepts of culture vie with concepts found in nature. In modes of traditional thinking these categories are often intertwined. Increasingly, moderns too realize that actual human life is made up of mixtures of nature and culture in addition to brews of subjective and objective perspectives. Modern folk are taught to distinguish between how one *speaks* about knowledge (objective) and how knowledge is *embedded* (subjective) in real-life practices. But modern practitioners often forget that these categories of objective and subjective are purely heuristic, and our lived reality is not sliced into such neat categories.

Take, for example, a description of a unique teacher-student relationship that illustrates the blended binary quite effectively. The renowned Shah Waliyullah left India in the eighteenth century to study prophetic traditions, hadith, in Arabia with a notable scholar called Tahir bin Ibrahim Kurdi. Kurdi records his interactions with his student in these words: "He [Waliyullah] took the authorized transmission (*sanad*) of the words [of hadith] from me, while I often stood corrected about the meaning of the prophetic reports (*hadith*) from him!"[5] Kurdi admits the difference between facts and meanings. He objectively certified the prophetic reports that established one kind of knowledge. At the same time, he praises Waliyullah for his superior intelligence and intuition to grasp the deeper meanings of these prophetic reports. Hence, for Kurdi, as well as for Waliyullah, scholarship involves both the facts and the subjective meanings of the facts in a seamless manner.

Alongside questions about the classification of knowledge itself, Muslim thinkers were equally interested in *how* we know *what* we know, and *how* knowledge is constituted. In modern parlance we describe these debates surrounding knowledge as *epistemology*, which simply means the branch of philosophy that studies the nature of knowledge. A parallel group of debates would fall under the heading of *ontology*, which means the branch of metaphysics that deals with the nature of being or the literally real.

In many of the old texts on logic, philosophy, and certain strands of theology studied in the madrasa, an objective (empirical and verifiable) ontology of a very antique vintage is frequently discussed. The question asked in those texts is this: how do we perceive a thing as it is ("the thing in itself," the way Immanuel Kant asked), or how do we perceive the true reality of things? Surely discourses of a subjective (personal, existing only in individual experience) ontology (existence or the real) and as a result a subjective encounter with knowledge (epistemology) prevail in the contemporary madrasas alongside the questions of objectivity. Since the top priority of the madrasa is to be engaged in the work of salvation, and since each believer's relationship with the divine is, by definition, deeply personal, it might appear that the subjective ontology of knowledge is the dominant one. In contemporary South Asian madrasas, there is a great deal of self-searching and questioning happening precisely because faith has to survive in a constantly changing world, and hence knowledge about faith has to be regularly updated. Yet change elicits anxieties and dilemmas.

Take the example of faith claims, which are often embedded in practice. However, the fact that faith claims come together with practices does not mean that they are not theoretically and abstractly refined. Theologians—Muslim theologians are no exception—do spend a considerable amount of time talking about faith. They heartily theorize about it. So while theologians pursue knowledge that leads to salvation, it is often the case that the knowledge picture tilts toward matters that might be described as being based on personal and community experiences (subjective). The keyword to shed light on this phenomenon is "cosmography." Literally, "cosmography" refers to a science that describes the general features of the universe—heaven and earth—without impinging on the domain of astronomy or geography. Features of a cosmographic universe include providential events, symbolic orders, myths, hidden meanings, and unknowable powers—in short, fantastic universes.

Even in societies that pride themselves as subscribing to a rational-technological universe, beliefs of all kind are present. With the help of science fiction and digital technology, even moderns subscribe to mythologies of love, happiness, wealth, health, and perfection that are replete with extraterrestrials and mysteries. Despite the mythologies of modern life, the objective conditions and circumstances under which knowledge is created are not entirely ignored. Similarly, in societies where the cosmographic elements might be more accented, there are clear notions of objective descriptions. Hence we witness that subjective experiences and objective descriptions blend to work in tandem.

In the eleventh century, the great theologian, jurist, philosopher, and mystic Abu Hamid al-Ghazali (d. 1111)—considered by some historians such as William Montgomery Watt to be the single most influential Muslim after the Prophet Muhammad—created several taxonomies of knowledge. His bifurcated (two-part) taxonomy gained the widest currency. Knowledge is of two kinds, Ghazali explains. One kind of knowledge addresses worldly interests; the other type addresses both worldly interests *and* matters related to salvation. Over time, the latter of Ghazali's categories of knowledge came to enjoy greater prestige, since it addressed the ultimate questions of truth for human beings.

Rhyming and alliterative Arabic aphorisms capture this binary dynamic. One says: "Knowledge is of two kinds: knowledge of medicine for the body; and knowledge of religion for salvation."[6] In another formulation, offered by an early pious figure, Hasan al-Basri, "knowledge of the heart" is contrasted with "knowledge of the tongue." The former is seen as "beneficial knowledge," while the latter is viewed as "superficial knowledge." Over time this binary expands to beneficial knowledge versus harmful knowledge, ethically advantageous knowledge versus onerous knowledge.

To be fair, Ghazali encouraged communities to cultivate a range of talents for their own flourishing. A well-resourced community, he argued, needs people who have knowledge of farming, trade, medicine, engineering, or the crafts—among many other "worldly" skills. When a community lacks certain skills that are crucial to its social well-being, it becomes morally mandatory, he argues, for at least some people to acquire those vital skills in order to advance the welfare of society at large.

Other leading Muslim theologians of the caliber of ʿAdud al-Din al-Iji (d. 1356) and al-Sayyid al-Sharif al-Jurjani also admitted that communities needed an immeasurable amount of knowledge in order to functionally flourish. A large palette of learning, disciplines, crafts, specializations, and technologies is exactly what the Prophet Muhammad meant, Jurjani says, by his statement, "Disagreement [difference] among my community is a source of mercy."[7] How does Jurjani derive that implication from this prophetic utterance? The Prophet, Jurjani explains, intended to encourage competition among a range of experts in knowledge—from those adept in the religious sciences to experts in social affairs—in order to maximize intellectual diversity for the Muslim community.

But Ghazali and Jurjani together with a number of Muslim thinkers in the medieval period understood *all* references to knowledge as primarily referring to knowledge of God, as the loftiest and the most transcendent form of knowing. Unfortunately, knowledge about the world and how to improve it was often subservient to knowledge of faith, and in terms of prestige, expertise in worldly knowledge enjoyed a secondary status.

THE KNOWER AND THE KNOWN

Open the popular textbook on logic taught in the madrasas, a primer called *The Ladder* (*Mirqat*) by Fazl-i Imam Khairabadi (d. 1828).[8] On the second page the reader encounters multiple definitions of knowledge. Of the many objective definitions, one explains knowledge as the perception of an object *in* the mind. Knowledge, a second definition goes, is an image of a thing as it *appears* to the mind. A third definition says knowledge is what becomes *present* to a rational person, without telling us how it becomes present. A fourth definition says that when a person *acquiesces* to a specific image of a thing, then that constitutes knowledge. A fifth definition of knowledge is intriguing: "knowledge is that *relation/attachment* that connects the knower [subject] to the known [object]."[9] All of this suggests that there is a rich opportunity to explore a phenomenological approach to knowledge in the Muslim tradition. So if, for example, you have a *book* in front of you, what makes it possible for you to know *it* is a *book*? All that matters, classical Muslim philosophers argue, is the *relation or attachment* between you and the book. If you can visualize your mental *connection* to the book, then surely you can grasp how knowledge works.

Muslim philosophers and theologians all agree that it is extremely difficult to define knowledge and how it works, as the examples given above show. Yet these subtle definitions offered convey different pictures of reality or of what exists. Some definitions allow one to *describe* the picture of reality and to imagine its existence independent of the observer, in what is called an objective ontology of knowledge. Other definitions show how reality is intimately embedded in connections and relationships to the knower and the known, between a subject and an object, in what can be described as a subjective ontology of knowledge.

So the next question to consider is this: What links the knower (a person) and the known (the thing or object)? Well, Muslim theologians say knowledge comes with a *desire* to know: often, to know God or to know the truth. Knowledge and the desire to know cannot be separated; the one exists for the other. Most Muslim thinkers will agree with Michel Foucault's claim that "the desire to know is in its nature already something like knowledge, something belonging to knowledge."[10] In other words, knowledge in itself is an object of desire.

Scholars in the madrasas explain that one's relationship with objects, with ideas (real or imagined), with other humans, and with animals is a result of a particular *quality* within us humans. This property or attribute within us is called *ʿilm*, an ability "to know," or the existence of the attribute of cognition within us. This unique ability to know separates us humans from other biological species as well as from cosmic beings, like angels. It is our ability *to know* that makes it possible for humans to cultivate relationships with others.

Exhibit number one is our primordial human ancestor, Adam. He stood apart from all creation, including angels, according to the Muslim tradition, because he had the ability *to know*, a quality not even God's angels possessed. Muslim thinkers explain that we each have within us an indivisible "illuminating" attribute that discloses, and unveils the verities or essences of things to us.[11]

Muslim philosophers do not dwell much on whether space (extension—length, breadth, and depth) and time are properties or attributes of, say, a book or a chair; they are more likely to assume that space and time are properties in the knower (the human person). Since the knower establishes a connection to the book, the properties of space and time

Children in the town of Deoband in India going to elementary school in traditional clothing, an image that is often confused as their attending madrasa. (Picture: Rodrigo Dorfman)

are projected *onto* the book; in this way we *know of* the book and have knowledge *of* the book. The German philosopher Immanuel Kant too points out that the properties of space and time do not belong to, say, the examples of a book or to the cat. Rather, he argues, that you—the person trying to grasp the difference between a book and a cat—inhabit perceptions of space and time.

Muslim philosophers figured out that the connection or relation with objects is how awareness of space and time is transmitted to an observer. In fact, some go so far as to say that it is impossible to define knowledge, since one knows things intuitively, through one's soul.[12] In other words, one knows things through one's existence, not only through one's mind.

Without grasping the subjective and interior aspect of knowledge, one would miss much of the debate about how people who live in the madrasa communities value and appreciate knowledge. Recall that even in the objective picture of knowledge, the attribute of cognition is located in the human body, albeit in the heart/mind. Cognition is the crucial link between the complex physical and mental activities of humans and an object, by which knowledge attains a distinct character. It does not pertain only to mundane observations such as, What is a book? What is a cat? Rather, more importantly, knowledge is the *path*, the connection or the relationship by which human beings understand themselves and

"I Exist Therefore I Know"

At least two centuries before René Descartes made his famous statement *cogito ergo sum*, "I think; therefore I am," the Persian polymath of a scholar al-Sayyid al-Sharif al-Jurjani (d. 1413) wrote, "Each person knows by necessity or axiomatically that he exists. Therefore he also knows, that he knows by means of that existence" (al-Sayyid al-Sharif al-Jurjani, Commentary on the *al-Mawaqif* of al-Iji, 1:48). One could paraphrase the statement of Jurjani to say, "I exist; therefore I know."

their place in the world. In other words, knowledge plays a critical role in grasping the ultimate truth or at least mediating the truth. It is a function that takes on a sacred character in this world beyond any other, lower function of knowledge. However, both sacred and mundane forms of knowledge often are embodied in practices.

EMBODYING KNOWLEDGE THROUGH PRACTICE

"In truth, knowledge on its own means nothing," writes Mufti Taqi ʿUsmani, a prominent figure in Pakistan's madrasa-sphere.[13] "Knowledge only becomes a source of virtue or excellence when it is matched by action," in his view; he adds that "knowledge without practice is worthless."[14] Given the twinning of knowledge and practice, a feature of a traditional Muslim education is the inculcation of practice: students are required to embody the knowledge they acquire.

Unlike the Cartesian formulation of knowing for knowing's sake, in madrasas one learns in order to know *how* to act. The "secret" of madrasa education is a disciplined life and apprenticeship to a master-teacher, a dimension that surpasses learning from books, dismissed as merely "letters and imprints on paper" (*huruf va nuqush*) if learning is bereft from exemplary action.[15] Frequently the following lines are cited to reinforce this wisdom.

Neither from books, colleges, nor wealth, is faith created
Rather, the visage of the pious creates faith
Courses instruct only bland words
Only a "person" shapes another person of worth.[16]

The vocabulary for the multiple technologies of learning and moral formation includes one or more prevailing concepts: "moral discipline" (*ta'dib*), "moral cultivation" (*tarbiyya*), and "ethical instruction" (*taʿlim*). Interchangeably used in Muslim moral discourses, these keywords denote the somatic features of knowledge, the processes by which knowledge inhabits bodies, becomes internal to bodies, and finally, bends bodies to the rhythms of learning, which is the desideratum of madrasa education.

When the learned Qasim Nanautvi, one of the cofounders of the Deoband school, sought spiritual guidance from the mystic Haji Imdadullah, who himself had very little training in the high discursive tradition of Islamic learning, many people were astonished by Nanautvi's decision. Rather, Imdadullah should be reaching out to you, some people told Nanautvi, since you are the person of learning. Nanautvi's reply was instructive. "I have knowledge of faith but I have yet to experience the joy of 'tasting' [experiencing] the practical application of that learning," Nanautvi admitted. "It is in search of tasting the joy of practice that I have come to serve Haji Imdadullah," he announced his discipleship.[17]

For a long time now, humanity has struggled to configure how knowledge becomes part of the human body and psyche. How do learning and faith, moral formation and belief become reflexive and habitual? But also, more importantly: why does knowledge have to be ingrained into us? To get a sense of why this is important, we need to consult a very influential North African thinker of the fourteenth century.

IBN KHALDUN ON HABITS AND THE BODY

Born in Tunis in the year 1332, ʿAbd al-Rahman Ibn Khaldun (d. 1406) lived for a remarkable seventy-five years. A statesman and a scholar, he was a refined man and a thinker who toyed with big ideas. Aspiring to write a comprehensive compendium of world history, he wrote prolifically and left behind a very valuable piece of writing. It is called the *Prolegomena* (*Muqaddima*), meaning an introduction to world history he planned to write. His work brims with details, and he captures a good number of relevant themes of world history up to his day.

Knowledge, Ibn Khaldun points out, is something cumulative. We eagerly embrace the knowledge of our predecessors because as humans we have the unique ability to reflect on things beyond our immediate selves. Once the senses grasp tangible things, we can then also project and

Students in class at Jamiʿa Naeemia, Lahore, Pakistan. (Picture: Amjad Pervez)

imagine abstract things based on our experience. What makes this imagining possible is a certain habit that becomes ingrained in us over time. In Ibn Khaldun's view, this habitus or ability (*malaka*), what we moderns would call power, grows within us and enables us to effortlessly make sense of disparate experiences and bundles of information. Recall our discussion about the attribute of cognition we humans possess. Well, when cognition becomes a natural part of our unconscious habit-in-action, then we call it knowledge.[18] But we not only hoard this knowledge; we also desire to transmit it to subsequent generations by way of instruction.

Ibn Khaldun also provides some enduring insights as to *how* humans learn. We just do not learn things automatically; rather, he says, we learn only after we acquire certain skills. Those vital skills too are a product of habit. When it comes to a discussion of habits, Ibn Khaldun seems to have anticipated debates that moderns only came to grips with recently: how we do we *know with* our bodies? "Habits are corporeal," he writes, "irrespective whether they [inhabit] the body, or, whether they [inhabit] the brain, like arithmetic, a result of thought and other such impulses. All corporeal things are sensory (*sensibilia*). Hence, all corporeal things require instruction."[19]

Memory and understanding in matters of learning, says Ibn Khaldun, pale in terms of importance when compared to habit and ability. Why? Habit and ability are more durable qualities. Ibn Khaldun long ago deflated the shibboleth that Muslims and Easterners learn things only by rote. In fact, possession by memory and cultivating understanding of what one had learned, in his view, are intuitive traits common to all humans.

By contrast, habit is a quality that requires meticulous nurturing by means of careful training and discipline. Habit for Ibn Khaldun thus resembles in many ways what the French sociologist Pierre Bourdieu identified as the *habitus*: those durable dispositions and primal structures that unconsciously enable one to accomplish certain tasks and gain mastery over them.[20] In the words of another prominent French thinker, one can actually say that habit is a form of capillary power, namely, power that permeates one's body in the same way as one's veins. Power, like habit, Michel Foucault clarifies, "reaches into the very grain of individuals, touches their bodies and inserts itself in their actions and attitudes, their discourses, learning processes, and everyday lives."[21] Therefore it is not at all surprising to hear people say that knowledge is a form of power. What they mean is that our abilities and habits *in-habit* our bodies through a process of learning; knowledge-making processes, then, are acts of power, which, if collectively harnessed, enable civilizations to flourish. It is precisely in order to facilitate civilization and civility among peoples, Ibn Khaldun explains, that the profession or "the craft" of instruction has become indispensable to human flourishing.

So before we study anything, it is crucial for certain habits to be ingrained into us humans by means of one of the most natural of processes we are accustomed to, namely, *instruction* (*taʿlim*). Even prophets were not exempt from this instruction, although their education occurred by way of divine tutorship. "My Lord *instructed* me," the Prophet Muhammad once proclaimed, "and perfected my *education*." The keyword in this remembered saying is the verb *addaba* and its verbal noun *taʾdib*, here translated as "instruction" and "education," respectively.

All of madrasa education is about ingraining certain habits through instruction and education. Habits are changed, comportment is regulated, and character is cultivated. Daily prayers and strictly following as many of the prophetic practices is one way to educate the body. Decorum is everything. One never addresses one's teacher by his name, but always in a respectful and humble tone as "sir" (*hazrat*). Furthermore, one never sits in the lotus position in the presence of a teacher, but always with one leg or both tucked underneath. That is a difficult posture to be seated in for a long duration, but it is also a respectful posture. Instructing the body to comply with norms, it is believed, also opens the body to receive the light of education.

Literature too in Arabic is called, *adab*: artistic creation that one reads, hears, or performs for enjoyment or moral refinement—in short, to become erudite. The literary use of the term is not insignificant, since in the broader Muslim humanist tradition, *adab* as literature offers paradigms for action and the refinement of character.[22]

RIGHT AND WRONG: THE MORAL DIMENSION OF KNOWLEDGE

Ta'dib, moral instruction and discipline, are the desiderata of education in the madrasa. In fact, madrasas are perhaps the world's last remaining educational redoubts where learning is still steeped in moral discipline. Students here are constantly reminded that their mastery of robust debates about the finer points of law and lofty theological arguments are indeed all commendable deeds; yet as students they should never lose sight of the ends of learning. The goal is to recognize God and become morally upright and exemplary human beings. To submit to moral instruction also means to be open and be vulnerable to correction and improvement.

There was a time when an educated person was referred to as a "cultured" or "refined" person, although today we prefer the term "ethical" person. It is therefore instructive to learn that some Muslim authors identified an "erudite person" (*adib*) in almost ethical terms, as "someone who possesses every commendable trait."[23]

NURTURING AND SUSTAINING: A DISTINCTIVE ISLAMIC EDUCATION

There has been much debate as to what is truly distinctive about an Islamic education. Some argue Islam's theistic notion of moral learning is unique. Others argue that the Muslim tradition as developed over time is distinctive as an archive of moral learning. Another group argues that the scriptural imprimaturs provided by the Qur'an and the teachings of the Prophet Muhammad are the repositories of unique learning.

Despite the diverse responses, everyone agrees that education is intimately tied to Islam's moral and ethical imperatives, known as the Shariʿa. As one medieval writer put it, "All ethical paradigms (*Sharaʾiʿ*) [sing. *Shariʿa]*, are effectively disciplinary signposts erected by God for [the guidance of] His servants."[24] Modern-minded Muslims differ profoundly as to how they understand and interpret the Shariʿa, while madrasa authorities are more unified around their understanding of Shariʿa doctrine.

In theory, tradition-based models of Shariʿa ought to be more sensitive to time, place, and history, while scripture-based approaches should be more limiting and restrictive. In reality, these typologies and their methods do not often unfold so neatly. Often it turns out that practitioners wedded to the authority of the canonical law schools are unable to unshackle themselves from the methodology they acquired and feel bound to uphold the authority of the past. Surprisingly, those who give lesser importance to the canonical schools often offer new interpretations of scriptural sources that are relevant to new contexts even though their opinions might lack authenticity.

"Nurturing" or "nourishing" (*tarbiyya*), a crucial term for moral cultivation set to the rhythm of the Shariʿa, is the raison d'être of South Asian madrasas. Even Urdu-language users frequently use the more common English word "training" in order to explain what they mean by *tarbiyya*. Etymologically the word derives from the word *rabb*, the Arabic word for the sole Nurturer and Sustainer of the world, God. The imagery signals the process of moral discipline. And as a fourteenth-century lexicographer put it, the goal is to produce "a scholar intimately tied to the pursuit of the Divine."[25]

God-fearing individuals are the true bearers of learning and piety. Students are not only encouraged to look to the founders of the scholarly tradition with great reverence, but they view their teachers as models for imitation in an education programmatically tied to pious purposes. A professor does not only teach the text of the prophetic tradition (hadith) but also embodies the teaching in his lifestyle. In doing so he infuses in the student a love for the path (*sunna*) of the Prophet Muhammad.

The teachings of the Prophet are in turn intimately tied to the teachings of the Qurʾan. If the Qurʾan—the lodestone of Muslim teaching—is both the inspiration for and the goal of pious pursuits, then how, precisely, are Muslims nurtured and sustained with inspiration from it? How, in other words, does the Qurʾan communicate to its audiences—reciters, readers, listeners, active and passive observers of the holy book—in different times and places?

Some scholars say one can distinguish between at least two modes of speech in the Qurʾan: one mode is called the homily or sermonic (*waʿz*) mode; the second is marked as ethical instruction (*taʿlim*).[26] Both modes of speech are deployed in the madrasas, but it takes the form of an elaborate program of ethical instruction involving the study of multiple disciplines, texts, and languages and an intimate familiarity with various methods and philosophies in order to appreciate the Qurʾan in the full panoply of its breadth and depth. So it is not so much the reading of the Qurʾan that is stressed in the madrasa as the desire to equip the student to understand the multiple worlds the Qurʾan navigates. In other words, the goal is to equip the student with a knowledge program as well as to inculcate a respect for the profound complexity of the Qurʾan's message. To do so successfully requires access to both knowledge and information.

ON KNOWLEDGE AND INFORMATION

Knowledge as a concept, in the view of most madrasa authorities today, must be understood as something quite distinct from information. Knowledge is intimately committed to truth-claims, verities regarding faith and issues related to ultimate reality. Information, on the other hand, is about ascertaining the facts and describes the conditions under which knowledge is produced. But information does not necessarily advance one's understanding of the facts, in the view of madrasa authorities. By contrast knowledge is seen as an attainment, something that has been personally wrested from the sources and connected to the possessor of learning. Information, in turn, is something merely obtained, something that can be passed on like a commodity, from hand to hand, usually in response to a question. At best it is a form of background knowledge that enables us to understand under what conditions knowledge was produced.

Information might not contribute anything significant to the meaning and purpose of life. The purpose of life, in the madrasa-sphere, is to live a life compliant with God's will—a life of obedience and piety. So anything that ostensibly poses as knowledge and learning but really does not prevent one from committing sin does not qualify as knowledge.

To qualify as knowledge, information has to effectively undergo a process akin to alchemy: it must be subject to the discipline of the mind and body in order to serve higher transcendent purposes—in the way copper supposedly turns into gold in the hands of the alchemists of old.

Much of the classical and preclassical conceptions of knowledge and its relation to faith thrive in the madrasa system of South Asia. Key figures from a variety of madrasa trends actively promote these knowledge traditions, which remain hegemonic. Yet parallel to it is a soul-searching process of a countervailing tradition existing at the margins of the madrasa tradition.

FAITH AND LEARNING

For Muslim thinkers, something as deeply personal and unfathomable as faith is incomplete if it is not anchored in a certain kind of learning. The acquisition of knowledge leavens the quest for faith and deepens one's participation in a desirable and prescribed moral life. Knowledge opens the door for humans to adore and serve God with sincerity in order to reach a heightened sense of self-awareness. Ultimately, the goal of learning is to earn God's pleasure and approval, a point made relentlessly by madrasa representatives.

Acquiring knowledge is thus a privileged activity because it paves the way to God. Here providential grace is decisive. To be deserving of the intimate knowledge of God and become a beneficiary of that treasure first requires an act of divine grace. In order to become a recipient of this benevolence and grace, a learner works continuously on her or his inner self to become worthy of divine illumination. In more mundane terms, one could put it like this: knowledge is a process; it begins with learning and ends in laudable deeds. Knowledge and deeds both in the end illuminate the devout, providing them with this-worldly success and promising salvation in the afterlife. How? Knowledge is closely tied to grasping what Muslims called *din*, a term that I translate as "salvation practices" but is often mistranslated as "religion," with its modern ring of private beliefs. If one were to scour the Muslim tradition, one would get the sense that *din* is not a belief but a grammar.

Indeed, *din* is a grammar of how one performs all the practices of salvation. To follow one's *din* means to perform those acts of redemption that both mediate and constitute the life-world. Once I broached this subject with Sayyid Salman Husayni Nadvi, an established scholar at the Nadwatul ʿulama seminary in Lucknow, India. "Knowledge of salvation," he said full of animation, "is the essential business of the life-world."[27] Hence, knowledge of faith paves the way to salvation. Thus, knowledge is an end in itself, and therefore it cannot be used as a means. Any use of this knowledge for the purposes of advancing one's material conditions, explains Husayni, echoing age-old Islamic wisdom, is frowned upon as a moral flaw in its bearer.

Three towering religious thinkers who left deep imprints on the madrasa landscape in the nineteenth and twentieth centuries were strong advocates of knowledge as a salvation project. Obscure in Western scholarship until quite recently are Siddiq Hasan Khan Qannawji (1832–1889), Ahmad Raza Khan (1856–1921), and Ashraf ʿAli Thanvi (1863–1943). All three men were key figures in different madrasa networks and spiritual circles that began in prepartition India but continue to this very day. Each wrote prolifically, and all established loyal audiences and accumulated broad support through print, preaching, and personal contact with myriads of disciples. In the view of all three men, all knowledge derives from God, and only the Qurʾan and the prophetic tradition constitute true knowledge.

SIDDIQ HASAN KHAN QANNAWJI (1832–1889)

Siddiq Hasan Khan Qannawji hailed from a North Indian family of religious notables. Marriage into the royal household of Bhopal provided him with a platform to advance his religious ideas, a moderate form of puritanism (*salafi*), and the privileges of marriage helped to promote his extensive transnational scholarly network. For him, as for all *salafis*, it is paramount to proclaim the conviction that the Qurʾan and the prophetic traditions (*Sunna*) are the *only* legitimate sources of religious inspiration in Islam. All else is a degradation of tradition and antithetical to true faith and practice. Especially suspect in *salafi* circles are Sufi practices and the requirement that lay Muslims commit to the authority of one of the canonical schools of Islamic law.

While Qannawji enjoyed respect for his scholarship, his adversaries were also critical of his affiliation to an unsophisticated trend of Salafism. Salafism in the Indian subcontinent went by the label of "Folk of the Prophetic Tradition" (*Ahl-i Hadith*). Qannawji's stern critiques of the authority of the ancient canonical schools of law that many non-*salafis*, broadly the Sunni mainstream, earnestly follow earned him notoriety among his peers.

In keeping with the ancient tradition of knowledge, Qannawji wrote, "The meaning of knowledge (*ʿilm*) as mentioned in all the prophetic reports means the knowledge of the faith and the elucidated normative tradition (*sharʿ*). It means simply, the knowledge of the Noble Book, the immaculate tradition and nothing else."[28]

AHMAD RAZA KHAN (1856–1921)

The renowned scholar Ahmad Raza Khan was the highest-ranking voice and most muscular ideologue of a trend that would later become known to its rivals as the Barelvi theological school. But Barelvis view themselves as truly orthodox Muslims and self-identify themselves as those who "Adhere to the Prophetic Tradition and a United Community" (*Ahl-i Sunna wal Jamaʿat*), the generic academic designation of Sunnism.

A quick study whose brilliance was widely acknowledged at an early age of twenty-four, Ahmad Raza visited Mecca several times. There he received investitures to narrate hadith from distinguished scholars, among them the reputed Sayyid Ahmad Zayni Dahlan (d. 1886), the doyen of Shafiʿi authorities, and from the official Hanafi jurisconsult of Mecca Shaykh Abdurrahman Siraj (d. 1896) and Shaykh Husayn ibn Salih Jamal al-Layl (d. 1967). In Mecca, Ahmad Raza impressed the scholars of that holy city with his extensive knowledge of Islamic law and a talent to rapidly compile treatises. Some 500 treatises are attributed to him. This includes a multivolume collection of legal and moral rulings, called fatwas, lucidly and knowledgeably written in addition to many medium-sized and smaller treatises. All his biographers acknowledge that he surpassed many of his contemporaries with his expertise in Islamic law and theoretical jurisprudence. And many admired his firm grasp of mathematics, astronomy, and timekeeping techniques.

"I can produce endless proofs from the Qurʾan and the prophetic tradition (*hadith*)," said Ahmad Raza, "that the meaning of the virtues of knowledge was exclusively limited to knowledge of salvation (*din*)."[29] Ahmad Raza was even more forthright. He invoked the esteemed classical scholar Shafiʿi, who said, "Every form of learning apart from the Qurʾan is frivolous."[30] Ahmad Raza dismissed early Muslim philosophers as "imbeciles" in claiming that knowledge is an "image acquired *from* a thing as it appears in the mind."[31] Rather "the image of the known object is acquired," Ahmad Raza argued, adding, "knowledge is an illumination (*nur*) that unveils whatever appears in its perimeter and whatever connects to it, so that the image becomes illustrated in our minds."[32] While Ahmad Raza was critical of the Salafis, his pungent loathing was reserved for the founders of the Deoband school. He singled them out and anathematized their views for endorsing a theology that in his view was irreverent to the Prophet Muhammad, and among them was Ashraf ʿAli Thanvi.

ASHRAF ʿALI THANVI (1863–1943)

Ashraf ʿAli Thanvi was indisputably the most influential scholar affiliated to the Deoband school.[33] Born in the town of Thana Bhavan not far from the city of Saharanpur and in close proximity to towns like Deoband, he hailed from a prosperous family. There were no immediate religious scholars in his family. His father managed an estate for a North Indian notable, and his younger brother joined the colonial bureaucracy.[34] Thanvi left behind an impressive scholarly oeuvre and hundreds of influential disciples in his role as a Sufi master, and his influence radiates to this very day in Deobandi circles. Thanvi held traditional and decisive views on knowledge like Qannawji and Ahmad Raza.

He distinguished between information and knowledge. Ponder the analogy he offers, which renders the difference quite stark. Person A, he says, travels widely in the world and sees many places, visits historical sites, and meets many interesting people. But Person A, Thanvi continues, is unable to offer any account of what lessons he can gain from his voyages. By contrast, Person B travels to fewer places and meets even fewer people. But Person B is gifted with an intuitive capacity to offer insightful comments. The result is that he can explain the significance and meaning of his travels and also share these insights with others. The minimal traveler, B, possesses an intuitive ability to grasp the essence and truth of events and the things he encounters, whereas the celebrity globe-trotter, A, despite possessing a surfeit of information and frequent-flyer miles, is unable to recruit his internal resources to enlighten him as to what his journeys mean. In this latter scenario, the copper of information does not turn into the gold of knowledge.

Information is no substitute for insight in Thanvi's view. "Knowledge requires a sound and strong [interior] perception in order to rapidly reach correct conclusions," he writes, adding, "This is the transcendent reality of knowledge, attained not only by study and teaching. Other ways of reaching perception includes supplication and cultivating God-consciousness. To attain God-consciousness, one should abstain from all transgressions. Adopt God-consciousness and then watch; words cannot express the true perfections of the soul."[35]

Contrasting the person who received madrasa training with one who received modern education, Thanvi is acidly critical of the latter. "These days modern educated [Muslims who are] English-speakers deem themselves extremely competent," Thanvi writes, "but in reality they completely lack any capability."[36] "I frequently meet these types during my travels," he continues, "and from my interactions with them I realized that they command only a few phrases, but in reality they know absolutely nothing!"[37]

For Thanvi, knowledge is, at its core, metaphysical.[38] Therefore, Thanvi states polemically, if information is the sum total of all learning, then "knowledge can cohabit with unbelief too." "But that is not true," he asserts, "since the Christians of Beirut and Germany are also highly literate and expert in Arabic, possessing great memories and sharp minds. But what they possess, we know, is not called knowledge."[39]

People of other faiths who study Islam, in his view, surely possess information about Islam as a faith, but they lack the ability to assent to the truth claims of their knowledge and own it personally. Knowledge, in his view, is tied to some deeper and transcendent cosmic reality where the truth of things becomes manifest and serves as the driver of the soul. The Deobandi point of view, which Thanvi represents, acknowledges that Islam advances the pursuit of knowledge, *ʿilm*. But it is an understanding of knowledge in a specific sense. True knowledge opens a path to salvation, in Thanvi's view, following twelfth-century theologian Abu Hamid al-Ghazali, who held a similar view.[40] Thanvi often gave the example of his own spiritual master Haji Imdadullah, who did not have recognized scholarly credentials but was an accomplished mystic. Thanvi confesses that his own book learning is no match for his master's superior intuitive insight of the transcendent reality of all things in ways that he, Thanvi, can only aspire to reach.

Knowledge, Ghazali held, must lead to salvation. However, Ghazali did not reduce all of knowledge to salvific ends. Ghazali, unlike Thanvi, also engaged in a fairly elaborate project to reconstruct and revitalize the Muslim discursive tradition. He freely borrowed from philosophy, logic, political theory, and ancient knowledge traditions in order to creatively revitalize the foundations of thought that affected Muslim life in the worldly sphere. The additional disciplines he studied and adapted into the Muslim knowledge tradition were in his view part of his elementary literacy and life world in the eleventh and twelfth centuries. Ghazali's interventions in legal theory, ethics, and law were not reductive to personal salvific ends. In fact, he anticipated a public sphere in which Muslim moral and ethical teachings could discursively flourish in order to advance the common good and public welfare. Knowledge as personal salvation was effective only at the individual level and was qualitatively different from discursive knowledge that was designed to promote the worldly and common good.

Thanvi and some twentieth-century Muslim traditionalists in South Asia failed to provide the Muslims of the subcontinent a viable and robust public discursive tradition steeped in an Islamic alphabet. Instead, they tried to engage the public sphere with the intuition-based discursive knowledge of individual salvation. It was a category mistake and proved to be limiting, isolationist, anachronistic, and ineffective at the public level. In fact, Thanvi repeatedly and with utter disdain discredited secular learning as the very antithesis to what the tradition stood for.

However, some traditionalists like Mahmood Hasan, ʿUbaydullah Sindhi, and Husayn Ahmad Madani, among the Deobandis, at least showed some awareness of the fact that Islam's public discourse needed a cosmopolitan and socially relevant component. They reached for knowledge that advanced the common weal, even if they did not always succeed in providing an effective one. Mahmud Hasan was among the founders of the Jamiʿa Millia Islamia, a university established in 1920, with the express purpose to furnish Muslims with skills and knowledge that were relevant to their life world. For them engagement in the political sphere alongside people of other faith traditions enabled them to broaden Islam's theological horizon in the public sphere. In that sense it came closer to Ghazali's project of promoting the public good while they might differ in the details.

PLURALISM IN THE PUBLIC SQUARE

What accounts for this construction where people like Thanvi regard faith-based knowledge as the only form of meaningful knowledge? The primary reason is clear enough: the historical classification of knowledge in the Muslim tradition sets up this dichotomy between knowledge of faith and knowledge of the world. The underlying Aristotelian structure identifies the chief good and the primary master narrative. Once salvation is identified as the highest good, all else becomes secondary.

There is, however, another critical factor to consider why the faith-based knowledge tradition became hegemonic in the nineteenth and twentieth centuries: the Muslim encounter with the West. Whether through colonialism or other forms of social and political contact, traditional Muslim religious scholars viewed Western knowledge systems with suspicion. Modern education was not seen as an advance but rather as bait for cultural conversion, a ruse aimed at colonizing Muslims politically and dominating them socially and culturally. In such contexts exclusivist Islamic discourses served as bulwarks for the preservation of religious identity.

More difficult to analyze but equally important is the emergence of a secular public square in many postcolonial Muslim societies. The very success of the secular public square anticipates and requires the emergence of an exclusive religious sphere. Hence the madrasas fill that exclusive religious sphere with consummate ease and enable the discourse of individual religious salvation to morph into identity politics.

Even though representatives of the madrasas in South Asia diagnose this growing public sphere to be crudely materialistic, secular, and prone to libertine indulgence, yet these very conditions pluralize the public sphere for them. Hence, Muslim traditionalists can claim to have access to this very same public square and, of course, offer drastic alternatives to the secular utopia advanced by their opponents. Instead, theirs is an ideal of austerity, piety, and a preoccupation with personal salvation, modeled on that of the Prophet Muhammad himself.

Gradually, the madrasa in South Asia transforms itself from earlier incarnations as an academic institution with multiple sources of knowledge into a religious institution with a single source of knowledge and a standardized madrasa curriculum.[41] Identifying larger public trends, the prescient Ashraf ʿAli Thanvi predicted, "I think as the absence of [social] restraint [i.e., libertinism] and atheism grow so too will the importance of the madrasas proportionately increase."[42] Thanvi saw the madrasa as a traditional Muslim bulwark or a counter-utopia (*heterotopia*) to advance the project of individual salvation, in contrast to the utopian ideals of the modern nation-state, its secularizing and social salvation project as advanced by Muslim supporters of the secular state.[43]

While many people in the madrasa community share Thanvi's view, it is certainly not the entire picture. Thanvi was unsympathetic to the idea that knowledge of the world provided by the secular educational system was part of a modern person's elementary literacy in order to flourish. Muhammad Nazim Nadvi in Pakistan understood the need for a new basic literacy and applauded the introduction of modern subjects in the curricula of a tiny minority of madrasas.[44]

DISSENTING VOICES

Within madrasa circles there are those who challenge the dominant interpretation of knowledge, criticizing its restriction to exclusively being only knowledge of salvation. In fact there is an identifiable group of curriculum scolds consisting of former madrasa graduates, university professors, modernists, and political elites, each proposing changes for their own reasons. Shahabuddin Nadvi, himself a madrasa graduate, believes the reference to knowledge (*ʿilm*) in the tradition broadly conceived, including the Qurʾan and the hadith, refers to both knowledge of the moral tradition (Shariʿa) and knowledge of nature (*tabiʿa*).[45] In his view, worldliness receives a great deal of attention even in the Qurʾan's description of knowledge and spiritual matters.

In an exhaustive discussion but without directly criticizing any of the major figures in the madrasa tradition, Salman Husayni at the Darul Uloom Nadwatul Ulama in Lucknow makes a similar point. The great theologian Fakhruddin al-Razi, explains Husayni, clarified that everything from "knowing God to knowing all his creation—angels, planets, elements, mineral, plants, and animals"— qualified as knowledge.[46]

Pushing the envelope even further is the traditionalist scholar Muhammad Aslam Qasmi, himself a madrasa graduate and the great-grandson of Nanautvi, a cofounder of the Deoband seminary. Aslam Qasmi today commands a crucial voice in a breakaway Darul Uloom Deoband Waqf seminary, also in the town of Deoband. The knowledge project of the madrasa, he argues, has become hostage to an unfortunate "historical error of dividing knowledge into two parts: worldly and religious."[47]

Challenging Ghazali as well as the major voices in his own school's hierarchy, Aslam Qasmi boldly contests the gloss on references to knowledge in the Qurʾan and the prophetic traditions to mean only knowledge of faith. Some early scholars did not make a distinction between different types of knowledge, and saw all knowledge as divinely mandated, he argues. Aslam Qasmi is critical of contemporary madrasa authorities who believe that their sole purpose is to produce clerics who will become leaders to serve mosque communities. Madrasas must also, in his view, fill the knowledge gap evident in the construction of religious thought. Yet, despite spearheading a new madrasa, Aslam Qasmi's own institution is identical to other madrasas where his views have yet to make an impact.

Madrasa representatives often claim they are committed and qualified only to serve a very discrete religious discourse. They often refute accusation that they prevent Muslims, especially madrasa graduates, from expanding their intellectual horizons into other domains of knowledge. However, the reality is that very few madrasa graduates are encouraged to access learning beyond what the madrasa offers. There is a fundamental absence of grasping the fact that knowledge of science, math, civics, sociology, politics, economics, and history in addition to languages and skills is all part of one's basic equipment and literacy in today's world. Many madrasa authorities misunderstand and think calls for curricular reform means they have to become specialists in science or politics. In parts of the Middle East, a modicum of reforms to religious education has taken place.[48]

Aslam Qasmi tells of witnessing bias within madrasa circles against acquiring modern education. A friend, Aslam Qasmi reports, informed his madrasa professor that he was going to continue his education at the secular Aligarh Muslim University. In what seems to be a widespread and representative perspective, the professor disapproved of the student's choice to pursue modern education and deemed it a downgrade. "It seems," the professor sarcastically remarked to Aslam Qasmi's friend, "you dismounted from a horse in order to ride a donkey."[49] Secular education was derided as inferior as a donkey.

In contesting the otherworldly approach of madrasa education, Aslam Qasmi makes the following argument. Monasticism has no place in Islam, he argues, citing a hadith of the Prophet Muhammad. This leads Aslam Qasmi to critically question why the madrasas "have adopted intellectual monasticism." Even worse is when the madrasas refuse to provide any serious curricular options in order to equip students with modern knowledge and life skills. This level of asceticism has been harmful to Muslim interests at large and has reduced religious thought to mediocrity, in his view. He laments the narrow-minded approach to knowledge adopted by the majority in the madrasa circles and invokes a few lines from the renowned prepartition poet Muhammad Iqbal, who mockingly reveals the limited knowledge of clerics. In biting sarcasm Iqbal asks,

> *What is a people? What constitutes the leadership of a people?*
> *What will a poor imam, only knowledgeable in the rituals of two prayer genuflections, know about this?*[50]

My own experience is that those students who choose higher education elsewhere, especially at universities, are frequently viewed with suspicion. While madrasa authorities sometimes honor the additional qualifications of madrasa graduates, no credit is given, or praise extended, to the insights those graduates gained from modern knowledge. Often, more orthodox elements within the madrasas view it as their duty to counter modern interpretations generated by their former graduates in bruising polemics and futile apologetics.

CONCLUSION

If representatives of contemporary madrasas in South Asia and beyond were to admit that they face a major crisis, then the brave among them would acknowledge the epistemological crisis in Muslim religious knowledge. For a minority of madrasa administrators, the crisis of knowledge and how to equip their graduates to meet the needs of their ever-modernizing societies is quite real. The battle between those who would amend the curriculum and those who favor the status quo is far from resolved.

Some believe that the safest method would be to create a parallel track of secular education—high school and even college education—functioning alongside madrasa education, the model that Mawlana Ghulam Vastanvi established at his madrasas in the state of Maharashtra or the approach adopted at a madrasa in Jaipur in India. Others have thought about integrating modern education with madrasa education but with very minimal, if not zero, dividends. For the majority of madrasa administrators, however, the tried-and-tested madrasa system—with its traditional syllabus and accompanying knowledge framework—can only be modified at the cost of the integrity of the entire system itself. Change is thus off limits. It is taken as an article of faith that the successful experiences of madrasas in the past prove that they will save the present. This approach is daunting and courageous, but lacking in conviction.

PART FOUR

Madrasas in Global Context

Media and political commentators frame madrasas as malevolent institutions. Madrasas have become the casualties in the fog of the war on terror and its aftermath—against the Taliban, terrorists, and any number of Muslim cultural institutions in both the West and the non-West. This jaundiced view of the madrasas as bastions of extremism is at odds with reality, and Western publics remain uninformed about these orthodox Muslim institutions.

CHAPTER NINE

Talking about Madrasas

MEDIA, MADRASAS, AND MULLAHS

In the twenty-first century Western imaginary, countries like Afghanistan, Pakistan, Iraq, and Iran, and perhaps most Muslim majority countries, are viewed as the iconic symbols of Muslim otherness. As a people, according to this imaginary that is sustained by some sectors of scholarship and the media, Muslims are purported to lack both comparative and critical value because they adhere to a faith called Islam. And the term "madrasa" epitomizes only one aspect of an iconography of Muslim weirdness.

In Euro-America's war against the Taliban, madrasas—long-standing Muslim religious institutions with ancient pedigrees—have been turned into scapegoats by Western governments with the aid of despotic Muslim governments in order to sustain a narrative of Muslim weirdness. Western publics and institutions of civil society with few exceptions follow this viewpoint uncritically. This attitude goes both ways. Most Muslims, as studies conducted worldwide show, view Western governments to be especially hostile to Islam as a faith. A good number of Muslims view the West's hostile pursuit of the Taliban and al-Qaeda to

What Pakistan Knew About Bin Laden

By CARLOTTA GALL MARCH 19, 2014

The New York Times

Shortly after the Sept. 11 attacks, I went to live and report for The New York Times in Afghanistan. I would spend most of the next 12 years there, following the overthrow of the Taliban, feeling the excitement of the freedom and prosperity that was promised in its wake and then watching the gradual dissolution of that hope. A new Constitution and two rounds of elections did not improve the lives of ordinary Afghans; the Taliban regrouped and found increasing numbers of supporters for their guerrilla actions; by 2006, as they mounted an ambitious offensive to retake southern Afghanistan and unleashed more than a hundred suicide bombers, it was clear that a deadly and determined opponent was growing in strength, not losing it. As I toured the bomb sites and battlegrounds of the Taliban resurgence, Afghans kept telling me the same thing: The organizers of the insurgency were in Pakistan, specifically in the western district of Quetta. Police investigators were finding that many of the bombers, too, were coming from Pakistan.

Taliban recruits in 2008 in Quetta, Pakistan, where leading organizers of the Afghan insurgency are based. Alex Majoli/Magnum

One of many madrasas in Quetta in 2008. Alex Majoli/Magnum

New York Times magazine story giving the impression that all madrasas are run by the Taliban and are linked to terrorism.

be mere smokescreens for their anti-Islam campaigns. This mutually sustaining paranoia provides slim dividends for intercultural understanding and cooperation.

Madrasas fit nicely with attempts to raise the specter of Islam as a dangerous ideology, not a faith, to Western political interests. Self-appointed pundits often sound half-intelligent at cocktail parties in Washington and Whitehall if they can sprinkle their conversations with reference to the dangers posed by madrasas.

The conflict in Afghanistan engulfs neighboring nuclear-armed Pakistan. Yet, in Afghanistan and Pakistan as well as in Iraq and Syria, few analysts acknowledge that religion is an overblown singular analytical element in complex and volatile political theaters, where competing ethnic and class elements are also at play. In the vocabularies of the Western media and government, the conflict is remorselessly painted as a standoff between incompatible cultural and religious idioms, the modern versus the nonmodern, tradition and orthodoxy versus change and progress. The truth of the matter is that the issues involve historical developments as well as political and economic considerations that cannot merely be reduced to cultural issues. A sound analysis requires one to look beyond the smokescreen of murderous activities in the name of Islam.

VOCABULARIES OF DIFFERENCE

In America and Europe, the word "madrasa," along with keywords like "terrorism," "Islamic fundamentalism," "suicide bomber," "Taliban," and "Bin Laden," make up the narrative for a clash-of-civilizations rhetoric. Even terms like "Islam," "mosque," and "minarets" are now advertised as anti-Western viruses that must be expunged from European societies. Feverish, anti-Islamic propaganda now emboldens Western neo-Nazi extremists to act on their anti-Muslim rage. Norwegian terrorist Anders Behring Breivik confessed to killing ninety-three people because of his hatred for Muslims. Breivik is a Christian extremist who was manifestly motivated by religion, yet his deeds did not provoke public discussions about the extremist nature of Christianity.

Islam, however, is frequently painted in extremist colors as a religion that must be treated as an exception. Almost instantly the word "madrasa" together with "Taliban" became synonymous with the West's fears of scary Muslim actors, trafficking in terror, who look as if they stepped out of a medieval time capsule. As a result all madrasas, in a post-9/11 world, have suffered whiplash at the hands of media campaigns fomented by a diverse range of actors.

Sure, it is fashionable to brush the Taliban in dark colors. Yet it is important to recall that these rustic clerics once were held out as the best hope for Afghanistan after the mujahidin, the group of fighters who expelled the Soviets but later brutally turned on each other. As the mujahidin fomented a civil war, the Kalashnikov-toting Taliban, sporting

Sunni and Shiʿa

Sunni and Shiʿa are terms that indicate the political and theological schism in early Islam. Sunnis are those who believe that succession after Muhammad was a fact decided by the community of early believers and that the order of the first four leaders was Abu Bakr, ʿUmar, ʿUthman, and ʿAli. The Shiʿa believe that the Prophet had designated ʿAli, his son-in law and cousin, as his successor. Some Shiʿa polemics used the term *nasibi* (pronounced *naa-si-bee*), meaning "despisers," to denounce hostile Sunnis. With this term they mean to indicate that Sunnis harbor ill-will toward ʿAli by not acknowledging him as the political and spiritual successor to Muhammad. Sunni writers in their literature refer to Shiʿa with a denunciatory term, *rafidi* (pronounced *raa-fi-dhi*; plural *rawafid*), meaning "rejecters," for their refusal to accept the legitimacy of the first three caliphs preceding ʿAli.

long-beards and turbans, emerged from their refugee camp redoubts in Pakistan in 1994 in order to put Afghanistan back on the road to stability. That was, of course, before the Taliban self-imploded and turned into a carnival of religious tyranny.

The Islamic emirate of Afghanistan scripted itself as the benign standard bearer of authentic traditional Islam and filled the power vacuum with brutal measures. Some in the Muslim world, especially Deoband-inclined orthodoxy, were prepared to give the Taliban the benefit of the doubt, not least because some of them claimed a madrasa lineage. But Taliban malcontents undermined their own cause with draconian applications of the Shariʿa, which effectively placed women under house arrest, preventing them from attending school, and culminated in the gratuitous destruction of the treasured Buddha statues in Bamian, a cultural vestige that survived centuries of Muslim rule.

Viewing secular education for females as part of a campaign of Westernization, the Pakistani Taliban has destroyed dozens of schools in Pakistan's Swat region, as have their counterparts in Afghanistan. A targeted assassination attempt on a young female education activist, Malala Yusufzai, on a school bus must count as one of the most craven acts in a series of atrocities committed by the Pakistani Taliban to date.

Most authorities on the subject acknowledge that a little more than a third of the Taliban's fighting force came out of the makeshift madrasas in Pakistan's North West Frontier Province, alleged to be affiliated to the Deoband school. To call these institutions "madrasas" is to make the term into a euphemism for boarding schools. In none of these "madrasas" are the students trained in curricular and self-formation activities described in this book. Apart from these madrasas on the Afghanistan-Pakistan border along with a few proper madrasas elsewhere in Pakistan, which are openly pro-Taliban, there is very little reason to persist with the libel that all madrasas are redoubts of terror and conduits for militant Islam. Few observers are even aware that madrasas affiliated with the Barelvi, Ahl-i Hadith, Shiʿa, and even some Deobandi theological orientations among the orthodox groups despise the Taliban and do so vocally and publicly. The story linking madrasas to terror is simply more sensational.

MEDIA, CULTURE, AND POLITICS

Media pundits and shoddy journalism only harden the cultural differences between the West and the Rest. Needless to say, Western consumers of culture have succumbed to the impulse to etch Islamic difference through metaphors and images of demonization in public discourse.

In the West, media representations create the impression that madrasa education defines the totality of Muslim culture. Culture experts tell us that it is an effective strategy to mention only a part of something when you really mean to telegraph much more. The figure of speech used to do this is called synecdoche (pronounced *se-neck-de-key*). "The daily press," argues media and culture analyst Bruce Jackson, ". . . is superb at synecdoche, at giving us a small thing that stands for a much larger thing."[1] The strategy works perfectly. Like the word "jihad," the term "madrasa" has become a stand-in keyword to suggest that the whole of Islam has demonically gone viral. Not only are madrasas projected as malevolent places, but the mere mention of the term triggers negative visceral reactions in consumers. America's occupation of two major Muslim countries resulted in war propaganda that cast the culture, history, and institutions of Muslim peoples in the worst possible light.[2]

In propaganda wars, high culture sometimes offers a critique of muscular government propaganda, but often culture also reinforces stereotypes. A few minutes into David Hare's play *The Vertical Hour*, theatergoers will hear the following dialogue:

"Listen. Listen," yells the combative professor Nadia Blye.

"This is a school," she aggressively tells her student Dennis Dutton.

"It's not a madrasa."

Western universities, Professor Blye asserts, promote the free discussion of ideas, whereas madrasas only teach a dogmatic and suffocating "one path." Even the *Economist* magazine can recklessly write, "America's spies after a year of lurking by madrassas [*sic*] and in dark corners of towns . . . will start working again with the Pakistani military spy outfit, the Inter-Services Intelligence directorate (ISI)."[3]

Playwrights and scriptwriters, journalists and novelists utilize the word "madrasa" without providing any translation. Nor do they feel the need to supply any evidence to support their claims that madrasas promote obscurantism and are part of a dangerous religious underworld. When this happens it is proof that the term "madrasa" has slinked into the Euro-American political lexicon to signify the demonic. Bruised by military encounters in Afghanistan and Iraq, the open-ended war on terror has also spawned a closing of the Western cultural imagination. Americans during foreign misadventures and domestic crises of adversity happily abandon cosmopolitanism and reach for isolationism. Isolationism is apparently a move that imitates America's enemies, as the Yale student, Dennis Dutton, seems to think in *The Vertical Hour.* "For me," the ardent libertarian and isolationist Dutton snaps, "politics is about the protection of property and of liberty."[4] In a telling riposte, he asks Blye,

DUTTON: Why? Why would I want an open mind?
BLYE: Why would you not?
DUTTON: Our enemies don't have open minds.

This exchange captures the dilemma of a section of the liberal West in relationship to other cultures and religions. Are the commitments to the much-vaunted credos of a liberal education—dispassionate comparison and open-mindedness—held by the Iraq war–supporting political science professor Blye a smoke screen or a genuine attempt to understand the "other"? Or is the crude, property- and liberty-hugging student's tit-for-tat credo more genuine if his views are summarized neocon-style, "I do what my enemies do and so don't ask me to be nice"?

Blye, in cavalier fashion, denounces the cultural assets of another civilization as unreflective, narrow-minded "madrasas" on the grounds of media stereotypes, not credentialed scholarly research. But which madrasas was she referring to? Did Blye know that, in the Arabic-speaking world, every secular school is called a madrasa? Perhaps she had in mind the seminaries of South Asia linked to the Taliban. Blye might yet rupture an aneurysm when she discovers madrasas flourish in the United States, Britain, and Canada. And she might be even more perturbed to learn that now more potential imams are studying in British madrasas than the number of Christian priests being trained in the seminaries of the United Kingdom!

If Professor Blye visited *Gates of Vienna*, a right-wing website, all her prejudices would be reinforced. The website is determined to deny madrasas any scholarly and academic credentials and refutes the claims of this book. It proclaims, "The description of Pakistani madrassas [*sic*] as 'Islamic seminaries' is an ingenious feint, evoking as it does Western institutions in which science, history, literature, and art are studied in addition to theology and scripture. But 'students' in madrassas memorize a single book, the Koran, and the only additional knowledge that is considered proper is derived from the sayings and commentary found in the hadith and the sunna. Nothing else goes on in madrassas. No ballet, no history club, no local chapter of Students for a Sustainable Future. Just the Koran, the hadith, and the sunna. The Five Pillars of Islam. And jihad."[5]

Such stereotypes coupled with media images of young children squatting on mats and swinging rhythmically while memorizing the Qur'an only reinforce a monolithic picture of the madrasas. In fact, these are often images of the equivalent of Sunday schools put on display. Captions associated with images often assert that Muslim kids are rote-learners and ask, do madrasas train students in modern science, math, and the humanities? Since the answer is no, the gross implication is that Muslim youth have no critical skills and can hardly be active participants of the modern nation-state.

Euro-American pundits view madrasas as the anti-Christ, bent on destroying Western civilization. Meanwhile, governing elites in India, Pakistan, and Bangladesh index madrasas as a sign of backwardness and nuisance. In media caricature "Muslims" and "madrasas" have replaced the bad Russians of Cold War fame. "Not Moscow but the Mullahs," reads a CNN headline, referring to Muslim clerics who graduated from madrasas as clerics, colloquially called mullahs. *New York Times* columnist and pundit Thomas Friedman repeatedly implicates the madrasas in his warnings to Americans. Feverishly advocating less dependency on Arab oil, he scares his readers into believing that their oil money will finance mosques and madrasas that keep Muslims backward: "We can shrink the piles of money we send to the worst regimes in the world . . . take away money from the people who finance the mosques and the madrassas [*sic*] that keep many Muslim youths backward, angry and anti-American."[6]

Unsurprisingly, to Western ears, the word "madrasa" is now a trope for malignancy, thanks to a repeated and consistent process of disinformation. The former U.S. secretary of defense Donald Rumsfeld and CNN's chief international correspondent Christiane Amanpour gratuitously bandy about terms like "madrasa" or "Salafi" in order to exhibit their expertise. Their purpose is clear: to find a sensational link between madrasas and trends of religious thought to a mutating list of code words for the "war on terrorism."[7] In a confidential memo leaked to the press, Rumsfeld posed his question like this: "Are we capturing, killing, or deterring and dissuading more terrorists every day than the madrasas and the radical clerics are recruiting, training, and deploying against us?"[8]

Even President Barack Obama's 2008 presidential campaign came perilously close to being derailed under a cloud of scurrilous charges claiming he was educated in a madrasa in far-off Indonesia as a teenager. The charge was rebutted in a timely manner, but for a while it looked ominous for his presidential bid, just as rumors still make the rounds that he is a closet Muslim.

A former leftist-turned-right-leaning pundit-grise, the late Christopher Hitchens, shamelessly used the word "madrasa" to naturalize a trope of Muslim malevolence. In a review of John Updike's novel *The Coup*, Hitchens, in his rebarbative style, critiqued Updike for not specifying, "how madrassas [*sic*] train their suicide bombers."[9] In short, "madrasa" is a code word for not only fanaticism but worse: a training ground for suicide bombers. If left unchallenged, the claims made by Rumsfeld and others with the help of a cottage industry of scabrous journalism might succeed in dehumanizing a complex but imperfect network of institutions in significant parts of the Muslim world.

Anti-madrasa fervor reached a fever pitch of hysteria when the London underground bombers in July 2005 were alleged to have trained in the madrasas of Pakistan. British prime minister Tony Blair weighed in by prosecuting the madrasas in a blanket condemnation and charged madrasa leaders for imparting extremist views to young students. "These roots are deep," Blair said, posing at a Downing Street meeting with Afghan president Hamid Karzai, adding, "They are coming about [*sic*] by people indoctrinated at a very, very early age . . . [who] go to some of these schools, these madrasas, and they get extreme teaching taught at them."[10]

Blair's allegations linking the London bombers to madrasas in Pakistan were never verified, yet the allegations continue to filter through Western and some non-Western intelligence and media sources. Among Euro-American writers only William Dalrymple took pains to investigate these charges.[11] "According to sources at the prime minister's offices in Downing Street," Dalrymple writes,

> There is in fact no evidence that any madrasa was visited by any members of the [Yorkshire] cell at any point on their journey. Still less is there any proof that madrasas were responsible for "brainwashing" the trio, as the British press assumed after the bombings. Instead there is considerable evidence to show that the trio were radicalized in Yorkshire through the Islamist literature and videos that were available beneath the counter of their local Islamic bookshop. And while it is now certain that the group made contact with al-Qaeda in Pakistan, there is no reason to assume that a madrasa acted as the conduit. In this case, as in so many others, the link between madrasas and international terrorism is far from clear-cut, and new research has been published that has challenged the much-repeated but intellectually shaky theory of madrasas being little more than al-Qaeda training schools.[12]

None of these allegations were ever retracted or corrected by the media or by British and American government spokespersons.[13]

What Dalrymple correctly identified as a "shaky theory" has pre-September 11, 2001 antecedents. One source is Harvard terrorism expert Jessica Stern's widely cited article in *Foreign Affairs* linking the jihad in Kashmir against Indian occupation to madrasas in Pakistan. But the article only identified one madrasa, the Deoband-aligned Darul Uloom Haqqania, as a culprit. In a condemnation of breathtakingly generalized proportions, Stern labels all madrasas as "schools of hate."[14]

Stern's report is based on interviews with solitary individuals and echoes certain government officials of Pakistan who, seeing themselves as modernized elites, often intensely dislike the Muslim clergy and their madrasas. Stern cites no other evidence as to how the diverse and complex array of madrasa networks are all actively, if ever, linked to the jihad in Kashmir or terrorism for that matter. Madrasa Haqqania, run by one Mawlana Sami ul-Haqq, in a place called Akora Khattak in Pakistan's

North West Frontier Province, proudly self-identifies with causes of jihad. Sami ul-Haqq is an open supporter of the Taliban and is joined by a few supporters with madrasa backgrounds who actively engage in sectarian violence. Another instance of madrasa militancy was the 2007 standoff at the Red Mosque in Pakistan's capital, Islamabad, and the affiliated women's madrasa, Jamiʿa Hafsa. The madrasa leadership led by the Ghazi brothers confronted the army and resulted in over 150 fatalities. Prosecuting an entire system for the deeds of a few would be as bizarre as saying that all American universities are dens of terror because Harvard University and University of Michigan graduate Ted Kaczynski turned out to be the notorious urban terrorist known as the Unabomber.

ANOTHER PERSPECTIVE

The film *The Clay Bird* attempts to give a more complex account of life in a madrasa.[15] Set in the civil war of Bangladesh in the 1960s, the film depicts how a family is caught in a maelstrom of competing and contested cultural and political narratives.

The father, Kazi, undergoes a religious transformation and is attracted to the evangelical Muslim group known as the Tablighi Jamaʿat, founded in prepartition India in the early part of the twentieth century. Globally dispersed, the Tablighi Jamaʿat serves as a nonviolent and nonpolitical vehicle for individual piety and adherence to the basic teachings of Islam. But the Tablighi Jamaʿat is also the popular backbone of the Deoband movement and is fiercely opposed by the Barelvis.

In his turn toward an "authentic" expression of Islam, Kazi is attracted to alternative medicine, Unani medicine. Literally, "Unani" means something that is derived from Greece, the Galenic medical system adopted by early Muslims. Today Unani medicine is widely prevalent in the Indo-Pak subcontinent. The fusion of Unani and modern Western medicine is also widely available.

Kazi not only dispenses Unani medicine but also adopts a more strict interpretation of Islam. His newfound religious zeal brings a gloomy pall to a once joyous family's social life. His austere lifestyle and religious perspective cause him to ban the use of photos, music, and dance for recreation. He even goes so far as to forbid his daughter, Asma, from playing with dolls in his home! This latter measure goes beyond what is allowed in traditional Islam, since tradition reports that the Prophet

Muhammad's young wife ʿA'isha entertained herself with dolls and enjoyed music during festivities.

The film's title, *The Clay Bird*, is derived from his daughter, Asma's heart-wrenching relationship with her toy clay bird. Kazi's religious strictures even deprive Asma from playing with a clay bird. Refusing to be cowed into subservience, she hides the clay bird from her father and buries her love and companionship for the bird in her heart.

Seized by religious passion, Kazi decides to send his son Anu, short for Anwarul Islam, to a madrasa. He hopes Anu's madrasa education will transform his family into an Islamically compliant one. But his plan backfires. Anu's mother is anxious about her husband's decision. Neither is the son pleased with his father's choice affecting his future. Reluctantly yielding to his father's wishes, Anu ends up in a madrasa in a far-off town, where he is totally alienated. He establishes a friendship with another boy who feels equally displaced in the madrasa. In the madrasa Anu encounters different types of teachers. Some are harsh and sadistic in their conduct and in their treatment of students, reminiscent of English boarding schools in decades past. Yet other teachers are gentle and kind: they promote a theology of love and compassion.

It is here that the film begins to lose some of its potency, even in a well-intentioned move to show diversity within madrasas. It ends up in being a bipolar portrayal of madrasa life. The message is simplistic: good teachers are those who follow a mystical or Sufi brand of Islam; the bad teachers are protagonists of a soulless Shariʿa-centered interpretation of Islam with austerity and harshness as its sole outcome.

Back home, Anu's sister, Asma, falls ill. Her father persists in his brand of traditional Unani medication, refusing to admit the child to a hospital for emergency treatment. Tragically, she dies as a result of the father's unfathomable hostility to modern medicine. As the civil war engulfs Bangladesh, the family disintegrates and is scattered.

On his return home, Anu confronts the news of the death of his sister. Only days before he witnessed his best friend die at the madrasa as a result of abject living conditions, administrative brutality, and the criminal neglect of students. In the end the film drives home the pathos of religion-gone-berserk. Just as the civil war in Bangladesh wreaks havoc on the nation, another war fueled by religious fervor tears apart a normal and once happy family.

Unfortunately, only the mosque and the madrasa are identified as the sites where misplaced religious zeal plays out. *The Clay Bird* fails to give the multiple shades of how people live their lives of piety but do not end in the tragic and the grotesque. Thousands of families send their children to madrasas for religious education. For them this experience is fulfilling and gives meaning to their lives and is very different from the unsparing tragedy the documentary portrays. *The Clay Bird* misses the ordinary but complex everyday lives of the inhabitants of the madrasas, students and their families, even though these aspects partially shine through and perhaps redeem the cinematic venture.

CONCLUSION

Western cultural portrayals of the traditional centers of Muslim learning are gross distortions generated by the fogs of military and cultural wars. Madrasas vary in ideological orientation, but they are far from the dens of malevolence that media, cultural, and political portrayals assert. Clinging to such claims only harms intercultural understanding and unnecessarily raises suspicion about Islam as a faith tradition. After all, the madrasas are the most orthodox representatives of Islam. To falsely discredit them only raises more suspicion among the madrasa leadership about Western motives.

As Mawlana Abu Saʿud, a prominent scholar at the Matliwala madrasa in Bharuch, Gujarat, told me, "The Americans are very intelligent. There is a reason why they target madrasas. Madrasas are the true representatives of Islam and therefore they must eradicate these institutions. For their [America's] fight is with Islam; it is Islam that they fear!" In Mawlana Abu Saʿud's view, the West's antimadrasa propaganda is not an effort to combat terrorism, but a mere fig leaf to undermine Islam itself. Millions of people who follow the orthodox teachings provided by the madrasas, in his view, felt the same. They ask, he said, why do Americans target our most hallowed institutions where our scholars are dedicated to the study of the Qurʾan and the teachings of faith, Islamic law, and theology?

The future of the madrasas is hobbled by the inability of madrasa communities to make informed decisions about the complex world they inhabit. Trapped in an ideological bind, hesitant about the merits of Western knowledge production and its potential synthesis with the Islamic knowledge tradition, madrasas are unable to harness their full intellectual strength in order to make a meaningful contribution to broader society.

CHAPTER TEN

The Future of Madrasas

UNSOLVED OLD QUESTIONS

In a meditation titled "Education: Old and New," comparing madrasa education with modern education, the literary-minded genius and proinnovation traditionalist thinker Shibli Nuʿmani (d. 1914) poses the following questions. "Are one of these two systems superfluous?" "Are these mutually contradictory educational systems?" he asks.[1]

Nuʿmani's questions might sound redundant, but almost a century later they remain contentious. The content of madrasa education is the hinge-question today. The topic is riven with deep divisions and risks for stakeholders. Perhaps the future of South Asia's madrasas depends on a resolution of this pressing problem. Or, if one is skeptical, then paradoxically the future of the madrasas as we know it is tethered to the nonresolution of this debate.

Debates and disagreement are periodically heightened over whether the old madrasa curricula should be retained, altered or blended with a curriculum that consists of modern disciplines. Responses vary. They range from those who oppose an iota of change to madrasa syllabi to some who tolerate cosmetic amendments, to others who favor a syllabus that integrates the old and the new. Decades and scores of conferences later, reform to madrasa curricula in India, Pakistan, and Bangladesh and their satellites elsewhere is a grim story. The stakeholders agree on the spectrum of options available to them as outlined above. There is no one to bell the cat, so to speak, on a scale that would alter the character of madrasa education enough to make a difference. The absence of will and the lack of bold, innovative, and clear thinking capture the problem. Innovative approaches adopted by a few madrasas have yet to become the norm.

ELEPHANT IN THE ROOM: MUSLIM IDENTITY

The elephant in the room is the question of Muslim identity. This is a challenge so insurmountable that it successfully wrecks any potential solution. Put differently: Which two Muslims agree on the outlines as to what constitutes Muslim identity? Answer: "What was the question again?" What fuels the identity debate is this: "Who is authorized to shape Muslim identity?" "What legitimates Muslim identity?" "And what ends does Muslim identity serve?" Muslim identity is a hotly contested domain. It goes beyond being an observant Muslim who practices Islam's five pillars. The fault lines envelop multiple contested interpretations and meanings of Islam. There are several contenders, yet in the madrasa sector only two polar views seem to shape the problem: a mild form of cosmopolitanism and uncompromising orthodox authenticity.

Community identity or nationhood (*qawmiyyat*), purports Nuʿmani, is central to the educational concerns of Muslims.[2] Those of Nuʿmani's persuasion view Muslim identity to pivot on Islam in two ways: as a faith tradition and as a cultural tradition. Most are clear on what it means to identify with Islam as a faith tradition, although the content and presentation of that faith tradition in the modern world have come under tremendous strain. Madrasa communities and Muslim intelligentsia are even less clear on what it means to identify with Islam as a cultural and civilizational tradition. With the rise of scripture-based religiosity in the twentieth century, much of the cultural assets of Islamic theological discourses have suffered. Robust discussions about faith and culture in contemporary settings have yet to occur.

A modern, multireligious society involving citizenship and a version of political representation, possibly even democracy, is what Nuʿmani envisages, but he is not clear on the specifics. Many conservative ʿulama will agree with him on the centrality of Islam as a faith tradition and as an ingredient of identity. On the question of Islamic culture, however, he has fewer supporters among the ʿulama. Why? Nuʿmani believes in some amount of intellectual hybridity on the cultural question. His opponents among the ʿulama persist in pursuing an unmolested notion of tradition, and they will accent a notion of culture that is hemmed in by the requirements of premodern theology and effectively renders culture impotent.

A biopsy of Nuʿmani's rhetoric, "Are these educational systems [modern and traditional] in need of reform? Can they be combined in order to be effective?" reveals his own answers to his rhetorical questions are an irrefutable yes.[3] Muslim exposure to both modern secular and religious education is indispensable, in Nuʿmani's view, even if both were to his mind in need of reform, correction, and adaptation. While he rebukes early twentieth-century modern educated Muslims for lacking in "broad-minded ideas, true freedom, bold aspirations and an enthusiasm for progress," he is certainly not dismissive of the utility and value of modern education.[4] In a severely mocking coup de grâce he describes modern educated Muslims as people only interested in "a fashion parade to exhibit their exquisite [fashionable Western] jackets and trousers!"[5]

On the other side, even the ʿulama do not escape his lash. The attempt to "reform the curriculum [of madrasas] only interests a few open-minded ʿulama while the majority," Nuʿmani laments, "are 'slaves of prescribed texts' (literally, "slaves of written lines," *lakir ka faqir*)."[6] "Slaves of prescribed texts" is a comic euphemism for the ʿulama's slavish attachment to ancient texts and their equally stubborn refusal to consider new curricular proposals. Nuʿmani would be even more depressed to learn that since he wrote these lines decades ago, there has been very little curricular reform.

An impassioned advocate of Islamic education reform, Nuʿmani proposes a solution. "I have said it repeatedly, and say it once more," he writes, and then adds, "For us Muslims mere English [modern] education is not sufficient, nor does the old Arabic madrasa education suffice. Our ailment requires a 'compound panacea' (*maʿjun-i murakkab*)—one portion eastern and the other western."[7]

The person whose views won the day, the influential Deobandi thinker Ashraf ʿAli Thanvi, is also the one who poured cold water on Nuʿmani's remedy to the education and identity crisis of Indian Muslims. Thanvi always viewed Nuʿmani's freethinking with some alarm. Very early on, Thanvi turned away from the educational initiatives spearheaded by the Nadwatul ʿUlama in which Nuʿmani played a premier role.

Thanvi leans on the theological authority of tradition as a shield against Western learning. He weighs the difference between tradition-based religious education and modern education that yields material and secular benefits by using an interesting analogy. Each educational system, in his view, espouses a different telos and is thus incommensurable to the other. His example uses the utility of cash versus the utility of credit in business to illustrate his point. Surely, businesses accustomed to cash sales, he says, will find credit transactions to be less attractive. Pushing his analogy, he states, "So therefore understand also that religious learning and knowledge of the hereafter is like credit, while the disciplines related to worldly knowledge is like cash transactions."[8] In Thanvi's mind the dividends of knowledge linked to salvation are deferred, like credit to be collected later in the afterlife, whereas secular knowledge, in his view, is like cash, bringing instant gratification.

Interestingly, Thanvi uses the demonstrative expression "compound panacea," the same one that Nuʿmani deployed to rebut the latter's view in a game of shadow boxing but in a negative direction. A compound solution in education that mixes Western with Eastern learning traditions, in Thanvi's view, is a bad remedy. "When two [types of learning] are combined," he writes, "then of course, people will be more inclined towards cash [modern secular education] while knowledge of faith [credit], linked to salvation in the hereafter, will be left behind, and, in fact, it will be totally ignored."[9] Thanvi's preference for separate education systems is not innocent but rather ominous. Graduates from the madrasas who reach for modern education, he severely predicts, will invariably be misguided and end in perdition.

LEGACIES AND OUTCOMES

Two antithetical paths and visions for Muslim identity crystallize from the preceding discussion: Islamic cosmopolitanism and Islamic parochialism. Nuʿmani believes an efficient educational system combining the old and the new will preserve Islamic values and enable Muslims to be self-sufficient and allow them to flourish in the modern world. He is certain that a cosmopolitan approach to learning blended with the best practices of Muslim civilization will steel the spine of Muslim identity.

Thanvi, on the other hand, believed the ʿulama are not only the repositories but also the genuine carriers of the DNA required for Muslim identity, namely, faith-based teachings. Parochialism, with strong doses of ʿulama paternalism and orthodoxy, was Thanvi's panacea to the challenges of a modern Muslim identity. Prevalent in most madrasas are Thanvi-type views, irrespective of Deobandi, Barelvi, or Ahl-i Hadith affiliations, groups that might otherwise be hostile toward him on theological grounds.

An heir to Thanvi's line of thinking with regard to madrasas and their role in Muslim identity is the previously mentioned Mufti Taqi ʿUsmani, a Pakistani religious scholar. Few ʿulama in contemporary South Asia can rival ʿUsmani's esteem in learning and international exposure and experience. Contrary to Thanvi's caution about modern education, ʿUsmani did attend secular universities in Karachi and Lahore, where he acquired degrees in law and an MA in Arabic literature after completing his madrasa education. Thanvi would, of course, be relieved to know in his grave that ʿUsmani came out relatively unscathed from Western education.

Despite his own exposure to some measure of cosmopolitan education, ʿUsmani displays a strong repugnance toward Western learning. "It is no secret," ʿUsmani confidently claims, that "at present all the intellectual misguidance found among Muslims can be traced to its source, the West."[10] Without being specific, ʿUsmani claims Western thought corrupted the "social mindset" of Muslims and therefore efforts to rehabilitate and correct the Muslim "mind" was an urgent priority for both the ʿulama and the madrasas. Just as medieval Muslim theologians expunged Greek influences from Islamic thought, so too contemporary madrasa scholars, ʿUsmani believes, must of necessity combat the negative influences of Western thought and its impact on Muslims.

Scholars of ʿUsmani's persuasion invoke the authority of the medieval scholar Abu Hamid al-Ghazali (d. 1111) and his polemical and occasional hyperbolic combative stance toward Greek learning. ʿUsmani, of course, omitted the fact that Ghazali was just as appalled by ignorant theologians who rejected the a priori truths of natural science as he was apprehensive about the ability of Greek learning to charm uncritical students.[11] Ghazali nevertheless was not closed to cosmopolitan learning of his time.

Yet it appears that to ʿUsmani, ideas are like steroids. In order to strengthen the intellectual combat-kit of the ʿulama, he proposes, they should learn English and also acquire knowledge of modern disciplines like Western philosophy, economics, politics, and legal studies. "Modern learning in itself," he gingerly demurs from Thanvi's severities on the same topic, "is not antithetical to faith and the knowledge traditions that are linked to faith."[12] But after making this explicit claim, ʿUsmani hastily makes a u-turn. He qualifies his proposal by inexplicably hitting a pause button, to put it generously.

"Pakistan's leading madrasas of late have recognized the need to supplement the curriculum with modern disciplines," he admits. "Despite the gratifying intellectual temperament of these madrasas, it would be absolutely intolerable if they adopted modern disciplines in their current guise," ʿUsmani warns. Western knowledge has to be filtered of its harmful effects. Why? "Those who compiled the modern disciplines" in ʿUsmani's view "are well-known non-Muslims who have designed this knowledge with the purpose to only sow the seeds of doubt in the hearts of students and to foster skepticism in the cumulative authority of the narrators of the Muslim faith tradition."[13]

So who can access the unfiltered knowledge? Only discerning ʿulama, he argues, who have a firm grasp of the modern disciplines, can effectively combat and refute the threat posed by Western ideas. Instead of exposing madrasa students to the corrosive risks of modern institutions, ʿUsmani proposes that Western disciplines be taught within madrasas. What is required, he argues, is an in-house vetting program where modern disciplines are cleansed of their odious effects before incorporation into madrasa curricula.

At ʿUsmani's own Darul Uloom Karachi, where he is vice-president, even a modest version of supplementary modern learning is yet to be realized, apart from the offerings in English and a few subjects in civics. But the conflicted attitude toward upgrading madrasa education and the inclusion of modern subjects is not only about Muslim identity but which segment among the Muslim community will have the power to inaugurate change. For a long time this battle has been identified as the "mister-versus-Mawlana" conflict, which pits the Westernized and cosmopolitan "mister" against the traditional and religious "Mawlana."

MISTER VERSUS MAWLANA

ʿUlama antipathy toward modern secular education is fueled by what the ʿulama perceive to be the monstrous values advanced by the culture of modern universities and colleges. Dreaded is the tolerance for permissiveness and promiscuity, especially the mixing of the sexes, unmitigated freedoms, and the lack of deference for professors. Heightened wariness that the poisonous well of Western scholarship will bleed into Muslim societies via disreputable educational institutions is their central objection.

So why are even Muslim intellectuals at modern institutions of learning unworthy of giving leadership? Because the ʿulama view modern educated Muslims to be "uncritically in thrall" (*marʿub*) of Western ideas, a derisory label frequently used with rhetorical surfeit.[14] As holders of the keys to leadership in their societies, modern educated Muslims remain a "confused" bunch whom ʿUsmani pungently accuses of distorting Islamic teachings and discredits as the enablers of Western hegemony over Muslims.[15]

While the alliterative phrase "mister versus Mawlana" is partly true, the tensions have become more complex. Now the secular educated class is also divided between a religiously devout but secularly educated segment of Muslims and ultrasecular elites. The tensions between these groups are more social than ideological. While it is easy for the ʿulama to dismiss the ultrasecular elites for their ideological antipathy for Islam, the real challenge to ʿulama authority comes from secular-educated pious Muslims. The best the ʿulama can do is to discredit them as lacking a proper understanding of faith. Often members of the latter group get their instruction from self-help books and from inspirational figures who operate outside the ʿulama's circles, figures like Abul Aʿla Mawdudi, Javed Ghamidi, Dr. Israr Ahmad, and others who are influential for their advocacy of Islam in an idiom that differs from the ʿulama's orthodox discourse.

Mutual recriminations between these factions feature regularly in the public media of Muslim-majority societies, including those of South Asia. Of course each side feels victimized by the other. A triumphant ʿUsmani as a partisan of the ʿulama camp claims victory for the ʿulama who counter the "flood of westernization" that washes into Muslim societies. Both Muslim secularists and devout Muslims who follow a non-ʿulama interpretation of Islam, in ʿUsmani's view, only enable the Westernization of Muslim societies. And, at the barricades, ʿUsmani proudly trumpets, it is the madrasas who guard the citadel of orthodox Islam.

In bruising sarcasm, ʿUsmani boasts the power of the madrasas. If critics characterize madrasas as institutions that are "despised by time" or "colorless and without sparkle" and ridicule scholars as "old fashioned and narrow minded," then they do so because the madrasas and scholars have, in his view, effectively diminished the impact of Westernization.[16] Sayyid Salman Husayni Nadvi also claims the ʿulama and madrasas protect Islam in South Asia and therefore earn the full support of the Muslim elites. Without empirical support, this is a claim hard to verify, but given the size of support the ʿulama receive in order to build and run their institutions, there is more than a grain of truth to their claims.

When madrasa graduates pivot toward modern educational institutions, their choices are interpreted as turning their backs on madrasa education and opting to become "misters." Nevertheless, annually hundreds of madrasa graduates, still an insignificant minority, heed Shibli Nuʿmani's call to pursue cosmopolitan learning.

In choosing to attend secular institutions, they face tortuous dilemmas to which I, and several others, can testify. Often such a move is a one-way ticket out of the madrasa world and an exit from ʿulama circles. Madrasa peers view graduates who proverbially "made it" in secular society with a combination of deep suspicion and envy. Changes in the ideas and lifestyles of former madrasa graduates as a result of their new learning environments only confirm the fears of the ʿulama.

When many madrasa graduates trade in their regulation-size, unkempt, fist-length beards for manicured facial hair, an alteration to bodily comportment that signals a break from orthodox teachings, the die is proverbially cast. Madrasa peers view a change in beard length and the adoption of Western dress as major character defects. Adopting Western dress or slightly fashionable variations of traditional South Asian dress only completes the ultimate nightmare scenario of a loss of orthodox faith that Thanvi and many other conservative authorities predicted. In fact, any adjustment or alteration in ideas and bodily comportment from the standard madrasa regulations are without exaggeration viewed as a form of mini-apostasy.

Soon these graduates with additional secular qualifications find themselves stigmatized, marginalized, subject to whisper campaigns. The madrasa network issues proverbial health warnings, admonishing students about the poisonous effects of secular viruses embedded in modern knowledge. The ultimate betrayal is, of course, accepting better-paying jobs outside madrasa circles in education or industry. Such moves not only signal a turn toward despised materialism but also semaphore an end to their membership of the ascetic community of "coarse rug-dwellers."[17] The latter is a frequently used euphemism to signify the madrasa culture of piety, which esteems poverty and frugality of almost monastic proportions.

Only rarely are graduates who were certified in the two traditions of learning—madrasa and modern university education—welcomed back to madrasa circles. It depends on the amount of Western poison they can expel on rehabilitation. Disowning their modern learning and adopting the standard paraphernalia of the ʿulama's comportment are the beginnings of rehabilitation. Joining the cottage industry of Islamic apologetics and anti-Western polemics is a sure way to win back favorable status in madrasa circles. But most of those who leave the madrasa circles rarely find their way back.

LAMENTATIONS AND HESITATIONS

Psychic ambivalence among Muslim intellectuals and elites has contributed to the stalemate over the use of modern knowledge in order to advance Muslim religious thought. I refuse to condemn the madrasas with the absurd generalizations made by the Islamophobes and will not ignore the need for long-overdue intellectual reforms. I personally made some hard choices in navigating these difficult shoals.

Illustrations from epochs over two centuries apart will highlight the dilemma. Mughal Emperor Aurangzeb also had a traditional education in precolonial India and studied subjects similar to the ones students encounter in today's madrasas. One of his tutors, Mulla Salih, once made the rounds at his court in order to gain some favors. A bitter and irked emperor lamented to Mulla Salih, as recorded by the French traveler François Bernier. He chided Mulla Salih for the deficits of his education. In an unusually acrimonious tone he berated the Mullah for the inferior education that was not only self-servingly triumphant but also unbearably irrelevant. Ironically, the same question about the relevance of madrasa education to Muslim life in the twenty-first century was broached three centuries ago.

The second viewpoint comes from the poet-philosopher Muhammad Iqbal, who received a traditional Islamic education in the Punjab followed by advanced studies in England and Germany. Iqbal was an Islamo-nationalist who had an agonistic relationship with both colonial modernity and orthodox Islam. A poet and an idealistic romantic, Iqbal enjoyed high visibility in public life. Many of his views resonated with Muslim

Aurangzeb's Lament on His Education

"What is it you would have of me, Doctor? Can you reasonably desire that I should make you one of the chief Omrahs [ministers] of my court? Let me tell you, if you had instructed me as you should have done, nothing would be more just; for I am of this persuasion, that a well-educated and instructed child is as much, at least, obliged to his master as to his father. But where are those good documents you have given me? In the first place, you have taught me that all that Frangistan [Europe] . . . was nothing . . . telling me that the kings of Indostan [India] were far above them all together. . . .

"You should rather have taught me exactly to distinguish all those different states [governments] of the world, and well to understand their strength, their way of fighting, their customs, religions, governments, and interests; and, by the perusal of solid history, to observe their rise, progress, decay, and whence, how, and by what accidents and errors those great changes and revolutions of empires and kingdoms have happened. . . .

"You had a mind to teach me the Arabian tongue, to read and to write. I am much obliged to you, forsooth, for having made me lose so much time upon a language that requires ten or twelve years to attain to its perfection; as if the son of a king should think it to be an honor to him to be a grammarian or some doctor of the law, and to learn other languages than those of his neighbors, when he cannot well be without them; he, to whom time is so precious for so many weighty things, which he ought by times to learn. . . .

"Do you not know, that childhood well governed, being a state which is ordinarily accompanied with a happy memory, is capable of thousands of good precepts and instructions, which remain deeply impressed the whole remainder of a man's life . . . ? The law, prayers, and science, may they not as well be learned in our mother-tongue as in Arabic? You told my father . . . that you would teach me philosophy. It is true, I remember very well, that you have entertained me for many years with airy questions of things that afford no satisfaction at all to the mind, and are of no use in humane society . . . they are very hard to understand and very easy to forget . . . all I retained of it was a multitude of barbarous and dark words, proper to bewilder, perplex, and tine out [shut out] the best wits, and only invented the better to cover the vanity and ignorance of men like yourself, that would make us believe that they know all, and that under those obscure and ambiguous words are hid great mysteries which they alone are capable to understand.

"If you had seasoned me with that philosophy which forms the mind to ratiocination, and insensibly accustoms it to be satisfied with nothing but solid reasons, if you had given me those excellent precepts and doctrines which raise the soul above the assaults of fortune, and reduce her to an unshakeable and always equal temper, and permit her not to be lifted up by prosperity nor debased by adversity; if you had taken care to give me the knowledge of what we are and what are the first principles of things, and had assisted me in forming in my mind a fit idea of the greatness of the universe, and of the admirable order and motion of the parts thereof; if, I say, you had instilled into me this kind of philosophy, I should think myself incomparably more obliged to you than Alexander was to his Aristotle and believe it my duty to recompense you otherwise than he did him. Should not you, instead of your flattery, have taught me somewhat of that point so important to a king, which is, what the reciprocal duties are of a sovereign to his subjects and those of subjects to their sovereign; and ought not you to have considered, that one day I should be obliged with the sword to dispute my life and tit [seize] crown with my brothers? . . . Have you ever taken any care to make me learn, what it is to besiege a town or to set an army in array? For these things I am obliged to others, not at all to you. Go and retire to the village whence you are come, and let nobody know who you are or what is become of you."

—François Bernier in *Travels in the Mogul Empire A.D. 1656–1668.*
The text was slightly edited for coherence by the author.

audiences around the globe, especially madrasa communities who have since become his greatest admirers. Anti-curriculum-reform madrasa communities favorably cite Iqbal's views in support of the status quo even though the same ʿulama will viscerally disagree with Iqbal's unorthodox interpretations of religion and his often-sarcastic criticism of Muslim clerics. Engaging in double-critique, Iqbal bruisingly criticized the Muslim clerics for being immune to change while he simultaneously was very pessimistic and suspicious that change would take place according to a Western agenda. After encouraging people to embrace innovation, renew themselves, and throw off the mantle of imitating (*taqlid*) the past in a famous poem, Iqbal concludes darkly,

> I fear this cry for modernism
> Is only a ruse to make the East imitate the Franks [the West].[18]

Madrasa authorities align with this thread in Iqbal's writings. Iqbal once told a friend, Hakim Ahmad Shuja, not to modernize prepartition India's madrasas and traditional early learning Islamic schools, known as *maktabs*. "Leave these traditional schools (*maktabs*) as they are, let the children of poor Muslims study there," Iqbal allegedly implored his friend. "If there are no clerics (*mulla*) and dervishes, do you know what will happen?" he rhetorically asked Shuja. Iqbal's ostensible turn toward the need to retain orthodoxy apparently stemmed from his traumatic visit to the ruins of Muslim Spain during one of his visits to Europe. "What I witnessed with my own eyes will happen here!" he told Hakim Shuja. "If Indian Muslims are deprived of these traditional schools then their [Muslims'] fate will be similar to that of the Muslims of Hispania despite their eight centuries of Islamic rule there," he explained.[19] For some elements in the madrasa-sphere, it is Iqbal who helped them frame madrasas and traditional schools as cultural barricades against a rising Westernization. Alteration to traditional Muslim culture, madrasa audiences seem to hear Iqbal saying, will in the *longue dureé* undo Muslim identity, as he implies also happened in Muslim Spain. Iqbal's ambivalence and multiple critiques of both Muslims and their adversaries make it difficult to clearly say where exactly he would come down on calls for madrasa reform. After citing Iqbal's communication discouraging the reform of traditional schools, one madrasa authority virulently dismissed engagement with modern knowledge and deemed it a conspiracy to undermine the madrasa tradition.[20]

A disgruntled Aurangzeb nearing the end of his life and centuries later Shibli Nuʿmani too pleaded for a cosmopolitan, socially relevant, and realist version of Muslim education. Being at the helm of an empire, Aurangzeb realized in hindsight the deficits of his own education; he was unhappy that he was not furnished with the requisite skills and relevant knowledge that were required to govern and flourish in the world. His late life lamentations predictably sealed the fate of the Mughal Empire when his equally ill-prepared successors failed in governance and paved the way for the disintegration of Mughal power, which opened the path to European colonization. Yet the moral of Aurangzeb's experience is lost on later generations of Muslims in South Asia.

Suspicious of Western culture and power, Ashraf ʿAli Thanvi and later Taqi ʿUsmani took refuge in a hypercultural narrative of authenticity. They viewed, for reasons still unclear, Islamic classical education as superior to Western learning. Do Muslims only have a choice between Aurangzeb and Shibli Nuʿmani's cosmopolitan ideals and Thanvi's authentic parochialism? Why are these impulses presented as antithetical to each other, as an either/or? Is this not a false dichotomy? Why can Muslim education not embrace both authenticity and cosmopolitan instincts in education and matters of identity and foster their unique life-world at the same time?

THE WAY FORWARD IS ALWAYS A FAUSTIAN BARGAIN

Many critics as well as well-wishers of madrasa communities believe the deficits in madrasa education can be remedied if elements of modern education and skills are integrated into the curriculum. Equipping madrasa graduates with skills and professions in order to attain financial independence is proposed as one remedy. Plus, modern learning, they say, will enable graduates to provide contextually relevant religious guidance to their audiences.

Madrasa authorities in favor of retaining the status quo find such suggestions laughable. In their view, the madrasas are purveyors of a transcendent truth, and claim to advocate a picture of reality in accordance with that truth. Some would not be opposed to the use of technology and aspects of modernity, but only if science, technology, and modernity served the grand purposes of their understanding of religious truth. Many are not opposed to the use of computers, motor vehicles, and other modern technologies. However, many madrasa authorities are alarmed at the lack of control over the Internet and have banned the use of smartphones in madrasas, fearful of the deluge of pornography that might titillate young men. Yet, ironically, many madrasas have active websites, a cyber-presence for fatwas, and pastoral guidance sites. Even more worrisome to madrasa authorities is the inability to control and regulate contact between men and women through instant text messaging on phones and computers. Technological modernity is viewed only as an instrument to further

Islamic ends, as if the good outcomes and bad outcomes can be tightly regulated.

Some in the madrasa world embrace aspects of modern technology and resist other aspects of cultural modernity in order to pursue their way of life. Yet they are unaware that all technology, experts say, comes in the form of a Faustian bargain, in which one thing is traded for another. So acquiring conveniences and luxuries with the aid of technology often means one has to be prepared to make an exchange for a loss of privacy and absence of control over freedoms.

The same necessary Faustian bargain will be evident if the madrasas engage with modern knowledge to the petrification of Thanvi among past figures and someone like ʿUsmani among contemporaries. But the growing voices in favor of modern knowledge in madrasa curricula might well determine the prospects of madrasas, their graduates, and the nature of the ʿulama of the future.

CONCLUSION

The future of madrasas hinges on the kind of Faustian bargain the ʿulama and their institutions are prepared to make with modernity and its knowledge systems. It appears that an attempt to filter a Faustian bargain is being proposed by figures like ʿUsmani. A cautious approach, the ʿulama hope, will, in the end, make the knowledge tradition of the West "Islam-friendly." While such proposals betray an insecure, mechanistic, if not naïve, understanding of how knowledge functions, it has yet to be tried. The attempt to impart certain skills to madrasa students is a well-intentioned gesture but does not sufficiently address the crisis of religious knowledge that affects values, ethics, and theology. Whether Islamic orthodoxy can provide substantive religious advocacy in terms of the place of faith in a world driven by scientific prowess, democratic politics, and runaway capitalist economics remains to be seen. A progressive, cosmopolitan, and knowledge-friendly movement within the madrasa-sphere is the best hope in order to effectively transform and rejuvenate Islamic thought.

CHAPTER ELEVEN

Letter to Policy Makers

Often policy makers execute decisions based on media impressions or faulty intelligence reports. If I were to explain the role of the madrasas in Muslim religious life and advise the president of the United States and members of the U.S. Congress or any government around the world, I would send them a copy of my book, *What Is a Madrasa?*, along with the following letter.

Dear Mr. President of the United States and Members of the United States Congress:

Imagine a major attack on U.S. forces in South Asia, or God forbid, a terrorist attack on the United States mainland that was planned in Pakistan succeeds. Will the United States this time go to war and destroy madrasas in Afghanistan and Pakistan (the Af-Pak region), or launch drone attacks on madrasa facilities? This scenario is eminently possible. Judging from past performance, America's political leadership always found it necessary to find a scapegoat to heal its wounds in defeat—Vietnam after the failure of the Bay of Pigs, the invasion of Iraq after the September 11 attacks. So an intensified, remote-controlled drone war in the Af-Pak region is not entirely unforeseeable, since a low-intensity drone war is already underway.

Intelligence sources and the pundit classes have successfully painted the madrasas of South Asia as not only America's sworn enemies but also the sworn enemies of the West and the civilized world. Several journalists and columnists made lucrative careers in manufacturing links between terrorism and the madrasas without any proof.

I hope that no catastrophic scenario will tempt the White House, lawmakers, and members of the American public to embark on such an erroneous path of attacking madrasas. My book, *What Is a Madrasa?*, will surely inform you, but you will also have to ignore the utterances on record by people like Donald Rumsfeld and even the level headed Colin Powell who demonized the madrasas. You might recall that both men committed serious errors of judgment during George W. Bush's administration in preparation for and during the invasion of Iraq.

Sure, Taliban insurgents have tarnished the reputation of both the madrasas and the Muslim clerics, the ʿulama. But the Taliban is only one segment of madrasa affiliates. The majority of Muslims in South Asia view the madrasas as places of religious learning, not of terror. They support the madrasas, because these institutions provide religious services to communities. Generally, Muslims do not view madrasas as menacing or toxic institutions as many Americans and Europeans have come to believe madrasas to be.

It is time for the United States to hit the reset button when it comes to dealing with Muslim communities around the world. Waging a cultural war against Muslim societies is not the answer; it only aggravates the situation. The invasions of Afghanistan and Iraq have eroded trust with Muslims globally—middle classes and elites included. Many Muslims, especially the youth, feel wronged by the international community for being singled out as pariahs who deserve discrimination on the grounds of their faith commitments. Anti-Muslim discrimination has now morphed into lethal forms of Islamophobia.

Treating the madrasas with hostility would be a monumental failure of U.S. public diplomacy. Hostility will only aggravate relations with the Muslim communities of South Asia, and it will have a domino effect on South Asian Muslim communities all over the world, especially those in Europe, North America, and Africa, where they have numbers and influence.

Everything secular elites or the military classes in Muslim countries say must be viewed through the prism of their self-interests. These elites are experts in double-speak: they badmouth the madrasas as troglodytes in conversation with Euro-American interlocutors, but at home they engage in appeasing Muslim orthodoxy. Instead of relying on secondhand information, it's time to know who these so-called madrasa adversaries are, learn more about them, and engage them in order to build bridges between cultures.

As decision makers you should know the role and place the madrasas and the ʿulama play in Muslim societies. The ʿulama are the clerics who serve people of the Muslim faith. They are trained in madrasas, as clerics are trained in seminaries in the United States and elsewhere. Imagine the fallout when Country A targets the clerics of a particular religion in their war with Country B because a few clerics are engaged in subversive political activities. Such a move would only succeed in alienating the global religious community of that faith. Well, this is what happens when America targets the madrasas in their military and cultural wars in the Af-Pak region.

South Asia as a region is crucial to Muslim demographics. With a combined population of 489 million, spread over India, Pakistan, and Bangladesh, the Muslim population of this region alone is projected to grow to 679 million by 2030. With a growth in population, one can also assume a significant increase in the religious sector. Bear in mind the millions of Muslims who follow their ʿulama on a daily basis. They pray behind the ʿulama at mosques around the world five times a day. They listen to them during weekly sermons and annual festivals. On a daily basis, individuals and communities consult their ʿulama on matters of moral and ethical importance. And they appeal to pious ʿulama for prayers in times of crisis. Often, the faithful expect a member of the ʿulama to be present at their side at the time of death and to perform the burial rituals. Serving as learned authorities in matters of faith and salvation in the afterlife is one major role of the ʿulama. At the same time, the ʿulama also inform, guide, and instruct their audiences on topics as diverse as global politics and ethical issues related to the family—contraception, marriage, and finance and inheritance matters. When issues related to national political protests and elections come up, the ʿulama are not far away. Many ʿulama address vast audiences on television, on radio, in recorded sermons on the Internet, and in print, in places as far and varied

Muslim Demographics in South Asia

The total population of Muslims in the three countries of South Asia is at present 489 million (Pakistan 174 million, India 161 million, and Bangladesh 145 million), far surpassing the Muslim population of the Arab world. The Muslim population of all three countries is projected to reach 679 million by 2030, all things being equal. By the year 2030, a Pew survey projects, Pakistan will surpass Indonesia as the most populous Muslim country, growing from 178 million to 256 million people. Pakistan will represent a tenth of a projected 2.2 billion global Muslim population according to the Pew Survey. The country is a strategic player in the politics of the larger Muslim world with growing influence as the only Muslim majority nation possessing nuclear power and being an industrialized nation.

—*The Future of the Global Muslim Population: Projections for 2010–2030*, Pew-Templeton Global Religious Futures Project, January 2011

as Bandung in Indonesia, Baltimore in the United States, Kashgar in China, and Cape Town in South Africa.

A cleric in Malaysia or Mali might have studied in Cairo, yet he, and sometimes she, can intuitively understand the religious worldview of a cleric trained in any madrasa in South Asia and vice versa. Madrasas and the ʿulama form a global network, and they speak a common language. The common language is one of juristic theology, a combination of Islamic law and theological teachings. Yes, many Muslims agree that there are deficits in these discourses resulting in some ʿulama's espousing fairly distorted views on marriage, sexuality, and family life, and wield an authority that Muslims with modern sensibilities find offensive. Yet the ʿulama too represent a spectrum of views ranging from enlightened to obscurantist.

Some of the ʿulama enjoy a rock-star status. Shaykh Yusuf al-Qaradawi, the Qatar-based outspoken Egyptian cleric once popular on al-Jazeera, is just a good example of the many who air their views on thousands of radio stations and television channels throughout the Muslim world.[1] Yes, not all of the ʿulama are friendly to the United States or the West. This is precisely why dialogue with the ʿulama is so crucial. In order for this dialogue to happen, members of Congress, the White House, and foreign governments will have to ignore the naysayers among their advisers and show the courage to engage folk who hold different perspectives.

It is worth remembering that those who run the modern Muslim nation-states often relegate the ʿulama to the status of internal exiles. To these authorities, the ʿulama are largely invisible, except during election seasons and occasions when global religious crises erupt. Then the ʿulama are brought into the public sphere in order to mobilize votes or quell passions.

In a country like Pakistan, with its brittle political establishment, the ʿulama show an awareness of the worrying features of that society.[2] In 2008 they described the Pakistani military's collusion with the United States' war on terror as "deceptive and shameful." Pakistan's elite, the ʿulama said, is extravagant, corrupt, and vulgar in its efforts to undermine the country's judiciary. By all accounts, most patriotic Pakistanis welcome these statements made by the ʿulama. The ʿulama engage in double critique: they rail at what they view as a corrosive Western influence on their society on the one hand, and they serve as a buffer in order to curb religious extremism on the other.

Education is the cultural battleground in the view of the ʿulama. They recall with disdain the ambition of the eighteenth-century British administrator Lord Macaulay, who wanted to produce "a class of persons, Indian in blood and color, but English in taste, in opinions, in morals, and in intellect."[3] Secular education, if unchallenged, in the ʿulama's view is a threat: it is out to pervert Muslim identity and to enslave future generations to Euro-American authority. Even Yusuf al-Qaradawi, according to a recent study, views globalization itself as "a thinly veiled effort to spread Western norms throughout the rest of the world."[4] Qaradawi, I am aware, has a checkered record in the views of some, but in a Muslim context he is an orthodox thinker with some liberal sensibilities.

Some groups, like the Taliban, have gone to the extreme in outlawing Western education, especially women's education, by homicidal means. But in this matter the Taliban are outliers, and their perspective is not widely shared. Women's madrasas and regular schools are on the increase all over South Asia. Furthermore, most moderate madrasa authorities believe that as long as secular education does not disrupt their way of life and values, Muslims can benefit from it.

It will help if you showed some understanding for the theology that the madrasas and the ʿulama espouse. Belief in one God is integral to every Muslim's faith. Muhammad is not only God's final Prophet but also

His most revered Messenger. The Prophet Muhammad and his Companions, centuries ago, fought battles against polytheism and the rejection of God, opposed injustice, and sought to restore integrity to human life. Faith for the ʿulama is embedded in ways of living where it makes a difference if the inspiration is the Hindu avatar Ram, Jesus, the Buddha, or Muhammad, the Messenger of Allah. To grasp the role of the Prophet in Islam is to acquire a perspective of Muslim faith practices. Dealing sensitively with the image and persona of Muhammad enhances intercultural dialogue and efforts in religious tolerance and peace building.

The madrasas follow the authority of ancient theological authorities and also attempt to adapt their theology to a changing world, albeit conservatively and not always efficiently in my view. The same is true for their ethical practices, often called Islamic law or Shariʿa. Some madrasa authorities are more eager than others to be adaptive in matters of Shariʿa; again, you can find a spectrum of authorities with varied perspectives.

For instance, not all madrasa authorities encourage their followers to immolate themselves in paroxysms of rage against offensive images of the Prophet Muhammad. Often intra-Muslim competition and acts of demagoguery are the main motives for some to peddle violence with little regard to theology. Long ago a distinguished figure in the ranks of the Deoband school, Mahmud Hasan, reasoned that, for the better part, protests against blasphemy often revealed the wounded psyche of the Muslim community rather than a redemptive perspective of their faith.

Today the overwhelming majority of South Asia's orthodox Muslim leadership view the West as a mortal threat to their lifestyle, and they see the madrasa as a bulwark to predatory Westernization.[5] Just as the eighteenth-century madrasa networks held colonial designs at bay, similarly, today's madrasas attempt to fortify Muslim cultural resolve in a bid to combat Western neoimperial hegemony. Madrasas serve the "existence of Islam," one moderate figure wrote, "like veins nourish the body."[6] Another described madrasas as the "power houses" that sustain "Muslim cultural and community identity" and thus are essential to the survival of the moral values and religious life of Muslim society.[7] After the Cold War, several madrasa leaders solemnly believe that it "is Islam that remains the sole antagonist of the West."[8]

It would be a mistake to think that the ʿulama and madrasa communities are not well informed. They read vernacular and international news and are outraged by the way the United States conducts itself globally.

They are especially incensed by the United States' role in the Middle East and the invasions of Afghanistan and Iraq and for overseeing the detrimental treatment of Palestinians. The imbalance in global power between the hyperpowerful and the powerless creates conditions for multiple pathologies to flourish. An unfortunate and detrimental mindset now characterizes many religious decision makers in the Af-Pak region.

Be ready to expect a greater entanglement of religion, culture, and political life in complex ways in the Af-Pak region and beyond in the Muslim world. Also keep in mind that religiously colored violence is linked to deteriorating geopolitical realities in the region. In Pakistan, cross-border relations with India over the independence of Kashmir are a major source of instability. Whether Afghanistan will in the long term have a stable and inclusive government—-vital to regional peace and stability—is another. Secessionist movements and ethnic tensions utilize religious power to advance their agendas, and therefore the issues deserve close scrutiny.

Here are a few tips as to what policy makers must avoid if they wish to be successful in dialogue with elements of Muslim orthodoxy. The easiest way to thwart relations is to meddle in the affairs of orthodox Muslims and to be prescriptive in matters of madrasa curricula, values, and lifestyle. Demonizing madrasas amounts to rejecting the religious and cultural values and institutions of Muslims, a move that will be fiercely rebuffed. Telling people to abandon support for their madrasas is like dictating what religious and cultural preferences they should adopt.

A precondition for any dialogue with the orthodox sector is to end the ongoing U.S. drone strikes in South Asia and elsewhere. Targeting alleged terrorists without the oversight of the rule of law is morally perilous and results in the unjustifiable deaths of innocents. In addition, such practices erode the United States' credibility and undermine its commitment to human rights.

Informed dialogue is the only way forward, just as building confidence is a prerequisite. American and European political leadership faces many challenges in dealing with the future of this region. The most challenging question is how to engage in respectful conversation and interaction with societies who espouse radically different worldviews to those of the West. Can Euro-America imagine a world with radically pluralistic values? Disagreement over values becomes the basis for meaningful conversation. Dialogue with madrasa communities will teach respect for difference.

Most importantly, I discovered that madrasa folks just want to be left alone. They want to espouse a life of Islamic piety and to preserve their traditional scholarship that reinforces their religious convictions. In short, they don't want others to change their way of life. The question of others' changing their way of life should sound familiar to Americans in a post-9/11 world. Others around the world feel similarly passionate that strangers and foreigners should respect their ways of being in the world.

Meeting these prerequisites will require a total change in mindset in how America's political leadership deals with other nations, cultures, and values. Without these elementary changes, the road forward will be perilous. The globalizing world is a very delicate ecosystem. From the fragility of the air we breathe as a result of greenhouse gases to the treatment of others in international relations, diplomacy, wars, and human relations—all require sensitivity that is guided by the knowledge that our survival depends on the flourishing, not the elimination, of others. Building on the principle that the culture of others is as valuable as one's own is a great starting point. The West's relationship with Islamic orthodoxy, the ʿulama, and the madrasas is a litmus test for such coexistence.

Sincerely,
Ebrahim Moosa
Professor of Islamic Studies
Kroc Institute for International Peace Studies
University of Notre Dame

The madrasa leadership in South Asia and elsewhere don't fully comprehend that the negative image of the madrasa in the West also impacts the reputation of Islam as a faith tradition. The betterment of these institutions and their graduates can only add to the flourishing of Muslim communities globally. I share my own experiences with the leadership of the madrasas in a candid manner with a view to start a conversation leading to progress. I will provide a sketch of my madrasa career and also send a letter together with a copy of my book, What Is a Madrasa?, to my teachers.

CHAPTER TWELVE

Letters to My Teachers

Almost four decades ago, I landed on the shores of India, a wonder-struck youth from South Africa in search of the truths of Islam. I stubbornly shunned South African universities offering Islamic studies. I decried them as inauthentic, a view I would come to reconsider years later. My own life experience about the arrogance and self-righteousness of youth has taught me to eat my words and revise my positions. At the time, I searched for Islamic authenticity and enrolled at madrasas in India. Over a period of six years I completed my *ʿalimiyya* education.

The world was a very different place then. India taught me a great deal: about life, Islam, madrasas, and the ʿulama tradition. But it also gave me another gift. It taught me how to question. In many ways, I have moved on from the madrasa tradition. In others, I cling to some of its treasures. For one, I have battled the shadows of my exemplars that expected me to remain loyal to the orthodox tradition in the ways they taught me. However, I am sorry to say perhaps only in that respect I might be a disappointment as a student. For I too carry the burden to answer Ben Jonson's searching question: "how of late thou hast suffered translation, and shifted thy coat in these days of reformation."[1]

My teachers, I will always remain in your debt. You taught me with care, love, and sincerity. But I examined critically what I studied at your feet. So when curious people ask me what I learned at the madrasas such as Darul Uloom Matliwala in Bharuch, Gujarat, then Darul Uloom Deoband near Saharanpur, and graduating from Darul Uloom Nadwatul ʿUlama in Lucknow, my answer is instinctive.

I say: Madrasas taught me how to love knowledge and learning. Only the madrasas could make me so curious about everything from religion, philosophy, and ethics to politics and literature. In short, madrasa education taught me how to live in the world. These are lifelong assets I carry with me: an unslakable thirst for knowledge and a curiosity that served me wherever I went.

Madrasa education gave me the keys to access the Islamic tradition, its faith and dogmatic aspects. But its rich humanistic learning also prompted me to ask questions, to explore new vistas. Madrasas taught me how to navigate a path to God, in the colors of Islam. I suspect I was not always satisfied with what I read in the madrasa texts, so I explored other avenues of learning.

I never abandoned my madrasa texts, but I learned how to read them differently, with new eyes and experiences. It was a different "I" reading them decades later. Over time I changed, and it seems as though the texts I studied changed with me. The more I study the classical texts I was taught in the madrasas, the more I realize that the madrasas do not do a good job of mining all the gems these great classics contain. In fact, I discovered the gems and beauties of the classical tradition only after I left the madrasa. Perhaps that was my fate and not of others. But I am gratified.

I am now a professor of Islamic Studies at the University of Notre Dame. Prior to that, I taught at the University of Cape Town in my native South Africa, Stanford University, and for thirteen years at Duke University in the United States of America. Life is full of ironies. If I had avoided universities as venues to study Islam in my youth, I now teach at one. As I say, my ignorance and my passion for authenticity drove me to the madrasas. I now have graduate students, teach undergraduate students, and am engaged in a very rewarding and engaged world of global scholarship. But in hindsight, I often think I was fated to beat a path to the madrasas.

Let me now turn to two of my professors at different institutions and share with them some thoughts with a view to further conversation

New marble mosque on Darul Uloom Deoband campus. (Picture: Rodrigo Dorfman)

with each of them on critical matters related to the future of the madrasas.

Respected Mawlana Abdulkhaliq Madrasi, Vice-Chancellor, Darul Uloom Deoband

With Greetings and respect.

Sir, when I first met you in Deoband, decades ago, you were a newly minted professor. I fondly recall how we admired you as a dapper dresser, a man with a great literary taste in Arabic and an excellent sense of humor. Students were abuzz with praise for your gifts as a scholar and litterateur. In winter you wore neatly ironed *sherwanis* and well-pleated caps; in summer your immaculately starched white long shirts (*kurtas*) were the envy of all.

From among all my teachers, you kindled in me the fire to question and investigate. I recall how often, you would go off-topic in class in order to comment on an event within the madrasa or some national or global event. You showed a critical edge and often scoffed at the faux piety on display within the madrasas.

For instance, you frequently said that it was pretentious to use the second person plural of a pronoun or a verb in Arabic as a token of respect.

Your argument was simple and straightforward. It was eye-opening to hear you tell us that the most revered figure in Muslim history, the Prophet Muhammad, on whom be peace, was never addressed in the plural. He neither required his Companions nor asked them to address him in the royal plural. And the Companions with their unrivaled love and dedication to the Prophet merely addressed him as, "*You*, oh Messenger of God-*anta ya rasul allah*!" For me these were baby steps in my critical questioning of the tradition.

To be devout and to maintain hygiene were not incompatible qualities, you frequently said. You often took gentle digs at some students as well as professors whose hygiene was less than ideal. I now realize the wisdom of your saying that piety is compatible with simplicity but not with fouled air. As you led by example, your room was always the neatest, most elegant, and cleanest place on campus.

You also taught that it was vital to have a sense of humor. In class you often chided students whose piety clouded their sense of humor. Your favorite was a line dripping in sarcasm from Abu Tammam's *Diwan of Hamasa* aimed at the self-righteous among us.

> "As if, among all His creation, your Lord,
> Only created them—no one else, to revere Him!"

You should know the conversations you spurred actually punctured some of my youthful sanctimony and helped me to think clearly. Of course, I will not recite here the lines from the noted pre-Islamic poet Imraʾul Qays that often served as a pretext for the youthful titillation of us students. I fear that repeating some of those lines here might scandalize the sensibility of some readers, as it did folks in the medieval world who deemed it the "most obscene" verse in Arabic!

But I recall clearly how unforgivingly you criticized the curriculum and charged that it was outdated. I have since come to learn that many others, like you, have for decades made petitions for changes and upgrades to the Nizami curriculum.

So when I met you several decades later, I was pleased to witness that your spirited self was intact. Time did very little harm to your learning, energy, hospitality, and sense of humor. I am gratified to learn that you are now the deputy vice-chancellor of Darul Uloom Deoband, the citadel of South Asian seminaries, a great honor and responsibility indeed.

Everyone admires your efforts to give Darul Uloom Deoband a major facelift. The new all-marble mosque built under your supervision is an architectural masterpiece and an aesthetic feat, setting a new standard in class and efficiency. The ongoing construction of a major library and new residences will add to your legacy. All those who wish traditional Islamic education to advance thank you for your dedication to these causes.

Yet I also look forward to see how you plan to undertake curricular reform. At Deoband, the mother ship of contemporary madrasas, students and faculty all face the same challenges of a changing world that requires new skills, different approaches, and innovative solutions. In my book, *What Is a Madrasa?*, I have documented many of those challenges, and you will have a sense of my proposals.

The World Wide Web has brought about a revolution in information. Arabic, Urdu, and Persian texts dealing with Islamic thought and materials in European languages are now instantly available at one's fingertips on the Internet. Communication between your students and their counterparts elsewhere in the world opens up possibilities for collaborative learning on a global scale. It offers new possibilities for the mission of your institution.

Of course, technology, like any new thing, also requires its users to enter into a Faustian bargain: acquiring conveniences and ease in certain areas can, in exchange, also bring with it potential harms or unexpected consequences. But this is a challenge every age had to manage, rather than avoid. When people discovered ox-driven plows, it created unique challenges just as when cars replaced bullock carts. Agricultural production cycles, like travel, have become more rapid, yet we also emit greater pollutants. The challenge is to find motor vehicles that are environmentally friendly so that we can have both efficient transport and clean air. No one is proposing we abandon motor vehicles, tractors, or computers.

Similarly, one can anticipate a future in which cybertechnology will have an even more prominent role. The day is not far off when every house in Deoband will be connected to the Internet and every student will take notes on a laptop computer at your institution. So it's best to anticipate that future. It's futile to adopt the Chinese attitude of placing filters on the Internet. What the Chinese forget is that people are very resourceful and will find ways around censorship. It is better to improve the political environment of a country and reward the adoption of sound values that will in turn displace subversive ways.

The World Wide Web also challenges mainstream values on decency. Making quality literature and entertainment available to students in madrasas will, in my view, deflect their attention away from disruptive activities and toward constructive work and practices. Creating opportunities for students to pursue productive activities rather than threatening them with penalties appears to be a better solution to boredom and idleness that young people around the world frequently experience. Yet we have to concede that a percentage of students are going to make bad choices anyway. It is unavoidable.

It is my hope that you, sir, might spearhead a deliberative process in order to deliver to Darul Uloom's curriculum the necessary content upgrades, similar to the infrastructure upgrade taking place under your courageous leadership. Perhaps the time has arrived that those ideas you fostered during the early part of your career can now be discussed, since you are now part of the higher administration of Darul Uloom.

You should know that those of us on the outside and living abroad would indeed like to see your institution succeed. Your success at Darul Uloom Deoband will have a ripple effect. Your success will benefit the Muslim community on the subcontinent and in the world at large. If there is any work I can facilitate in terms of consultation and discussion regarding the curriculum, then feel free to call on me. I am sure many others within India and abroad will also be more than happy to make a contribution.

I write with gratitude for the intellectual nourishment you offered when I was still a young adult and the positive impact of your guidance on my life. For that and many other gifts, you will forever be in my prayers.

With good wishes and prayers,
Ebrahim Moosa
Professor of Islamic Studies
Kroc Institute for International Peace Studies
University of Notre Dame

To: Mawlana Sayyid Salman Husayni Nadvi, Head of Shariʿa Studies, Nadwatul ʿUlama

With greetings and respect.

It was a thrill to visit Nadwatul ʿUlama in 2006 for the first time after I graduated from this renowned institution in 1981. Reliving those environs I once inhabited brought on remarkable evocations of uncanniness. Perhaps the excitement in part was a quiver of astonishment as I realized that I did indeed study in prestigious madrasas like the Nadwa, and prior to that in Deoband. To express my visceral feelings is a way to acknowledge my eternal debt to both institutions. The tremendous strides Nadwa has made with a new library and new buildings all augur well for its future.

I was gratified by the opportunity to spend some time with you. And I thank you for your time and the insights you shared during our interviews. It was a real privilege, as always, to attend the hadith class you taught, namely, the lesson on the book of Bukhari. Memorable to me was your kind gesture in inviting me to share some thoughts with your students. In chapter 7 of my book *What Is a Madrasa?* I shared the lesson on hadith you gave with a readership interested in learning more about the scholarly life in the madrasas.

I realized that the tragic event of 9/11 has scarred the thinking of a section of South Asia's madrasa leadership. Overshadowing everything else are the anger and resentment generated against America in particular and the West in general for the unconscionable invasion, destruction, and loss of life caused in Afghanistan and Iraq. My visit to madrasas in India and Pakistan drove home a sense that many people in these circles believe that real-world events are shrouded in complex conspiracies. Many of the people I met believe that anyone who does not see the world through this distorted glass of conspiracies is either a stooge of American propaganda or worse, a sell out.

Yet I was struck by how many of the challenges madrasa education faced even before 9/11 remained unaddressed. I am sure one response to what I just noted will be to say that if the madrasas do not respond to the Western threat, then there will be no future left for madrasas to defend. This might be an exaggeration, but it is at least partly true. The question is whether the vital religious interests of Muslims in South Asia, especially the future of a robust and socially relevant religious education, should be sacrificed at the altar of unpredictable and catastrophic global political developments. The question is, what is the cost of becoming opponents of something, which is easy, instead of the more challenging task of proposing a constructive alternative?

Reading the Indian and international press, I have noted with alarm that some prominent madrasa scholars have issued heated statements on

Doors to mosque of Jamiʿa Naeemia, Lahore, Pakistan. (Picture: Amjad Pervez)

vastly complicated global situations, such as the unfortunate 2013 military coup in Egypt, or have pledged support for the Islamic State in Iraq and Syria (ISIS), also known as Islamic State (IS). I was saddened to read your public letter in which you unfortunately lauded the leader of ISIS in the same breath as you counseled him to refrain from killing others. Such comments only reinforce the negative stereotypes of madrasas, whereas the vast majority of madrasas can hardly endorse the brutality of ISIS in its murderous conduct of adversaries, fellow Muslims-Sunnis and Shiʿas alike, as well as religious minorities.

The founders of Deoband and Nadwa, men like Mawlana Muhammad Qasim Nanautvi and Mawlana Monghiri, respectively, looked beyond their immediate world and dreamed of a future. They took bold and unpopular steps in their time in order to sustain a network of madrasas. One looks forward to the day when South Asia's visionaries will once again step forward to take the madrasas of India, Pakistan, and Bangladesh to new futures to serve the global Muslim community with learning and moral teachings.

Nadwa's ambition was to combine the best of the old and the new. As a graduate of Nadwa, I believe the focus is today more on the old with very little evidence of the new in the curriculum. You have yourself eloquently written about the educational challenges facing madrasa education. I believe you have raised important questions, and I trust others will join your constructive proposals in a path forward.

With best wishes and prayers,

Ebrahim Moosa
Professor of Islamic Studies
Kroc Institute for International Peace Studies
The University of Notre Dame

Epilogue

South Asia's madrasa tradition presents potential opportunities for a serious renewal of religious scholarship, if such a moment is seized. For if serious reforms are not implemented then I fear the negative features of the current madrasa system will at some point in the future reach a breaking point and in the process undermine a great tradition. In writing this book I have been vaulting between two tensions within me. I vacillate between the impulses of a romantic humanist and that of a pragmatic realist. I suspect many, like me, are caught in this bind. One part of me continuously wants to treasure those great documents of the Islamic past: rich texts brimming with human experiences of other worlds that so indelibly shaped the Islamic tradition in all its civilizational complexity and diversity. The realist in me wishes to understand how this tradition can be put to work by drawing on the past without ignoring the realities of the present, a task that requires tradition to creatively speak in the idiom of our time. It requires creative interpretation and a need to draw on the intrinsic adaptability of tradition.

It is a messy past, and from where I stand today, not all aspects of it are equally appealing, for every document of civilization is also tainted and thus requires judicious readers. Most appealing, though, is the breadth of innovation evident in theological, juridical, literary, philosophical, political, and scientific thinking that men and women produced as a legacy for human civilization. It was impressive how past Muslims engaged with a prophet, a revealed book, a multiethnic and multilingual faith community, histories, and contexts in order to fashion a durable legacy in a little more than a millennium.

The realist in me struggles impatiently with the heirs of this kaleidoscopic civilizational past. Particularly those who represent Muslim orthodoxy, the ʿulama and the madrasas, in my view, could do better in their engagement with tradition. As I have shown in this book, the madrasas are very good at retrieving the pious version of the Islamic past, often at the expense of intellectual innovation, a feature of the Muslim past often forgotten. Today's heirs of the intellectual tradition have largely failed to find a formula where the worldly knowledge tradition is not antithetical to a personal salvation project. Furthermore, little effort is invested in enabling the madrasas to fully and intelligibly engage with the lived realities of the present.

In fact, it has been frustrating to communicate with the ʿulama and make them understand that a contemporary context requires a different literacy such as knowledge of the humanities, social sciences, and science in order to produce a competent theologian. If such an initiative is taken, then Muslim religious thought can be updated and South Asia's madrasas and ʿulama can lay the grounds for an enlightened Muslim orthodoxy.

The absence of an intellectually robust orthodoxy puts Muslim communities at great risk. Modernity spawns conditions where realist visions of orthodoxy clash with hyperidealistic versions of it, an outcome that produces a paralyzing ambivalence. Nothing captures this ambivalence more eloquently than the views of two important figures in South Asian history. The realist emperor Awrangzeb eloquently chastises his teacher for his poor education in an account preserved for us by the Frenchman Bernier. The romantic poet-philosopher Muhammad Iqbal, who is beloved in South Asia's madrasa circles, encourages innovation and change in thought, but he frequently erases that optimism with his dark poetic sirens of the dangers lurking behind the modern. For nearly a century, debates about reforms to orthodox madrasas on the Indo-Pak subcontinent are stuck between realists and romantics without reaching any meaningful proposal on a way forward.

Tradition, like any living organism, needs updating. Such updating can occur only when there is a serious engagement with the knowledge of the present. In all my interviews and discussions with madrasa leaders, I found many who realized that there was a need to engage with the present, but they were unable to find workable solutions. Some were triumphalist about tradition, or claimed to lack the capacity to engage with modern knowledge. Madrasa students should get modern knowledge elsewhere, they retorted, though they knew that students were ill-equipped to engage with contemporary knowledge systems without proper preparation.

In order to understand the Qurʾan, the *Sunna*, and the historical Muslim intellectual tradition, I said in my exchanges with the madrasa leadership, it was necessary to give the experience of contemporary Muslims a central role in the interpretative process. It was difficult to get many folks to understand my point. The posture was defensive. Few recognized that it was possible to approach the Qurʾan, hadith, theology, or jurisprudence in the light of a modern subjectivity where newer understandings of a human being, history, time, culture, nature, science, and meaning could play a central role. An unhealthy skepticism of modern knowledge produced in the minds of madrasa authorities the idea that a modern Muslim subject was at best questionable or only modern technology was usable. It was, in my view, a double jeopardy: the Muslim past was rendered a monument, as Nietzsche described it, and not as a source for critical engagement; and the present was too polluted with "otherness," in the view of the ʿulama, in order to qualify as a resource.

Hope lies with the voices at the margins of the madrasa tradition that do realize that it is necessary to provide an intelligible and enlightened orthodoxy for Muslims today. They understand that there is no need to make a choice between intellectual excellence on the one hand and spiritual advancement on the other, both desiderata of madrasa communities. Knowledge does not only have to serve the purpose of salvation and bypass the realities of the world in which believers live and flourish. Both the revelatory tradition and the humanistic tradition of knowledge can be fruitfully harnessed, rather than one at the expense of the other. The metaphysical legacy of the past could have a fruitful dialogue with the scientific heritage of the present in order to create a new metaphysical theology. But to achieve that goal a robust exposure to multiple knowledge traditions is a precondition. A refurbished Muslim orthodoxy in

South Asia can offer guidance to millions in an effective and realistic manner. Madrasas are the ideal social laboratories where these experiments with knowledge can successfully be undertaken.

The absence of a credible orthodox tradition opens the door for rank scripturalism and toxic versions of do-it-yourself Islam that jettison tradition in order to make self-serving instruments out of the tenets of faith and the teachings of scripture. Contemporary Muslim societies are exposed to dangerous distortions of faith and are paying a very high price. Constructive engagement with tradition in the madrasas holds out the promise for constructive religious thought and the opportunity to meaningfully serve humanity in the ways of faith and tradition.

Glossary

adab: An artistic creation that one reads, hears, or performs for enjoyment or moral refinement—in short, to become erudite; also refers to ethical conduct.
adhan: The call to prayer.
adib: Person who is erudite.
ʿalim (plural *ʿulama*): Arabic word meaning learned person; these days the term is often used to describe members of the Muslim clerical establishment.
ʿalimiyya: Program required for gaining the knowledge and skills of an *ʿalim,* the Arabic word for "a learned person."
ʿawra: Bodily privacy.

burqa: A loosely draped piece of outer clothing that covers a woman's entire body and face.

daʿwa: Inviting people to Islam; also evangelizing fellow Muslims to the faith.
din: A term that is often mistranslated as "religion," with its modern ring of private beliefs. If one were to scour the Muslim tradition, one would get the sense that *din* is not a belief, but a grammar of how one performs all the practices of salvation.
dupattas: Rectangular scarves worn by women.
durvesh: Ascetic.

fajr: Morning prayers.
fatwa (plural *fatawa* or *fatwas*): A nonbinding scholarly legal opinion.
fazilat: A degree issued to a graduate from a madrasa.
fiqh: Often translated as Islamic law; another term frequently used is Shariʿa.

hadith: A prophetic report.
hafiz (pl. *huffaz*): One who has memorized the Qurʾan.
haram: Acts that are forbidden.
hijab: A head covering worn by women that allows the face to be visible.
hijra: Migration, exile.
hijri: As in *hijri* calendar, calendar based on the date of the *hijra* starting in the year 622 A.D.

ijtihad: Independent legal reasoning; intellectual effort.
ʿilm: The Arabic word for knowledge.
ʿilm al-kalam: Dialectical theology.

imam: The prayer leader; sometimes used to refer to the leader of the community of Muslims.
ishraq: Optional after-sunrise prayers.

jahiliyya: Arabic word meaning ignorance used to describe the period before Islam. Some Muslim ideologues applied this term to describe the secular modern world.
jihad: Religiously sanctioned military efforts.
juzʾ (plural *ajzaʾ*): One of thirty portions of the Qurʾan to facilitate a monthly reading schedule of the Muslim scripture.

kurta: Long shirt worn by many in the madrasas.

madhahib (singular *madhhab*): Legal academies or guilds; law schools or rites lay Muslims follow in religious and moral practices.
madrasa: Secular school, Sunday school, religious seminary.
maʿjun-i murakkab: Compound panacea.
makruh: Strongly discouraged acts.
maktab: Sunday school equivalent.
mandub: Encouraged acts.
marʿub: To be in thrall of.
maslak: Describes how an institutional memory of virtuous conduct is constructed, sustained, and cherished by folk who follow tradition.
mubah: Permissable acts. This is the default mode for all human acts.
mufti: An expert authorized to issue scholarly opinions called fatwas.
mulla: Cleric.
mutun (singular *matn*): Primers or core texts studied in madrasas.

nawab: Honorific title bestowed by the Mughal emperor to rulers of princely states.

purda: The strict covering of women's bodies and the enforced segregation between the sexes; also describes a face veil worn by women.

qari (plural *qurraʾ*): Specialists who recite the Qurʾan in various melodious styles and will perform at special events in mosques, public events, and religious ceremonies.
qawmiyyat: Nationhood, community identity.

rakʿa: Genuflections that constitute the ritual prayer, or *salat*.

sadhus: Hindu ascetics.
salah: A set of bodily movements and pauses that are replicated in each prayer session and repeated several times a day.
sayyid: One who is a descendant of the Prophet Muhammad's family.
shahid: Martyr.

shalwar-kameez: An outfit consisting of baggy pants and knee-length shirts and also worn by women who adorn themselves with large shawls covering the hair.
sharh: A commonsense gloss on the meaning of a text.
shariʿa: often translated as Islamic law, but actually a moral discourse that proposes ethical guidelines for society.
sunna: A precedent established by the Prophet Muhammad.
sura: A chapter of the Qurʾan.

tafsir: Exegesis.
taʿlim: Generally means ethical instruction; also refers to a mode of Qurʾanic speech.
tarbiya: "Nurturing" or "nourishing"; a crucial term for moral cultivation set to the rhythm of the Shariʿa.
tawhid: Divine unity.
taʾwil: Expansive interpretation used in Qurʾanic and hadith interpretation.
tawjih: A "steered" interpretation of the Qurʾan.
taʿziya: A passion play in which Shiʿas commemorate the death of Husayn, the Prophet Muhammad's grandson.

ʿulama (plural *ʿalim*): Arabic word meaning learned person. These days the term is often used to describe members of the Muslim clerical establishment.

wajib: Obligatory acts.
waʿz: The homily or sermonic mode of Qurʾanic speech.
wudu: The ritual washing of specific limbs before the act of ritual communion with God.

Notes

PROLOGUE

1. Bergen and Pandey, "The Madrassah Myth," *New York Times*, June 14, 2005; Dalrymple, "A Largely Bourgeois Endeavour"; Winthrop and Graff ("Beyond Madrasas," 2), both affiliated with the Brookings Institute, lamented the exclusive Western focus "on madrasas and their role in the mounting violence." This approach, they argued, distracted attention from "how the education sector as a whole may be fuelling violence, over and above the role of the minority of militant madrasas."

2. ʿUsmānī, *Hamārā*, 16.

3. Colin Powell quoted in Dalrymple, "Largely Bourgeois Endeavour."

4. Donald Rumsfeld quoted from "The Charlie Rose Show: Interview with Donald Rumsfeld," *Charlie Rose Show*, transcript, August 20, 2005.

5. Chef 28 Restaurant, 28th Street, New York, between Park and Madison Avenues, 21 April 2010, 1 P.M.

6. Hamid, *Reluctant Fundamentalist*, 34.

7. See, for example, Sikand, *Bastions of the Believers*; Bano, *Rational Believer*; Ali, *Islam and Education*; Johnston, Hussain, and Cataldi, "Madrasa Enhancement and Global Security"; Fair, "Islamic Education in Pakistan"; Hartung and Reifeld, *Islamic Education, Diversity and National Identity*; Hefner and Zaman, *Schooling Islam*; Malik, *Madrasas in South Asia*; Ahmad, "Madrassa Education in Pakistan and Bangladesh."

8. Zaman, " 'Ulama of Contemporary Islam," 129–55.

9. Dubuisson, *Western Construction of Religion*, 21.

CHAPTER TWO

1. Ibn ʿArabī, *al-Futūḥât al-makkīya*, 7:89.

2. Nīsābūrī et al., *Ṣaḥīḥ Muslim bi Sharḥ al-Nawawī*, 2:101.

3. Asad, *Message of the Qurʾān*, 480n96.

4. Ghaurī and ʿAbdulḥaq, *Ashraful Savāniḥ*, 1:50–51.

CHAPTER THREE

1. Ibn Khaldūn, *Muqaddimah*, 1:15–16.

2. Ibid.

3. Khudā Bakhsh Oriyanṭal Pablik Lāʾibrerī (Ed.), *ʿArabī Islāmī madāris kā niṣāb va niẓām-i taʿlīm aur ʿaṣrī taqāẓe*, 1: 43.

4. See Zaman, "Commentaries, Print and Patronage."

5. Hodgson, *Venture of Islam*, 1:360.

6. Ṭayyab and Bigyānvī, *Shakhṣiyāt va tavārīkh ḥakīmul islām*, 1:178.

7. Kākā Khel, "Muslim Madarsa Students Not Terrorists Part 1."

8. Ibid.

9. Laknawī, *al-Ajwiba al-fāḍila*, 23.

10. Ibid.

11. Kākā Khel, "Muslim Madarsa Students Not Terrorists Part 1."

12. Kafawī, *al-Kulliyāt*, 610–11. Kafawī writes, "The word *knowledge* (*ʿilm*) means to grasp something in its true essence . . . [the verb] *ʿallama* derived from the root *ʿalima*, when it occurs as the strong form of the verb, signifies the fact that knowledge relates either to an individual or always connects to several persons."

13. Ibid., 610–11.

14. Ibid., 611.

15. Thānvī, *al-ʿIlm val ʿulamā*, 4.

16. Tahānawī, *Kashshāf*, 1:814.

17. Arberry, *Koran Interpreted*, 18.

18. al-Shāfiʿī, *Diwān al-imām al-Shāfiʿī*, 98.

19. *Ibid.*, 70.

20. Ṭayyab, *ʿUlamāʾ-i Deoband ka dīnī rukh aur maslakī mizāj*, 109.

21. See Tareen, "Polemic of Shahjahanpur."

22. Thanvī, *Arvāḥ-i s̱alās̱ah*, 254–55.

23. Ibid.

24. Asqalānī, *Fatḥ al-bārī*, 9:5816–18.

25. Nīsābūrī et al., *Ṣaḥīḥ Muslim bi Sharḥ al-Nawawī*, 1:290

26. Gīlānī, *Iḥāta*, 154–55.

27. Ibid.

28. Qāsmī, "Do bātyn̲," 64.

CHAPTER FOUR

1. Nuʿmānī, *Maqālāt*, 99.

2. Robinson, *ʿUlama of Farangi Mahall.*

3. Ḥasanī, *Nuzhat*, 5:158. One of his teachers, Mulla Daniyal Jawrasi, himself was privileged with an illustrious intellectual itinerary. How? Well, his spiritual master was one Shaykh Sakhi, the grandnephew of the renowned Delhi-based mystic and teacher Shaykh Nizamuddin Awliya of the early fourteenth century. Jawrasi was a foremost student of Mufti Abdussalam Diwi, an expert on the Hanafi rite of Islamic law. Diwi's expertise in Muslim moral philosophy coupled with his extraordinary courage allowed him to issue dissenting ethical rulings derived from his innovative research. In doing so, he occasionally ignored the black letter of the law, much to the chagrin of his peers.

4. Ibid., 5:350–53. Not only was Muhibbullah enchanted with the teachings of Ibn ʿArabi, but he was also a major interpreter of the Spanish mystic's ideas. Being a defender of Ibn ʿArabi also meant courting controversy with those scholars who held firmly to orthodox readings of traditional theology.

5. Ibid., 5:194.

6. Qannūwjī, *Abjad al-ʿulūm*, 3:233.

7. Anṣārī, *ʿUlamāʾ-i Farangī maḥall*, 14–15.

8. Ḥasanī, *Nuzhat*, 6:219–20.

9. Nuʿmānī, *Maqālāt*, 99.

10. Iṣlāḥī, *Taʿlīm ʿahd-i islāmī ke hindūstān main*, 82.

11. Malik al-ʿulamā and Baḥr al-ʿulūm.

12. Ḥasanī, *Nuzhat*, 7:313–18.

13. Sharar, *Lucknow*, 124–25.

14. Anṣārī, *Bānī-yi*. Abdul ʿAli used to say that "just as my father cared for my education during his lifetime he paid equal attention to me after his death helping me solve difficult passages."

15. Ḥasanī, *Nuzhat*, 6:249–50.

16. Rezavi, "Physicians as Professionals in Medieval India," 45.

17. Abdul ʿAli's son, Abdul ʾAʿla, also acquired quite a reputation as a scholar. It is thanks to his foresight and writings that some of the early history of his family's ordeals and successes were preserved for posterity. Bold and outspoken, he argued that new interpretations in Islamic law known as *ijtihad* could never cease to be practiced and strongly advocated it despite the howls of many naysayers. ʿAbd al-ʾAʿla died in 1793.

18. Ḥasanī, *Nuzhat*, 8:250–56.

19. Anṣārī, *ʿUlamā-i Farangī maḥall*, 137.

20. Notable among them was the Syrian hadith scholar Shaykh ʿAbd al-Fattāḥ Abū Ghudda and the Jordanian-Palestinian scholar Shaykh Salah Abu al-Haj.

21. Ismāʿīl, *Taqwiyatul īmān*.

22. Ibid., 29.

23. Ibid., 29–30.

24. Dihlawī, *Ḥujjat Allāh al-Bāligha*, 1:33.

25. Dalrymple, *Last Mughal*, 73; Nizami, "Islamization and Social Adjustment," 243.

26. Gīlānī, *Savānih*, 1:384–85n1.

27. Sanyal, *Devotional Islam and Politics in British India*, 231–67.

28. Ḥasanī, *Nuzhat*.

29. Gīlānī, *Savānih*, 1:107. Gīlānī cites Sir Sayyid Ahmad Khan's observations and defends the description of Mamlukul ʿAlī as unoffensive and realistic. It is erroneously reported that Muhammad Qasim and Sir Sayyid were both students of the same teacher. Sir Sayyid indeed frequently visited Mamlukul ʿAli at Delhi College.

30. Yaʿqūb Nanautvī, "Savanih-i ʿumri," 26. Muhammad Qasim's educational career paradoxically profited from a tragic family event causing him to be shuffled around neighboring towns and villages for safety. The story goes that before he reached the age of ten, a feud broke out between Muhammad Qasim's grandfather, Shaykh Ghulam Shah, and his business partner, Shaykh Tafaddul Husayn. (The title "Shaykh" does not signify a scholar or elderly person in the Arabic language, but rather indicates the family tree of the person's descent from ʿUmar ibn al-Khattab, the second caliph of Islam.) Shaykh Tafaddul Husayn had for some inexplicable reason abandoned the Sunni creed and adopted the Shiʿa doctrine. In doing so, he infuriated the sensibilities

of the village elders and provoked the ire of former friends in the village inhabited almost exclusively by persons aligned to the Sunni creed. In subsequent tensions Shaykh Tafaddul was mortally wounded by the violent actions of Muhammad Qasim's maternal uncle. Fearing that reprisals from the deceased man's family might harm the young and vulnerable, the patricians in Muhammad Qasim's family resolved to send him away to one of the nearby towns on the pretext of education but primarily to keep him out of harm's way. This turned into an opportunity for Muhammad Qasim to get an excellent education from teachers in nearby towns. In later years, for many in Muhammad Qasim's circle of friends and admirers, this event has cosmic significance, since it prefigured a divine plan to prepare him for a greater task to serve the Muslims of India.

31. In Deoband Mawlawi Mehtab ʿAli gave Muhammad Qasim a rudimentary education in Persian and other subjects, and he took Arabic with Shaykh Nihal Ahmad. In Saharanpur he studied with the reputed Muhammad Nawaz Saharanpuri. By then he had mastered the abridged primers in Islamic law, arithmetic, and geometry in addition to Arabic and Persian grammar.

32. Rashid Ahmad Gangohi also took classes from Qazi Ahmaduddin Punjabi Jhelumi and from descendants of the family of the previously mentioned Shah Waliyullah, including the distinguished Shah Makhsusullah, the grandson of Waliyullah.

33. ʿĀshiq Ilāhī, *Tazkiraturrashīd*, 1:28.

CHAPTER FIVE

1. The Arabic terms are species (*nawʿ*), genus (*jins*), difference (*faṣl*), particular accident (*ʿarḍ khaṣṣa*), and common accident (*ʿard ʿamm*).

2. Maybudhī, *Sharḥ Hidāyat al-Ḥikma*, 2.

3. Gangohī, *Ẓafarul muḥaṣṣilīn*, 259.

4. Ḥasanī, *Nuzhat*, 5:285.

5. Ibid.

6. Ibid.

7. Jāmīʿ, *al-Fawā ʾid*.

8. See Algar, *Jami*.

9. Jespersen, *Philosophy of Grammar*, 65.

CHAPTER SIX

1. The elements of a Muslim Republic of Letters are different from what is described in McNeely and Wolverton, *Reinventing Knowledge*.

2. Burke, "Erasmus and the Republic of Letters," 8.

3. See Makdisi, *Rise of Humanism in Classical Islam and the Christian West*.

4. Shāṭibī, *al-Muwāfaqāt*, 1:93–99.

5. Dihlawī, *Ḥujjat Allāh al-Bāligha*, 1:33.

6. Ḥasanī, *Nuzhat*, 4:227.

7. Munavvar Sulṭān Nadvī, *Nadvatulʿulamāʾ kā fiqhī mizāj aur abnāiʾ Nadvah kī fiqhī khidmāt*, citing Khalid Sayfullah Rahmani.

8. Fārūqī, “Dīnī madāris kī jadīd kārī ʿaṣrī taqāḍun ke āyīne main,” 44. Muftī Muḥammad Arshad Fārūqī teaches at the Maẓāhir al-ʿUlūm (Waqf) madrasa in the city of Saharanpur in North India and is a leading advocate for madrasa curricular change.

9. See Binnawrī, “Madāris-i ʿArabīya.”

10. See Mahmood *“Dars-e-Nizāmī* and the Transnational Traditionalist *Madāris.”*

11. Appadurai, *Fear of Small Numbers*, 131.

CHAPTER SEVEN

1. See Ghias, “Juristic Disagreement”; Jāmiʿat al-ʿUlūm al-Islāmiyya, *Murawwaja Islāmī baynkārī*;ʿUsmānī, *Ghayr Sūdī Baynkārī: Muta'alliqa fiqhī masā'il kī* taḥqīq *aur ishkālāt ka jā'iza.*

2. ʿUsmānī, “Barr-i ṣaghīr ke madāris,” 10.

3. Ibid.

4. Ibid.

5. Abū Bakr Rabīʿ bin Subayḥ al-Saʿdī al-Baṣrī; see Sayyid ʿAbd al-Ḥayy Ḥasanī, *Yād-i ayyām*, 46.

6. Ḥasanī, *Nuzhat*, 1:69–70.

7. Ḥasanī, *Yād-i ayyām*, 74–76.

8. Ṭaḥāwī, *Sharḥ maʿānī al-āthār*, 1:19

9. Ibid.

10. Ibid.

11. Ibid., 1:20

12. See Katz, *Body of Text.*

13. Winkelmann, *“From behind the Curtain.”*

14. Ibid., 82.

15. http://www.nytimes.com/2010/10/09/world/asia/09pstan.html.

16. ʿAsqalānī, *Fatḥ al-bārī*, 8:4672.

CHAPTER EIGHT

1. Madrāsī, “Interview,” February 20, 2006.

2. Ījī, *Kitāb al-Mawāqif*, 1:20.

3. Ibid.

4. Ismāʿīl, *ʿAbaqāt*, 170–71.

5. Gīlānī, *Tazkira*, 174.

6. Ghazālī, *Iḥya'*, 1:56; *“al- ʿilmʿ ilmān: ʿilm al-ṭibb li al-abdān wa ʿilm al-fiqh li al-adyān”*; recall that I translate *dīn*, pl. *adyān*, as salvation practice.

7. Ījī, *Kitāb al-Mawāqif*, 21.

8. Khairābādī and Shīrkūtī, *Mirqāt ma ʿḥāshiya jadīda al-Mir 'āt*, 3.

9. Ījī, *Kitāb al-Mawāqif*, 1:59.

10. Foucault, *Lectures on the Will to Know*; with *Oedipal Knowledge*, 16.

11. See Ansari's commentary on, 3, where this quality is described as “an indivisible attribute” (*ṣifa basīṭa*), which is an “illuminating or transfiguring condition” (*al-ḥāla al-injilā' īya*).

12. Rosenthal, *Knowledge Triumphant*, 49.
13. ʿUsmānī, "Barr-i ṣaghīr ke madāris," 11.
14. Ibid.
15. Ibid.
16. Ibid.
17. Ibid.
18. Ibn Khaldūn, *Muqaddimah Ibn Khaldūn* (Arabic), 401–2.
19. Ibid.
20. Bourdieu, *Logic of Practice*, 53.
21. Foucault, *Power/Knowledge*, 39.
22. Goodman, *Jewish and Islamic Philosophy*, 131.
23. Ibn ʿArabī, *al-Futūḥāt al-makkīya*, 6:380. "*jāmiʿ liʾl-khayr.*"
24. Ibid., 7:85. "*fa al-sharāʾi ādāb allāhi naṣabahā li ʿibādihi.*"
25. S.v. *rabb* Ibn Manzūr, *Lisān al-ʿarab* (*ʿālim rabbānī*).
26. Kashmīrī, *Fayḍ al-bārī*, 1:280. Homiletics is called *waʿz* and ethical instruction is *taʿlīm* and *tafqīh*, as the roles played by the teacher (*muʿallim*) and the jurist-theologian (*faqīh*).
27. Husayni, "Interview."
28. Qannūwjī, *Abjad al-ʿulūm*, 1:97–98.
29. Ibid.
30. Ibid., 23:630.
31. Khān, *Malfūẓ-i Mukammal*, 197.
32. Ibid.
33. Zaman, *Thanawi*.
34. Ibid., 11.
35. Thānvī and Nadvī, *al-ʿIlm val ʿulamā*, 6–7.
36. Thānvī, *Malfūzāt-i ḥakīmul ummat*, 1:218.
37. Ibid.
38. Thānvī's incisive observations strangely resonated with the ideas of the Chinese sage Laotze's *Tao te Ching*. The famous British pop group the Beatles, in the lyrics composed by George Harrison, popularized the Chinese sage's intuitions. The song entitled "The Inner Light" quotes directly from that core Taoist text.

Without going out of my door
I can know all things on earth
Without looking out of my window
I could know the ways of heaven
The farther one travels
The less one knows. . . .
Arrive without travelling
See all without looking
Do all without doing

39. Thānvī and Nadvī, *al-ʿIlm val ʿulamā*, 4.
40. Ibid.
41. Zaman, *Thanawi*, 19.

42. Thānvī and Nadvī, *al-ʿIlm val ʿulamā*, 24.

43. Foucault describes "heterotopia" in both linguistic and spatial terms; see Michel Foucault, *Order of Things*, xviii–xxii; Michel Foucault and Jay Miskowiec, "Of Other Spaces."

44. Ahmad, *Dīnī madāris*, 96.

45. Muḥammad Shahābuddīn Nadvī, *Jadīd ʿilm-i kalām Qurʾān aur sāʾins kī raushnī men̲*, 13.

46. Ḥusaynī Nadvī, *Hamāra niṣāb*, 57.

47. Qāsmī, "Do bātyn̲," 64.

48. See Hefner and Zaman, *Schooling Islam*.

49. Qāsmī, "Do bātyn̲."

50. Iqbal, Zarb-i Kalim, 'Taqdir,' *Āsān Kulliyāt-i Iqbāl* (Urdū), 660.

CHAPTER NINE

1. Jackson, "Media and War."

2. Ibid.

3. "Pakistan and India."

4. Hare, *Vertical Hour*, 6.

5. Bodissey, "Sheep to the Slaughter."

6. Friedman, "What 7 Republicans Could Do."

7. Dalrymple, "Largely Bourgeois Endeavour."

8. Ahmed and Stroehlein, "Pakistan." Rumsfeld said this in October 2003.

9. Hitchens, "No Way."

10. Mendenhall, "Pakistan's Religious Schools."

11. Dalrymple, "Inside the Madrasas."

12. Ibid.

13. *The Guardian*, London, July 30, 2005, Declan Walsh reports, "President Pervez Musharraf yesterday pledged to expel an estimated 1,400 foreign students from Pakistan's Islamic schools and arrest extremist leaders as part of a crackdown on militant groups. The network of jihadi groups has come under scrutiny since revelations that two of the July 7 bombers visited madrasas during a trip to Pakistan last winter. In the past week police have arrested more than 600 suspected extremists. Mr Musharraf promised to act against the 'bigwigs' of their organisations. All foreign students would be ordered to leave the madrasas. 'We will not issue visas to such people,' he said, adding that British intelligence had provided more than 100 phone numbers that were proving 'useful to the probe.' Mr Musharraf must overcome scepticism that he is serious about tackling Pakistan's militant nexus, something he has repeatedly promised but failed to deliver since 2001. Previous sweeps have sent militants scurrying only to re-emerge unscathed months later and resume business as usual. . . . Analysts and diplomats believe the president is reluctant to dismantle the groups because their activities in Kashmir provide useful leverage in talks with India. . . . British attention has partly focused on Jamaat-ud Dawa, an Islamic charity that runs a madrasa near Lahore that suicide bomber Shehzad Tanweer allegedly visited. About 115 of Jamaat's activists were arrested this week under anti-terrorist laws." Measure the absence of

any factual basis in an article by Waleed Ziad who on June 18, 2004, wrote an article in the *New York Times*, titled "How the Holy Warriors Learned to Hate." He indicts contemporary madrasas to recent activities of jihad based on a piece of graffiti which states, "Jihad of the sword, like prayer, is a religious obligation," which he then attributes to the madrasa tradition. This is such a distorted a presentation that it can hardly warrant a corrective.

14. Stern, "Pakistan's Jihad Culture."

15. Burr, " 'Clay Bird' Intelligently Explores Religious Faith."

CHAPTER TEN

1. Nuʿmānī, *Maqālāt*, 138.

2. Ibid., 140.

3. Ibid., 138.

4. Ikram, *Mauj-i kauṡar, 227.*

5. *Ibid.*

6. *Nuʿmānī, Maqālāt, 3, 126.*

7. *Ibid., 163.*

8. *Thānvī and Nadvī, al-ʿIlm val ʿulamā, 63.*

9. *Ibid.*

10. *Usmānī, Hamārā, 120.*

11. *See Moosa, Ghazali and the Poetics of Imagination.*

12. *Usmānī, Hamārā, 82.*

13. *Ibid., 83.*

14. *Ibid., 119.*

15. *Ibid.*

16. *Ibid., 130.*

17. *Ibid., 131.*

18. *Iqbal, "Ẓarb-i Kalīm," in Āsān Kulliyāt-i Iqbāl (Urdū), 798.*

19. *Shāhin, Aurāq-i gum gashtah, 374–75.*

20. *Raḥmān, "Ahl-i madāris ko ʿaṣrī taʿlīm ka mashwara nā wāqifiyat par mabnī," 38–42.*

CHAPTER ELEVEN

1. For his views on suicide bombing, Qaraḍāwī is banned from visiting the United States and Britain. Recently, Qaraḍāwī's own son challenged his father's use of his religious authority to reinstate the ousted Egyptian president, Mohamed Morsi. See Qaraḍāwī, "Risāla ʿAbd al-Raḥmān al-Qaraḍāwī ilā abīhi Yūsuf al- Qaraḍāwī."

2. *The News*, "Ulema Open Their Heart to MPs on Terror."

3. Macaulay's Minute on Indian Education, http://www.english.ucsb.edu/faculty/rraley/research/english/macaulay.html.

4. Zaman, *Modern Islamic Thought*, 156–57.

5. ʿUsmānī, *Hamārā*, 77; Maẓharī, "Fudẓalāʾ," 199–206; Manṣūrī, "Maghrib," 105–9.

6. Maẓharī, "Fudẕalā'," 199.
7. Miṣbāḥī, *Qur'ān awr jihād*, 63.
8. Manṣūrī, "Maghrib," 108.

CHAPTER TWELVE

1. Jonson, *Volpone*, Act 1, Scene 1, 1203.

Bibliography

Ahmad, Mumtaz. *Dīnī madāris: Riwāyat aur tajdīd ʿulamā kī nazar main*. Islamabad: Emel, 2012.

———. "Madrassa Education in Pakistan and Bangladesh." In *Religious Radicalism and Security in South Asia*, edited by Satu P. Limaye, Mohan Malik, and Robert G. Wirsing, 101–16. Honolulu: Asia-Pacific Center for Security Studies, 2004.

Ahmed, Samina, and Andrew Stroehlein. "Pakistan: Still Schooling Extremists." *Washington Post*, July 17, 2005.

Algar, Hamid. *Jami (Makers of Islamic Civilization)*. 1st ed. New Delhi: Oxford University Press, 2013.

Ali, Saleem H. *Islam and Education: Conflict and Conformity in Pakistan's Madrassahs*. Oxford : Oxford University Press, 2009.

Anṣārī, Muftī ʿInāyatullāh. *ʿUlamāʾ-i Farangī Maḥall: Mabnī bar taẕkirah-yi ʿulamāʾ-i Farangī Maḥall* [in Urdu]. Edited by Muḥammad Ḥāmid Anṣārī and Muḥammad Shāhid Anṣārī. Lucknow: Muḥammad Shāhid Anṣārī, 1988.

Anṣārī Farangī Maḥallī, Muḥammad Raẕā. *Bānī-yi dars-i niẓāmī*. Aligarh: Aligarh Muslim University Publications, 1973.

Appadurai, Arjun. *Fear of Small Numbers: An Essay on the Geography of Anger*. Durham, N.C.: Duke University Press, 2006.

Arberry, A. J. *The Koran Interpreted*. 2 vols. New York: Macmillan, 1969.

Asad, Muhammad. *The Message of the Qurʾān*. Bristol: The Book Foundation, 2003.

ʿĀshiq Ilāhī, Muḥammad. *Taẕkiraturrashīd: Savāniḥ . . . Rashīd Aḥmad*. Lahore: Idāra Islāmiyāt, 1986.

ʿAsqalānī, Ibn Ḥajar Aḥmad ibn ʿAlī, Muḥammad ibn Ismāʿīl Bukhārī, *Fatḥ al-bārī: Sharḥ Ṣaḥīḥ al-Bukhārī*. Edited by ʿAbd al-ʿAzīz ibn ʿAbd Allāh Ibn Bāz and Muḥammad Fuʾād ʿAbd al-Bāqī.15 vols. Ṣaydā; Beirut: al-Maktaba al-ʿAṣrīya, 1468/2007.

Bano, Masooda. *The Rational Believer: Choices and Decisions in the Madrasas of Pakistan*. Ithaca, N.Y.: Cornell University Press, 2012.

Bergen, Peter and Pandey, Swati. "The Madrassah Myth," *New York Times*, June 14, 2005.

Bernier, François. *Travels in the Mogul Empire, A.D. 1656–1668: Constable's Oriental Miscellany of Original and Selected Publications*, vol. 1. Edited by François Bernier, Irving Brock, and Archibald Constable. Westminster: Constable, 1891.

Binnawrī, Muḥammad Yūsuf. "Madāris-i ʿarabīya ka niṣāb va niẓām-i taʿlīm (1)." *Tarjumān-i DārulʿUlūm*, February 2001, 38–44.

———. "Madāris-i ʿarabīya ka niṣāb va niẓām-i taʿlīm (2)." *Tarjumān-i Dārul ʿUlūm*, March 2001, 33–43, 51.

Bodissey, Baron. "Sheep to the Slaughter." *Gates of Vienna*. January 8, 2010. http://tiny.cc/n725kx. Accessed 15 December 2011.

Bourdieu, Pierre. *The Logic of Practice*. Translated by Richard Nice. Stanford, Calif.: Stanford University Press, 1990.

Burke, Peter. "Erasmus and the Republic of Letters." *European Review* 7, no. 1 (1999): 5–17.

Burr, Ty. " 'Clay Bird' Intelligently Explores Religious Faith." *Boston Globe*, July 30, 2004. http://tinyurl.com/ntft2dr. Accessed 16 December 2006.

Dalrymple, William. "Inside the Madrasas." *New York Review of Books* 52, no. 19 (December 1, 2005).

——. "A Largely Bourgeois Endeavour: Al Qaida-Style Terrorists Are Not the Type Who Seek Out Madrasas." *Guardian Unlimited*, July 20, 2005. http://tiny.cc/oc35kx. Accessed 10 August 2005.

——. *The Last Mughal: The Fall of a Dynasty, Delhi, 1857*. New York: Knopf, 2006.

Dihlawī, Aḥmad bin ʿAbd al-Raḥīm Shāh Walī Allāh. *Ḥujjat Allāh al-bāligha*. Edited by Saʿīd Aḥmad bin Yūsuf al-Bālanbūrī (Pālanpūrī). 2 vols. Deoband: Maktaba Ḥijāz, 1426AH/2005.

Dubuisson, Daniel. *The Western Construction of Religion: Myths, Knowledge, and Ideology*. Occident et la religion. English. Baltimore, Md.: Johns Hopkins University Press, 2003.

Fair, C. Christine. "Islamic Education in Pakistan." Washington, D.C.: United States Institute of Peace, 2006.

Fārūqī, Muftī Muḥammad Arshad. "Dīnī madāris kī jadīd kārī ʿaṣrī taqāḍun ke āyīne main." *Tarjumān Dārul ʿUlūm*, January 2004, 43–47.

Foucault, Michel. *The Order of Things: An Archaeology of the Human Sciences*. New York: Vintage Books, 1973.

——. *Power/Knowledge: Selected Interviews and Other Writings 1972–1977*. New York: Pantheon Books, 1980.

Foucault, Michel, and Daniel Defert. *Lectures on the Will to Know: Lectures at the Collège de France, 1970–1971; With Oedipal Knowledge*. New York: Palgrave Macmillan, 2013.

Foucault, Michel, and Jay Miskowiec. "Of Other Spaces." *Diacritics* 16, no. 1 (1986): 22–27.

Friedman, Thomas L. "What 7 Republicans Could Do." *New York Times*, July 21, 2010. http://tinyurl.com/n39ubjb. Accessed 10 August 2011.

The Future of the Global Muslim Population: Projections for 2010–2030. Pew-Templeton Global Religious Futures Project, January 2011. http://tinyurl.com/l7bwvxz. Accessed 12 May 2012.

Gangohī, Muḥammad Ḥanīf. *Ẓafarul muḥaṣṣilīn bi aḥwālil muṣannifīn yaʿnī ḥālāt-i muṣannifīn-i dars-i niẓāmī maʿ qurratil ʿuyūn fī tazkiratil funūn maʿiẓāfāt jadīda*. Karachi: Dārul Ishāʿat, 2000.

Ghaurī, Khvāja Azīzulḥasan Majzūb, and ʿAbdulḥaq, *Ashraful savāniḥ*. 4 vols. Multan: Idāra Taʾlīfāt-i Ashrafiyya, 1427/2006.

al-Ghazāli, Abū Ḥāmid Muḥammad b. Muḥammad. *Iḥyāʾ ʿulūm al-dīn*. 5 vols. Beirut: Dār al-Kutub al-ʿIlmīya, 1421/2001.

Ghias, Shoaib A. "Juristic Disagreement: The Collective Fatwā against Islamic Banking in Pakistan." In *Contemporary Islamic Finance: Innovations, Applications, and Best Practices*, edited by Karen Hunt-Ahmed, 103–19: Hoboken, N.J.: John Wiley and Sons, 2013.
Gīlānī, Manāzir Aḥsan. *Iḥāṭa-i Dārul-ʿUlūm main bīte huwe din*. Deoband: Maktaba Ṭayyiba Deoband, c. 1416 AH.
——. *Savāniḥ-i Qāsimī: Yaʿnī sīrat-i Shamsul Islām*. 3 vols. Lahore: Maktaba Raḥmāniyya, 1980.
——. *Tażkira-i haẓrat Shāh Valīyullah: Haẓrat-i mujaddid-i aʿzam kī zindagī aur un kī fikr o naẓar kī tashrīḥ va tavẓīḥ*. Deoband: Ḥāfiẓī Book Depot, 2005.
Goodman, Lenn E. *Jewish and Islamic Philosophy: Crosspollinations in the Classic Age*. Edinburgh: Edinburgh University Press, 1999.
Hamid, Mohsin. *The Reluctant Fundamentalist*. Orlando: Harcourt, 2007.
Hare, David. *The Vertical Hour: A Play*. New York: Faber and Faber, 2006.
Hartung, Jan-Peter, and Helmut Reifeld, eds. *Islamic Education, Diversity and National Identity: Dīnī Madāris in India post 9/11*. New Delhi: Sage Publications, 2006.
Ḥasanī, ʿAbd al-Ḥayy bin Fakhr al-Dīn. *Nuzhat al-khawāṭir wa bahjat al-masāmiʿ wa al-nawāẓir*. 8 vols. Multan and Rae Bareli: Tayyab Academy/Dār ʿArafāt, 1413/1992.
——. (ʿAbd al-Ḥayy, Sayyid). *Yād-i ayyām*. Lucknow: Majlis-i Taḥqīqāt va Nashriyāt-i Islām, 1983.
Hefner, Robert W., and Muhammad Qasim Zaman. *Schooling Islam: The Culture and Politics of Modern Muslim Education*. Princeton Studies in Muslim Politics. Princeton, N.J.: Princeton University Press, 2007.
——, eds. *Schooling Islam: The Culture and Politics of Modern Muslim Education*. Princeton, N.J.: Princeton University Press, 2007.
Hitchens, Christopher. "No Way: John Updike's Latest Novel Reveals His Tin Ear for Critical Times." *Atlantic Monthly*, June 2006, 114–17.
Hodgson, Marshall G. S. *The Venture of Islam: The Classical Age of Islam*. 3 vols. Chicago: University of Chicago Press, 1974.
Ḥusaynī Nadvī, Sayyid Salmān. *Hamāra niṣāb-i taʿlīm kiyā ho*. Lucknow: Jāmiʿa Sayyid Aḥmad Shahīd, 1424/2004.
——. Interview, January 17, 2005.
Ibn ʿArabī, Abū Bakr Muḥī al-Dīn. *al-Futūḥāt al-makkīya*. Edited by Aḥmad Shams al-Dīn. 1st ed. 9 vols. Beirut: Dār al-Kutub al-ʿIlmīya, 1420/1999.
Ibn Khaldūn, ʿAbd al-Raḥmān. *Muqaddimah Ibn Khaldūn*. Edited by Darwīsh al-Juwaydī. Ṣayda [Sida] & Beirut: al-Maktaba al-ʿAṣrīya, 1460/2000.
Ibn Khaldūn. *The Muqaddimah: An Introduction to History*. Translated by Franz Rosenthal. 3 vols. New York: Bollingen Series 43. Princeton, N.J.: Princeton University Press, 1980.
Ibn Manẓūr, Muḥammad b. Mukarram. *Lisān al-ʿarab*. Edited by ʿAbd Allāh ʿAlī al-Kabīr. Cairo: Dār al-Maʿārif, n.d.
Ījī, ʿAḍud al-Dīn ʿAbd al-Raḥmān ibn Aḥmad, with commentary by al-Jurjānī, al-Sayyid al-Sharīf ʿAlī ibn Muḥammad. *Kitāb al-mawāqif*. Edited by ʿAbd al-Raḥmān ʿUmayra. 3 vols. Beirut: Dār al-Jīl, 1417/1997.

Ikram, Sheikh Mohamad. *Mauj-i kauṡar.* 22nd ed. Lahore: Idāra Ṣaqāfat-i Islāmīya, 2003.
Ingram, Brannon D. "The Portable Madrasa: Print, Publics and the Authority of the Deobandi ʿUlama." *Modern Asian Studies* 48, no. 4 (2013): 1–27.
Iqbal, Muhammad. *Āsān kulliyāt-i Iqbāl.* Islamabad: Alhamra Publishing, 2000.
Iṣlāḥī, Ẓafarul Islām. *Taʿlīm ʿahd-i islāmī ke hindūstān main.* Azamgarh: Dārul Muṣannifīn/Shiblī Academy, 2007.
Ismāʿīl, Shāh Muḥammad Shahīd Dihlavī. *Taqwiyatul īmān maʿ tazkīrul ikhwān together with Naṣīḥatul muslimīn by Mawlānā Khurram ʿAlī Balhūrī.* Multān: Kutubkhāna-i Majīdīya, n.d.
——. Shāh Muḥammad Shahīd al-Dihlawī [Dihlavī]. *Abaqāt.* Karachi: al-Majlis al-ʿIlmī, c. 1960.
Jackson, Bruce. "Media and War: Bringing It All Back Home." CounterPunch, http://tinyurl.com/qxhw5m4. Accessed 10 December 2004.
Jāmī, Nūr al-Dīn ʿAbd al-Raḥmān. *al-Fawāʾid al-ḍiyāʾīya sharḥ Kāfiya Ibn al-Ḥājib.* Edited by Usāma Ṭaha al-Rifāʾī. Baghdad: Wazāratul Awqāf wa al-Shu ʾūn al-Dīnīya, 1983.
Jāmiʿat al-ʿUlūm al-Islāmiyya, Rufaqāʾ Dār al-Iftā.ʾ *Murawwaja Islāmī baynkārī:tajziyātī muṭālaʿah, sharʿī jāʾizah, fiqhī naqd-o tabṣara.* Karachi: Maktaba-i Bayyināt, 2008.
Jespersen, Otto. *The Philosophy of Grammar.* Chicago: University of Chicago Press, 1992.
Johnston, Douglas, Azhar Hussain, and Rebecca Cataldi. "Madrasa Enhancement and Global Security: A Model for Faith-Based Engagement." Washington, D.C.: International Center for Religion and Diplomacy, 2008.
Jonson, Ben. *Volpone.* Act 1, Scene 1. In Burns Mantle and John Gassner, *A Treasury of the Theatre: An Anthology of Great Plays from Aeschylus to Eugene O'Neill.* New York: Simon and Schuster, c. 1940.
Kafawī, Abū al-Baqāʾ Ayyūb b. Mūsā al-Ḥusaynī. *al-Kulliyāt: muʿjam fī al-muṣṭalaḥāt wa al-furūq al-lughawīya.* Edited and annotated by ʿAdnān Darwīsh and Muḥammad al-Maṣrī. 2nd ed. Beirut: Muʾassasa al-Risāla, 1419/1998.
Kākā Khel, ʿAdnān. "Muslim Madarsa Students Not Terrorists Part 1." YouTube GeoTv interview, 2008. http://tinyurl.com/m7seey4.
Kashmīrī, Muḥammad Anwar. *Fayḍ al-bārī ʿalā Ṣaḥīḥ al-Bukhārī.* 4 vols. Peshawar: Maktaba Ḥaqqānīya, c. 1357/1938.
Katz, Marion Holmes. *Body of Text: The Emergence of the Sunnī Law of Ritual Purity.* Albany: State University of New York Press, 2002.
Khān, Aḥmad Raẓ̤ā. *al-ʿAṭ̤āyā an-Nabaviyya fī al-fatāvá al-Riẓ̤viyya: Maʿ takhrīj va tarjumah-yi ʿArabī ʿibārāt.* Lahore: Raẓ̤ā Fāʾūnḍeshan: Jāmiʿah-yi Niẓāmiya Riẓ̤viya, 1991–2006.
——. *Malfūẓ-i Mukammal.* Siddhartanagar: Maktaba Qādirīya, 2005.
Khairābādī, Faḍl Imām, *Mirqāt maʿ ḥāshiya jadīda al-Mirʾāt.* Edited by Muḥammad ʿImād al-Dīn al-Ansārī al-Shīrkūtī. Rawalpindi: Kutub Khāna Rashīdīya, n.d.
Khudā Bakhsh Oriyanṭal Pablik Lāʾibrerī, ed. *ʿArabī Islāmī madāris kā niṣāb va niẓām-i taʿlīm aur ʿaṣrī taqāẓ̤e: madarsah sisṭam par 1968 ke Dihlī simīnār kī*

rūdād, maqālāt aur baḥas̱ (Report on the 1968 Delhi seminar on the madrasa system: essays and comments). 4 vols. Paṭna; New Delhi: K͟hudā Bak͟hsh Oriyanṭal Pablik Lā'ibrerī; Taqsīmkār Maktaba-i Jāmiʿa, 1995.
Laknawī, Muḥammad ʿAbd al-Ḥayy. *al-Ajwiba al-fāḍila: lil-as'ila al-ʿashara al-kāmila*. Edited by ʿAbd al-Fattāḥ Abū Ghudda. Ḥalab: Maktab al-Maṭbūʿāt al-Islāmīya, 1964.
——. *al-Fawā'id al-bahīya fī tarājim al-Ḥanafīya*. Benares: Maktaba Nadwatul Maʿārif, 1967.
Lane, Edward William, and Stanley Lane-Poole. *Arabic-English Lexicon* [in English]. 2 vols. Cambridge: Islamic Texts Society, 1984.
Macaulay's Minute on Indian Education. http://tiny.cc/5065kx. Accessed 15 December 2010.
Madrāsī, ʿAbdulkhāliq. "Interview." February 20, 2006.
Mahmood, Hamid. "The *Dars-e-Nizāmī* and the Transnational Traditionalist *Madāris* in Britain." MA thesis, Queen Mary University, University of London, September 2012. http://tiny.cc/5965kx. Accessed 14 June 2013.
Makdisi, George. *The Rise of Humanism in Classical Islam and the Christian West: With Special Reference to Scholasticism*. Edinburgh: Edinburgh University Press, 1990.
Malik, Jamal. *Madrasas in South Asia: Teaching Terror?* Routledge Contemporary South Asia series no. 4. London: Routledge, 2008.
Manṣūrī, Muḥammad ʿĪsā. "Maghrib ka fikrī chaylanj aur ʿulamā'-i kirām kī dhimme dārī." *Daʿwat-i ḥaqq* 2, no. 6–9 (1426/2005): 105–9.
Mantle, Burns, and John Gassner, eds. *A Treasury of the Theatre: An Anthology of Great Plays from Aeschylus to Eugene O'Neill*. New York: Simon and Schuster, 1935.
Maybudhī Ibn Muʿīn al-Dīn, al-Qāḍī Kamāl al-Dīn Ḥusayn. *Sharḥ hidāyat al-ḥikma: al-muḥashshá bi-taḥshiya mufīda*. Edited by al-Mawlawī Anwar ʿAlī and Bilāl Aḥmad. Delhi & Multan: al-Maṭbaʿa al-Mujtabāʾī/Kutubkhāna Majīdīya, 1334/1916.
Maẓharī, Wāris. "Fudẕalā' madāris awr maʿāsh ka mas'ala." *Daʿwat-i ḥaqq* 2, no. 6–9 (1426/2005): 199–206.
——. *Hindūstānī madāris ka taʿlīmī niẓām aur us main iṣlāḥ kī ẕarūrat: Īk jā'iza*. New Delhi: Global Media Publications, 2014.
McNeely, Ian F., and Lisa Wolverton. *Reinventing Knowledge: From Alexandria to the Internet*. New York: W. W. Norton, 2008.
Mendenhall, Preston. "Pakistan's Religious Schools in Spotlight Again: Crackdown Ordered, but Madrassas Promise Backlash of Hatred." *MSNBC*, July 25 2005. http://tinyurl.com/kxquf87. Accessed 6 September 2006.
Miṣbāḥī, Yāsīn Akhtar. *Qur'ān awr jihād*. Delhi: Dār al-Qalam, 1426/2005.
Moosa, Ebrahim. *Ghazali and the Poetics of Imagination*. Chapel Hill: University of North Carolina Press, 2005.
Nadvī, Muḥammad Shahābuddīn. *Jadīd ʿilm-i kalām Qur'ān aur sā'ins kī raushnī men̲*. Bangalore: Furqāniyah Ikaiḍamī Ṭrasṭ, 1989/1409.
Nadvī, Munavvar Sulṭān. *Nadvatulʿulamā' kā fiqhī mizāj aur abnāi' Nadvah kī fiqhī k͟hidmāt*. Lucknow: ʿAllāmah Sayyid Sulaimān Nadvī Akaiḍamī, 2005.

Nanautvī, Muḥammad Yaʿqūb. "Savanih-e ʿumri." In *Savanih-i Qasimi, ya'ni Sirat-i Shamsul Islam*, edited by Manāẓir Aḥsan Gīlānī. 23–48. Lahore: Maktaba-i Rahmanīya, c. 1980.

The News, "Ulema Open Their Heart to MPs on Terror," October 10, 2008. http://tinyurl.com/oeld7wr. Accessed 6 June 2009.

Nīsābūrī, Abū al-Ḥusayn Muslim bin al-Ḥajjāj. *Ṣaḥīḥ Muslim bi Sharḥ al-Nawawī*. Edited byʿIsām al-Ṣabābiṭī, Ḥāzim Muḥammad, and ʿImād ʿĀmir.1st ed. 9 vols. Cairo: Dār Abī Ḥayyān, 1415/1995.

Nizami, Farhan Ahmad. "Madrasahs, Scholars and Saints: Muslim Response to the British Presence in Delhi and the Upper Doab 1803–1857." PhD diss., Oxford University, 1983.

Nuʿmānī, Muḥammad Shiblī. "Mulla Niẓām al-Dīn ʿalayhi al-raḥma." In *Maqālāt-i Shiblī*, edited by Sayyid Sulaymān Nadvī. 8 vols. Vol. 3, 91–101. Azamgarh: Dārul Muṣannifīn, 1375/1955.

"Pakistan and India: A Rivalry That Threatens the World." *The Economist*, May 19, 2011. http://tiny.cc/d775kx. Accessed 16 July 2012.

Qannūwjī, Muḥammad Ṣiddīq bin Ḥasan. *Abjad al-ʿulūm: al-washī al-marqūm fī bayān aḥwāl al-ʿulūm*. Edited by ʿAbd al-Jabbār Zakkār. 3 vols. Damascus: Wizārat- al-thaqāfa wa al-Irshād al-Qawmī/Dār al-Kutub al-ʿIlmīya, 1978.

Qaraḍāwī, ʿAbd al-Rahman. "Risāla ʿAbd al-Raḥmān al-Qaraḍāwī ilā abīhi Yūsuf al- Qaraḍāwī." http://tinyurl.com/oedjr72. Accessed 15 September 2013.

Qāsmī, Muḥammad Aslam. "Do bātyn̠: dīnī madāris ke z̠immedārvn̠ se." *ʿIlmī ṣadá* 2 (2003): 61–65, 77.

Raḥmān, Ḥaqīqur. "Ahl-i madāris ko ʿaṣrī taʿlīm ka mashwara nā wāqifiyat par mabnī." *Riyāz̠yul jannat*, 2005, 38–42.

Reetz, Dietrich, "Change and Stagnation in Islamic Education." In *The Madrasa in Asia: Political Activism and Transnational Linkages*, edited by Farish A. Noor, Yoginder Sikand, and Martin van Bruinessen, 71–104. Amsterdam: Amsterdam University Press, 2008.

Rezavi, S. Ali Nadeem. "Physicians as Professionals in Medieval India." In *Disease and Medicine in India: A Historical Overview*, edited by Deepak Kumar, 40–65. Aligarh: Indian History Congress; Tulika, 2001.

Robinson, Francis. *The ʿUlama of Farangi Mahall and Islamic Culture in South Asia*. New Delhi: Permanent Black, 2001.

Rose, Charlie. "The Charlie Rose Show: Interview with Donald Rumsfeld." *The Charlie Rose Show*, transcript dated August 20, 2005.

Rosenthal, Franz. *Knowledge Triumphant: The Concept of Knowledge in Medieval Islam*. Leiden: Brill, 1970.

Sanyal, Usha. *Devotional Islam and Politics in British India: Ahmad Riza Khan Barelwi and His Movement, 1870–1920*. Delhi: Oxford University Press, 1999.

Shāfiʿī, Muḥammad b. Idrīs. *Dīwān al-imām al-Shāfiʿī*. Edited by ʿAbd al-Raḥmān al-Muṣṭāwī. Beirut: Dār al-Maʿrifah, 2005.

Shāhin, Rahīm Bakhsh, and Muhammad Iqbal. *Aurāq-i gum gashtah*. Lahore: Islamic Publications,1975.

Sharar, Abdul Halim. *Lucknow, the Last Phase of an Oriental Culture*. Edited by E. S. Harcourt and Fakhir Hussain. Delhi: Oxford University Press, 1989.

Shāṭibī, Abū Isḥāq. *al-Muwāfaqāt fī uṣūl al-sharīʿa*. Edited by ʿAbd Allāh Darāz. 4 vols. Beirut: Dār al-Maʿrifa, n.d.

Sikand, Yoginder. *Bastions of the Believers: Madrasas and Islamic Education in India*. Delhi: Penguin, 2005.

Stern, Jessica. "Pakistan's Jihad Culture." *Foreign Affairs* 79, no. 6 (November–December 2000): 115–26.

Tahānawī, Muḥammad ʿAlī (Aʿlā). *Mawsūʿa kashshāf iṣṭilāḥāt al-funūn wa al-ʿulūm*. Edited by Rafīq al-ʿAjam. 2 vols. Beirut: Maktaba Lubnan, 1996.

Ṭaḥāwī, Aḥmad ibn Muḥammad, *Sharḥ Maʿānī al-āthār*. Edited by Ibrāhīm Shams al-Dīn. 4 vols. Beirut: Manshūrāt Muḥammad ʿAlī Bayḍūn, Dār al-Kutub al-ʿIlmīya, 2001.

Tareen, Sherali. "The Polemic of Shahjahanpur: Religion, Miracles, and History." *Islamic Studies* 51 (2012): 49–67.

Ṭayyab, Qārī Muḥammad. *Shakhṣiyāt va tavārīkh ḥakīmul islām: Silsila-i taʾlifāt va ifādāt-i ḥakīmulislām haẓrat mawlānā qārī Muḥammad Ṭayyab ṣāḥeb mohtamīm-i sābiʿ dārul ʿulūm deoband: taḥqīqāt-i ḥakīmul islām*. Edited and compiled by Muḥammad ʿImrān Qāsmī Bigyānvī. 7 vols, New Delhi: Farid Book Depot, 2006.

——. *ʿUlamāʾ-i Deoband ka dīnī rukh aur maslakī mizāj*. Deoband: Maktaba-i Millat, c. 1990.

Thānvī, Ashraf ʿAlī. *al-ʿIlm val ʿulamā*. Edited and compiled by Muḥammad Zayd Mazāhirī Nadvī. Bānda: Idāra-i Ifādāt-i Ashrafiyya, 1410/c. 1989.

——. *Arvāḥ-i s̤alās̤ah: al-maʿrūf bah ḥikāyāt-i auliyāʾ*. Edited by Amīr Shāh Khān and Qārī Muḥammad Ṭayyab. Deoband: Kutub Khāna Naʿīmīya, n.d.

——. *Malfūzāt-i ḥakīmul ummat*. Edited by Mawlānā Shāh Abrār al-Ḥaqq, Muftī Jamīl Aḥmad Thānvī, and Dr. ʿAbd al-Ḥayy. 25 vols. Multan: Idāra-i Taʾlīfāt-i Ashrafiyya, 1416/1995.

ʿUsmānī, Muḥammad Taqī. "Barr-i ṣaghīr ke madāris." *ʿIlmī ṣadā: dīnī madāris nambar* 2, no. 4 (October 2003): 9–12.

——. *Ghayr sūdī baynkārī: mutaʿalliqa fiqhī masāʾil kī taḥqīq aur ishkālāt ka jāʾiza*. Karachi: Maktaba Ma ʿārif al-Qurʾān, 2009.

——. *Hamārā taʿlīmī niẓām*. Deoband: Zamzam Book Depot, 1995.

Walsh, Declan. Pakistan to expel foreign students in crackdown. The Guardian, July 29, 2005. http://tinyurl.com/myydcl4. Accessed 14 August 2006.

Winkelmann, Mareike. *"From Behind the Curtain": A Study of a Girls' Madrasa in India*. Amsterdam: Amsterdam University Press, 2005.

——. " 'Inside and Outside' in a Girls' Madrasa in New Delhi." In *The Madrasa in Asia: Political Activism and Transnational Linkages*, edited by Farish A. Noor, Yoginder Sikand, and Martin van Bruinessen, 105–22. Amsterdam: Amsterdam University Press, 2008.

Winthrop, Rebecca, and Corinne Graff. "Beyond Madrasas: Assessing the Links between Education and Militancy in Pakistan." In *Working Paper 2*: Center for Universal Education at Brookings, 2010. http://tinyurl.com/lsrfnea. Accessed 15 Aug 2014.

Zaman, Muhammad Qasim. *Ashraf ʿAli Thanawi*. Oxford: Oneworld, 2008.
———. "Commentaries, Print and Patronage: 'Ḥadīth' and the Madrasas in Modern South Asia." *Bulletin of the School of Oriental and African Studies, University of London* 62, no. 1 (1999): 60–81.
———. *Modern Islamic Thought in a Radical Age [electronic resource]: Religious Authority and Internal Criticism*. Cambridge: Cambridge University Press, 2012.
———. "The ʿUlama of Contemporary Islam and Their Conceptions of the Common Good." In *Public Islam and the Common Good*, edited by Armando Salvatore and Dale F. Eickelman, 129–55. Leiden: Brill, 2004.
Ziad, Waleed. "How the Holy Warriors Learned to Hate," *New York Times*, June 14, 2004. http://tinyurl.com/mb2z9ln. Accessed 10 November 2005.

Acknowledgments

I owe many debts to several people and institutions. I want to thank the Carnegie Corporation of New York for its generous Scholars Program grant that made this research possible. I especially want to thank Patricia Rosenfield, Vartan Gregorian, and Hilary Wiener for their support and guidance at different stages of this research and writing.

My colleagues at Duke University in the Department of Religious Studies were always encouraging. I want to thank Bruce B. Lawrence for his encouragement at an early stage, reading drafts and providing me with valuable feedback on the manuscript. Carl Ernst at the University of North Carolina at Chapel Hill strongly supported this project, and I thank him for his friendship and humanity. Orin Starn also read early drafts and provided advice; Engseng Ho has been an invaluable interlocutor and a sounding board for ideas. Srinivas Aravamudan is a good listener and compassionate adviser. Leela Prasad has throughout been a pillar of support. She tirelessly read drafts, provided feedback, and listened carefully to my anguish as she guided me through the writing process. My gratitude to her will always be deficient. Waris Mazhari has been an extraordinary friend, whose generous help and resources considerably lightened my burden. Scott Appleby at the University of Notre Dame's Kroc Institute is my friend for nearly a decade and now a colleague with whom I begin a new collaboration.

Brandon Yusuf Toropov, SherAli Tareen, Brannon Ingram, and Amir Hussain read the entire manuscript and gave valuable feedback. Ali Mian generously provided research support over the years and insightful feedback. Youshaa Patel, Brett Wilson, Saadia Yacoob, Mashal Saif, Nadia Inji Khan, Zaid Adhami, Daanish Faruqi, Sohaib Khan, Manzarul Islam, and Hunter Bandy at various stages provided me with help and research assistance. Sam Kigar not only tirelessly provided editorial support but also carefully prepared the graphics and the index. I want to thank two anonymous press reviewers for their valuable and productive feedback. All shortcomings are mine alone.

Close friendships and interlocutors sustained, inspired, and enriched me over the years. To Muneer Fareed, Rashied Omar, Sherman A. Jackson, Mohammad Fadel, Shamil Jeppie, Abdulaziz Sachedina, Ahmad Dallal, Richard C. Martin, Marcia Hermansen, Muhammad Qasim Zaman, Abdulkader Tayob, Saʿdiyya Shaikh, Abdul-Aleem Somers, Talal Asad, Muhammad Khalid Masud, Shabbir Banoobai, Zafar Malik, Ziauddin Sardar, Parvez Manzoor, Shuaib Manjra, Ahmad Manjra, Faizel Dawjee, Mohammed Saeed Kagee, Aslam Fataar, Ebrahim Rasool, Rosieda Shabodien, Kecia Ali, Hina Azam, and to countless others, I owe an immense debt of gratitude. Elaine Maisner, my editor at UNC Press, always treated me as her valued author, and I am grateful for her unwavering support and encouragement throughout the process. My thanks to Allison Shay and Paul Betz for editorial and production support, and to Ellen Lohman and Melody Negron whose excellent copyediting saved me from many infelicities.

My siblings, Sulaiman, Aisha, Nazeema, Faizel, and Zayboenisa, sustain me in multiple ways, as do my brothers-in-law, Sedick, Yusuf, and Nasier Pandit, and their families.

My wife, Nisa, is the gentle force in my life. Her love, care, and generosity are unrivaled. Lamya and Shibli are now adults who have reached memorable milestones, and their abiding love sustains us.

Index

Abbasids, 149
ʿAbdulhayy (of Lucknow), 90–92
Absolutism, 105
Abu Bakr (caliph), 170, 210
Abu Hanifa, 30, 106, 153, 157, 158
Academics. *See* Curriculum, madrasa; Disciplines, academic; Madrasas; Teachers
Adab, 48, 191, 255. *See also* Arabic: literature; Literature; Persian: culture
Adhan. *See* Call to prayer
Afghanistan, 79, 117, 207, 209–11, 212; Cold War and, 2; curriculum of, 136, 139; future of, 239; political Islam and, 25, 166; U.S. war in, 6, 7, 52, 164, 176, 233, 234, 247
Af-Pak region, 233–34, 235, 239. *See also* Afghanistan; Pakistan
Africa: Islamic orthodoxy in, 9; madrasas in, 2, 3; Muslim communities in, 234. *See also* South Africa
African National Congress, 24
Ahl-i Hadith, 67, 77, 90, 107, 136, 139, 223; history of madrasas, 49; law and, 195–96; orthodoxy and, 9; Taliban and, 211; theology of, 92, 97, 107
Ahmad, Sayyid (of Rae Bareli), 92, 96–98
ʿAʾisha (wife of the Prophet Muhammad), 174, 217
Alchemy, 6
Alcohol, 6, 65
Algebra, 5, 6
ʿAli (caliph), 210
ʿAli, ʿAbdul, 86–90
ʿAli, Mamlukul, 102–3
Aligarh Muslim University, 135, 202
ʿAlimiyya program, 20, 26, 162, 241, 255
Allah, 18, 34, 39, 77, 116, 148; mercy of, 36; Prophet Muhammad and, 95, 238, 244. *See also* God
Amulets, 92
Angels, 38, 93, 94, 185, 201
Anglo culture, 20, 88
Al-Ansari, Abu Ayyub, 79, 170
Al-Ansari, Muhibullah, 87, 112
Apprenticeship, 57–59, 67, 84, 121, 125–26, 152, 187
Arabic, 3, 6, 16, 22, 34, 116, 119, 120, 179, 180, 183, 192, 198, 244, 261 (n. 30), 262 (n. 1); author's experience with, 20–21, 45, 109; grammar, 45, 109, 110, 112, 114, 115, 117, 118, 132, 162, 243, 262 (n. 31); instruction, 2, 3, 54, 55, 109, 110, 112, 117, 132, 135–37, 139, 151, 154, 162, 177, 221, 228, 262 (n. 31); literature, 98, 102, 132, 163, 169, 176, 191, 223, 243; liturgy, 36, 42, 148; media, 28, 245; scholarship in, 103, 111, 122, 123, 135–36; scripture and, 63, 180; speaking world, 27, 122–23, 212–13
Arabs, 16, 25, 27, 90, 97, 100, 149, 178, 236
Arab Spring, 25, 105, 110, 122
Asad, Muhammad, 28
Asceticism, 202. *See also* Monasticism
Ashʿari, 106, 107, 113. *See also* Theology
Atheism, 200. *See also* Unbelief
Aurangzeb (emperor), 82, 227, 228–29, 230–31

Authority, 266 (n. 1); colonial, 68; competition and, 106; Euro-American, 237; of hadith, 91, 119, 146, 155, 156, 175; juristic, 90, 100, 126, 196; of law schools, 192, 195, 196; moral, 51, 57, 238; political, 51; of Qur'an, 90, 146; saintly, 107; scholarly, 9–10, 22, 26, 51, 54, 60–61, 72, 74, 79–80, 136, 138, 140, 141, 149, 159, 160, 192, 193, 202, 203, 225, 226, 230, 231, 235–36, 238, 252; of states, 142, 237; of teachers, 58; tradition and, 222–24
Autodidactism, 24, 59, 125–26
Al-Azhar University, 28, 109

Baghdad, 149; Mongol sack of, 112, 124
Bangladesh: civil war of, 216, 217; creation of, 27, 168; government of, 136, 213; madrasas in, 2, 8, 11, 34, 56, 136, 155, 220, 248; population of, 236; sectarianism in, 100; Sufism in, 85, 168
Banking, 10, 145
Al-Banna, Hasan, 25
Barelvi school, 28, 67, 77, 136, 139, 151, 166, 170, 173, 196, 216, 223; Deobandis and, 100, 101, 104–5, 106–7, 165, 166, 216; orthodoxy and, 9, 147, 196; Taliban and, 211
Al-Basri, Abu Bakr, 149
Battle of Uhud, 171–74
Beatles, 264 (n. 38)
Beliefs, religious, 92, 183, 188, 210, 237; knowledge and, 177; orthodoxy and, 9, 65, 106, 113, 133; popular, 93; private, 194; Prophet Muhammad and, 69; reform of, 57, 93; shared between faith traditions, 38. *See also* Faith; Theology; Unbelief
Bilgrami, ʿAbd al-Wahid, 116, 117
Bin Laden, Osama, 1, 11, 209
Binnawri, Yusuf, 138–39
Blair, Tony, 2, 214–15
Blasphemy, 68–69, 73, 165–66, 172–73, 238
Body, human, 183, 192, 194, 255; intentionality and, 35, 42; knowledge and, 46, 181, 186, 187–89; purity and, 155; Qur'an and, 63; ritual and, 33, 35; of women, 173
Bombay. *See* Mumbai
Buddhism, 6, 32, 38, 210, 238
Al-Bukhari, Muhammad bin Ismaʿil, 147, 149–50, 163, 170–73, 247
Burqa, 160–61, 255
Bush, George W., 2, 52, 234

Caliphate, 72, 210
Call to prayer, 34–35, 73, 255
Canada, 8, 213
Cape Town, 15–17, 26, 236, 242. *See also* South Africa
Chai, 19, 40, 44, 176
Chishti Sufi order, 81, 85, 103
Christianity, 6, 16, 33, 68, 104, 198, 209, 213
Citizenship, 11, 122, 140, 141, 220
Civics, study of, 132, 163, 202
Clash of civilizations, 8, 142, 207–8, 209, 213
Clay Bird, The (film), 216–18
Colonialism, 5, 134, 200, 237; anticolonialism and, 21, 68, 72, 97–98, 103, 105, 133–34, 238; French, 88; in India, 19, 24, 29, 51, 61, 68, 77, 89, 92, 98, 122, 127, 135, 197, 231, 237
Commentaries, 122, 129–30, 133; hadith, 103, 149–50; legal, 87, 119; lessons as, 155, 213; Qur'anic, 2, 148. *See also* Qur'an: exegesis of; Texts
Community, 4, 9, 57, 65, 112, 155, 183–84; of learning, 108, 109, 122–25, 127, 128; mosque, 52, 55, 202; South Asian, 100, 234, 236
—madrasa, 8, 134, 139, 165, 175, 239; contemporary pressures on, 136, 141, 176, 219, 220, 226, 229, 231; critique of United States, 12, 164; sense of, 45; view of knowledge, 61, 64, 177, 186, 201

—Muslim, 69, 135, 148, 151, 181, 220, 234, 235, 238, 241, 246, 248; diversity of, 164, 184, 251; early, 171, 210; orthodox, 138; reform of, 224; views of knowledge, 58; views of madrasas, 74, 234; in the West, 53
Companions of the Prophet Muhammad, 34, 64, 67, 68, 79, 85, 111, 148, 170, 171, 172, 238, 244
Cosmography, 183
Cosmology, 56, 64–65, 91
Cosmopolitanism, 10; American, 212; knowledge, 120, 134, 226, 230, 231, 232; Muslims, 72, 220, 222, 223
Council of Scholars. *See* Nadwatul ʿUlama
Counter-utopia, 200
Curriculum, madrasa, 22, 108–9, 119, 175; contemporary controversy over, 74, 122, 133–36, 177, 219–20; historical shifts in, 120–21, 132; for women, 162–63; modern debates over, 135–36, 139, 222–24; Nizami, 23, 28, 84, 108–9, 111, 122, 126–31, 138; reform of, 47, 51, 121, 122, 177, 219–20, 221, 229; subjects excluded from, 56, 175, 224. *See also* Education: religious and secular
Cyber. *See* Internet; Technology

Darul Uloom Deoband, 78, 176, 243, 244, 245, 246; author's experience at, 21, 26, 242; establishment of, 49, 97, 103–4; infrastructure of, 177; mosque at, 39; reforms at, 47–48; routines at, 38, 44. *See also* Deoband school
Darul Uloom Matliwala, 20, 218, 242
Darul Uloom Nadwatul ʿUlama, 27–28, 173, 195, 201, 242. *See also* Nadwatul ʿUlama
Daʿwa, 17, 18, 54–55, 162, 255
Decline narrative, of Islam, 5–6, 51, 57
Delhi, 17, 56, 72, 78, 85, 92, 94, 96, 98, 102, 103, 162, 163, 260 (n. 3)
Deoband school, 66–67; Ahl-i Hadith and, 136, 223; Barelvis and, 106–7, 136, 165, 166, 197, 216; founders of, 68, 134, 146, 248; leading authorities of, 44, 61, 68, 72, 73, 139, 145, 163, 165, 198, 199, 221, 223, 238; madrasas, 8, 38, 49, 67, 97, 106, 151, 215; Nadwatul ʿUlama and, 27, 28; orthodoxy, 9, 139, 210; social norms of, 26, 27; Tablighi Jamaʿat and, 17, 147, 216; Taliban and, 211; terrorism and, 210, 215; theological views of, 18, 100–101, 104–5, 106–7, 136, 166, 198. *See also* Darul Uloom Deoband
Derrida, Jacques, 118
Din, 53, 54, 58, 61–62, 69, 194, 255. *See also* Practice, religious; Salvation
Disciplines, academic, 2, 80, 121, 124, 127, 129, 136; distinctions between, 67, 83, 84, 86, 109–10, 118, 124, 130–32, 184, 222; faith-related, 20, 49–50, 132, 140; modern, 51, 73–74, 132, 135, 137, 139, 140, 199, 219, 224; rational, 84, 86, 130–31; specialization in, 77, 138; Western, 51, 133. *See also* Arabic: instruction; Curriculum, madrasa; Islamic law: study of; Philosophy: study of; Qurʾan; Theology: study of
Dogmatism, 134, 212, 221, 242
Dormitories, 45
Douglass, Frederick, 96
Dress, 26, 28, 66, 159–60, 170, 210, 221, 226, 243, 255
Drones, 234. *See also* War

East India Company, 88, 89–90
Eating, 19, 27, 41–42, 155, 156; abstinence from, 41, 180
Economics, 232; Islamic law and, 119; study of, 28, 175, 202, 224
Education, 40, 192–93, 199, 219, 222, 227; childhood, 74, 102, 228; women and, 210, 237

—national: American, 6; Indian, 54, 138, 170; Indonesian, 146; Pakistani, 54; phases of, on Indian Subcontinent, 127–28; South African, 17
—religious and secular: compound system of, 47–48, 202–3, 221–22, 227, 230, 231; Islamic, 27, 28, 29, 48, 57, 59, 127–28, 139, 141, 154, 175, 187, 190–92, 218, 221, 227, 245; liberal, 65, 212; modern, 127, 198, 200, 202, 203, 219, 221, 224–27; Muslim identity and, 220–22, 237; secular, 3, 47, 48, 65, 161–62, 201, 202, 203, 210, 221–24, 237
Embodiment. *See* Body, human
England. *See* United Kingdom
English, study of, 28, 65, 132, 133–34, 137, 163, 223–34
Epistemology, 182. *See also* Knowledge
Ethics, 35, 36, 123, 173, 177–78, 188, 191, 199, 232, 264 (n. 26); biological, 29; Islamic law as, 22, 23, 28, 49, 145, 192, 238; madrasas and, 10, 11, 65–66, 126, 163, 164, 175, 242, 260 (n. 3); Qurʾan and, 193; social context of, 28, 73; terrorists and, 7; ʿulama and, 235. *See also* Islamic law; Morality
Evangelism. See *Daʿwa*
Exegesis. *See* Qurʾan: exegesis of
Extremism, religious, 4, 11, 207, 209, 214–15, 237, 265. *See also* Terrorism

Faith, 36, 137, 175, 194–95, 238; author's journey of, 15–16, 18–19, 22, 242; declaration of, 116–17; education in matters of, 3, 10, 31, 110, 132–33; in God, 172, 179, 238; Islam as, 6, 7, 11, 43, 52–53, 55, 61, 97, 106, 113, 149, 150, 155, 162, 177, 207, 220; knowledge and, 9, 31, 57, 177, 181, 184, 187–88, 193–95, 196, 199–200, 201, 222, 224; other than Islam, 54, 65, 68, 97, 104, 198–99; theological discussions of, 182. *See also* Beliefs, religious; Salvation; Theology
Farangi Mahall, 77–84, 86, 87, 90, 92, 105; key scholars in, 80
Fast. *See* Eating: abstinence from; Ramadan
Fatehpuri, Kamaluddin, 86–87
Fatima (daughter of the Prophet Muhammad), 17
Fatwa, 145, 196; definition of, 152, 255; online, 231; specific examples of, 53, 98; as teaching tools, 122
Fiqh. *See* Islamic law
Five Pillars of Islam, 18, 41, 213, 220
Food. *See* Eating
Friedman, Thomas, 213–14

Gandhi, Indira, 15
Gandhi, Mahatma, 72, 105
Gangohi, Mahmood, 126
Gangohi, Rashid Ahmad, 101–4, 262 (n. 32)
Gates of Vienna (website), 213
Gender segregation, 146, 159–60, 163, 174, 225. See also *Purda*
Al-Ghazali, Abu Hamid, 19, 51, 183–84, 198–99, 201, 223
Gilani, Manazir Ahsan, 69, 72, 138–39
Globalization, 5, 10, 136, 141–42, 175, 237, 240
God, vi, 32, 33, 34–35, 45, 53, 54, 57, 63, 64, 67, 69, 77, 81, 92, 97, 105, 110, 112, 191, 192, 237, 242; attributes of, 106, 257; Christian views of, 16, 97; commandments of, 32, 46; declaration of faith and, 18, 39, 116; defense of, 150, 238; generosity of, 90, 133; giving thanks to, 42, 62; justice and, 19, 113; knowledge and, 60, 61, 178, 179, 180–81, 184, 185, 194, 195, 198, 201; love and, 148; power of, 93–94, 98–99; praise of, 36, 37, 38, 39, 111; Prophet Muhammad and, 93, 95, 98–99, 104, 116, 148, 156, 171, 237, 238, 244; remembrance of, 10, 18, 65; trust in, 172; truth of, 68; will of, 62, 113, 193. *See also* Allah

Hadith, 23, 37, 79, 90, 151, 152, 164, 170, 175, 181–82, 255; canonical Sunni books, 103, 147, 149–50, 163, 170, 173; collection and verification of, 91, 148; Qur'an interpretation and, 153, 171–72; status in South Asian madrasas, 145–48; study of, 49, 67, 72, 118–20, 131–32, 137, 138, 145–48, 151, 156, 159, 164, 174–75, 252; Western criticism of, 149, 213; women and, 159. See also *Sunna*
Hajj. *See* Pilgrimage
Hamdani, Mohammad Salman, 7
Hamid, Mohsen, 5–6
Hanafi school, 9, 30, 87, 90–91, 107, 119, 139, 153–56, 158, 163. *See also* Abu Hanifa; Islamic law: schools of
Hanbal, Ahmad b., 30
Hanbali school, 30, 119
Hasan, Mahmud, 68–69, 72, 73, 199, 238
Health care. *See* Medicine
Hifz, 19–20. *See also* Qur'an: memorization of
Hijab. *See* Burqa; Veil
Hijra, 41
Hinduism, 6, 18–19, 32, 38, 48, 64, 68, 96, 104, 138, 150, 168, 238
History, study of, 27, 48, 50–51, 90, 121, 123, 135, 137, 188, 202
Homosexuality, 21
Human beings, 94, 111, 158, 183, 252; abilities of, 188–90; agency and, 104–5, 106, 113; integrity of, 238; knowledge and, 180–81, 185, 186–87, 188, 194; potential of, 124, 178, 183–84, 191; relationship with God, 93; relationship with other existents, 35, 185, 186–87; sociability, 48, 124, 240
Humanities, 5, 50, 56, 79, 83, 123, 137, 140, 141, 191, 213, 242, 250–52
Human rights, 29, 239
Husayn, Haji Muhammad ʿAbid, 49, 103–4
Ibn Abdulwahhab, Muhammad, 97–98. *See also* Wahhabism
Ibn ʿArabi, 32, 81, 82, 260 (n. 4)
Ibn al-Hajib, ʿUthman b. ʿUmar, 114–18
Ibn Hazm, 125–26
Ibn Khaldun, ʿAbd al-Rahman, 49–50, 51, 124, 139, 188–91
ʿId al-Adha, 41, 102
Iji, ʿAdud al-Din, 113, 184
Ijtihad, 23, 95, 164, 255 (n. 17), 261 (n. 17). *See also* Islamic law: interpretation and
ʿIlm. *See* Knowledge
Ilyas, Muhammad, 17–18, 105
Imagination: cultural, 180, 207, 212; religious, 9, 127
Imams, 37, 53, 55, 64, 137, 151, 160, 202, 203, 213, 256
Imdadullah, Haji, 102–3, 188, 198
India: colonial history of, 25, 61, 77–78, 91–92, 96–97, 100–104, 122–23, 237; connections to other regions, 150, 181; education in, 127–28, 134–36, 138, 195; Islamic law in, 119; language in 27, 154–55; modern politics of, 48, 213, 215, 239; northern region of, 100, 102, 168–70; precolonial history of, 6, 227. *See also* Indo-Pak Subcontinent; South Asia
Indian National Congress, 72
Indonesia, 2, 19, 145–46, 214, 236
Indo-Pak Subcontinent, 32–33, 216; history of, 27, 89, 97, 127, 150, 168; Islamic geography of, 1, 78; Islam in, 18, 82, 92, 94, 145, 155, 195, 199; madrasas in, 8, 47, 101, 105, 159, 166, 175; politics in, 8, 25. *See also* India; Pakistan; South Asia
Innovation: in education, 50, 59, 83; in knowledge, 48, 130, 230, 251; resistance to, 51. *See also* Education; Knowledge
Intentionality, 35–36, 62, 116
Intercultural dialogue, 175, 236, 238, 239

Internet, 55, 59–60, 141, 231, 235, 245
Interpretation. *See* Qur'an: exegesis of
Iqbal, Muhammad, vi, 203, 227, 229–30, 251
Iran, 2, 25, 108, 111, 117, 130, 152, 207
Iraq, 26, 207, 209; militant rebels in, 25; premodern history of, 124, 153; U.S. war in, 7, 52, 174, 212, 233–34, 239, 247, 248
Islam: authenticity and, 138, 210, 231; as civilization, 6, 135, 221; egalitarianism of, 174; as faith tradition, 52, 150, 207; geography of, 1, 124; as ideology, 24, 208; as political order, 97; premodern history of, 124, 171–72, 173; relationship with other faiths, 54, 65, 68, 104; Western views of, 5, 7–8, 10–11, 207–9, 211–16, 218. *See also* Political Islam
Islamic banking. *See* Banking
Islamic law, 153; changes to, 192; definition of, 23, 255, 257; draconian uses of, 210, 217; interpretation and, 164, 174–75, 261 (n. 17); moral categories of, 158, 159; reverence for, 238; schools of, 30, 63–64, 90, 119, 124–25, 192, 195–96, 256; scripturalism and, 192; states and, 24; study of, 11, 22, 28, 49, 53, 84, 118–19, 132, 137–38, 140, 151–59, 162–63, 191. *See also* Ethics; Fatwa; Morality
Islamic revival, 17, 23, 25, 147
Islamic State in Iraq and Syria, 248
Islamophobia, 7, 15–16, 207–8, 211–16, 226–27, 234
Isma'il, Shah Muhammad, 92–94, 96–99, 100, 101, 111, 178

Jahiliyya, 24, 256
Jainism, 5
Jamat-i Islami, 24–25, 139
Al-Jami', 'Abd al-Rahman, 117–18
Jami'a Millia Islamia, 199
Jami'a Naeemia, 165–67
Jihad, 61, 78, 96–98, 150, 211, 213, 215–16, 256. *See also* Terrorism; War
Judaism, 5, 16, 28
Al-Jurjani, Mir Sayyid Sharif, 113–14, 178, 184, 187

Kalima, 116–17
Kant, Immanuel, 123, 182, 186
Karzai, Hamid, 214
Kashmir, 164, 215, 239, 265 (n. 13)
Kashmiri, Akram, 163–64
Kashmiri, Anwar Shah, 72, 138–39
Khairabadi, Fazl-i Haqq, 98–100, 101, 104
Khairabadi, Fazl-i Imam, 112, 184
Khairabadi school, 98–100, 101, 104
Khan, Ahmad Raza, 49, 100–101, 104, 172, 195, 196–97
Khan, Sayyid Ahmad, 134–35
Khomeini (Ayatollah), 152
Knowledge, 39, 45–46, 48–52, 130, 177, 181, 232, 255; classification of, 182, 183, 199–200; compensation and, 53; defense of, 140, 150–51, 260 (n. 12); definition of, 60, 177–81, 184–85; faith and, 6, 9, 31, 51, 53, 57, 133, 177, 184, 194–96; illumination and, 46, 61, 64, 197–98; information and, 32, 193–94, 197–98; knower and, 56, 58–59, 60, 61–62, 127, 184–87; modern, 50, 56, 73, 130, 134–35, 164, 252; morality and, 39, 129, 191; obligation to acquire, 178; politics of, 8–9, 190; practice and, 66, 126, 187–91; salvation and, 8–9, 48–49, 53, 56, 58, 61–62, 64–65, 73–74, 194–96, 199, 222; sources of, 79–80, 120; status and, 9, 21, 40, 56–57, 150–51; subjective, 181; transmission of, 58–60, 67, 125, 189; Western, 51, 123–24, 232; worldly, 48–49, 73–74, 140, 176, 177, 199–203, 251
Kurdi, Tahir bin Ibrahim, 181–82
Kurta, 26, 28, 243, 256. *See also* Dress

Lahore, 1, 27, 38, 56, 160, 162–63, 165–66, 223, 265 (n. 13)
Law. *See* Islamic law
Learning. *See* Community; Curriculum, madrasa; Education; Madrasas; Teachers
Linguistic philosophy. *See* Philosophy: language
Literature, 176, 189, 191; English, 28; study of, 2, 80, 102, 110, 121, 124, 132, 162–63, 213. See also *Adab*
Liturgy, 19, 32, 36–38, 42–43. *See also* Qur'an
Logic, 79, 80, 86, 90, 98, 169, 184, 198–99; study of, 2, 84, 110, 124, 127, 130–32, 163, 178, 182
Love, 69, 73, 148, 172, 183, 192, 217, 242, 244
Lucknow, 27, 28, 49, 77, 78, 82, 83, 87, 89, 90–91, 135, 173, 195, 201, 242

Madani, Husain Ahmad, 21, 72, 199
Madhhab, 124, 256. *See also* Islamic law
Madrasa ʿA'isha, 160, 162, 163
Madrasa orthodoxy. *See* Orthodoxy
Madrasas: aims of, 45–46, 58, 60, 110, 137, 163, 176, 187, 188, 190–92, 220; author's experience of, 19–30, 136–37, 150, 241–44; changes in, 140–42; crisis and, 140, 203; daily routines of, 31–46, 164, 217; definition of, 3; history of South Asian, 77–78, 83–84, 88–89, 97, 101, 103–7; internal debate and, 74, 201–3, 231–32; length of education, 132, 162; life after, 52–56; media coverage of, 2, 7, 11, 47, 207–9, 211–16, 218, 233; Muslim views of, 10–11, 74, 234–35, 238, 239; networks, 72, 238; physical spaces, 40, 154; sexual norms and, 21; Shiʿi, 49, 84; Taliban and, 210; types of, 49, 65; web presence and, 231; Western views of, 1–4, 7–9, 136, 207–8, 214–15, 234, 259 (n. 1); women's, 160–63, 237. *See also* Curriculum, madrasa; Education
Madrasa Sabilur Rashad, 19
Madrasi, ʿAbdul Khaliq, 176–77, 243
Majlis, 126
Maktabs, 230, 256
Malaysia, 2, 19, 236
Malcolm X, 28
Malik bin Anas, 30, 164. *See also* Maliki school
Maliki school, 30, 115. *See also* Islamic law; Malik bin Anas
Mandela, Nelson, 24
Marriage, 21, 33, 119–20, 161, 171, 235, 236
Maslak, 65, 68, 104, 256; narrative and, 54, 66–67
Master-disciple relations, 67, 81, 85, 103, 125, 197. *See also* Teachers
Maturidi school, 106, 107, 113. *See also* Theology
Mawdudi, Abul Aʿla, 24, 25, 27, 225
Mawlid, 91, 93, 166. *See also* Muhammad
Mazhari, Waris, 56
Mecca, 37, 41, 72, 95, 112, 134, 171–72, 196
Media: coverage of Islam by Western, 35, 152, 209, 211–16; coverage of madrasas by Western, 2, 7, 11, 47, 207–9, 211–16, 218, 233; electronic, 59; uses by Muslim clerics, 55, 137, 140, 163, 225; uses by Muslims, 141, 155
Medicine, 5, 18, 174, 175, 216–17
Medina, 41, 43, 164, 171
Memory, 64, 126, 141, 189–90; as educational tool, 3, 44, 130
Military: action, 7, 97; American, 235, 237; in early Islam, 171; Egyptian, 25, 248; Mughal, 96; Pakistani, 11, 164, 166, 212, 237. *See also* Jihad; Terrorism; War
Modernists, Muslim, 23, 26, 27, 146, 176, 201
Modernity, 48, 127, 128, 181, 231–32, 251

Modi, Narendra, 48
Monasticism, 2, 33, 51, 202, 227
Mongheri, Muhammad, 135
Morality, 113, 159, 188, 199; decline in, 56, 99–100; differences among Muslims, 146, 149; Islamic law as, 22, 95, 112, 118, 158–59, 192, 201; madrasa project of, 2, 9, 10, 39, 64, 65–66, 163, 191–92, 238, 248; responsibility and, 33–34; revealed, 61–62, 147–48; ʿulama and, 33–34, 51, 56, 235. *See also* Ethics; Islamic law
Morsi, Mohamed, 25, 266 (n. 1)
Mosques, 150, 168, 209, 214, 216, 217, 235; commemorative, 79, 90; madrasas and, 19–20, 34, 36–39, 43, 103, 166, 177, 244–45; South African, 16; Tablighi Jamaʿat and, 17–18, 31; work in, 52, 55, 137, 140, 151, 202, 256
Muftis, 145, 152, 256
Mughals, 27, 78, 85, 89, 92, 96, 127, 169, 227, 230–31
Muhammad (Prophet), 192; biography of, 41, 171–73; birthday celebration of, 91–93, 166; declaration of faith and, 18, 34, 116; example of, 33–34, 37–38, 64, 67, 85, 105, 119, 125, 148–49, 156–58, 174–75, 192, 200; insult to, 15–16, 68–69, 152, 165–66, 197; respect for, 146–48, 172–73, 192, 237–38, 244; study of, 2, 23, 110, 146–50; successors of, 210; traditions attributed to, 35, 56, 69, 178; uniqueness of, 98–100
Muhammadan Path, 92, 97
Muharram, 27, 87
Mujahidin, 2, 209–10
Mumbai, 15
Musharraf, Parvez, 165, 265 (n. 13)
Music, 26, 85, 216, 217
Muslim Brotherhood, 24, 25, 27
Muslims: demographics, 235; identity, 140, 220–24, 230, 231, 237–38
Muʿtazila, 106, 113, 114. *See also* Theology
Mysticism, 19, 65, 67–68, 81, 82, 87, 94, 96, 104, 116, 117, 120, 124, 140, 169–70. *See also* Sufism

Nadvi, Abul Hasan ʿAli, 27
Nadvi, Sayyid Salman Husayni, 173, 195, 226, 246
Nadwatul ʿUlama, 27, 135–36, 173–74, 195, 201, 222, 242, 246
Nanautvi, Muhammad Qasim, 49, 67–68, 101–2, 104, 134, 138, 188, 201, 248
Naqshbandi Sufi order, 85, 94
Nasser, Gamal Abdul, 24, 25
Nationalism, Islamic, 227
Nation states, 10, 51, 105, 127, 140–41, 152, 168, 176, 200, 213, 220, 235, 236, 237
Networks: madrasa, 2, 8, 11, 47, 49, 57, 72, 101, 105–6, 136, 139, 141, 214, 215, 226, 238, 248; scholarly, 55, 58, 77–78, 108–9, 122–24, 236; Sufi, 85, 92; terrorist, 10, 265 (n. 13)
News. *See* Media
Nizami curriculum. *See* Curriculum, madrasa
Nizamuddin (Mulla), 23, 77, 83–84, 86, 89, 90, 94, 113, 122, 123, 125, 127, 128, 130, 131
Nuʿmani, Shibli, 77, 83, 219, 220–22, 226, 230, 231

Obama, Barack, 52, 214
Oil, 213
Ontology, 65, 91, 182, 185. *See also* Human beings; Knowledge
Orthodoxy, Islamic, 23, 48, 148, 209, 230, 235, 251–53; challenges to, 135; definition of, 9; madrasa, 8, 78, 141, 147, 162, 210, 220, 238–39; South Asian, 174; women and, 159
Ottoman Caliphate, 72

Pakistan, 209, 235, 236; creation of, 24, 97, 127; government of, 145, 165–66, 212; India relations with, 239;

madrasas in, 1–2, 34, 51, 56, 136, 159, 163, 173, 220, 224; militancy in, 10–11, 105, 164, 166, 210–11; national education system of, 54; Northwest Frontier Province of, 211, 215–16; relations with United States, 4, 7, 207, 212–16, 233, 237; Shariat Appeal Court of, 145; Sufism in, 85
Parsees, 20
Pashtuns, 96, 100
Pedagogy, 23, 40, 44, 84, 127, 128, 134, 137. *See also* Education; Teachers
Persian, 123, 154–55, 245; culture, 112; study of language, 54, 110, 137; tradition of learning, 128, 130, 131, 132
Philosophy, 104, 124, 169, 178, 181–82, 198–99, 242; language, 116–18; modern, 137; moral, 28, 36, 67, 79, 95, 137, 260 (n. 3); Muslim contributions to, 5, 49, 117–18; study of, 2, 48, 84, 110–11, 127, 130–32, 163, 175, 224, 228–29. *See also* Disciplines, academic; Knowledge
Piety, 180, 240; gender and, 159–63; intellectual mediocrity and, 134, 140, 243; knowledge and, 32, 51, 139; madrasas and, 10, 29, 36, 45–46, 49–50, 145–48, 227; *masliks* and, 67, 105; material gain and, 48; Ramadan and, 41; religious movements and, 17–18, 216; Sufi, 105. *See also* Beliefs, religious; Faith; Salvation
Pilgrimage, 41, 72, 91, 112
Pluralism, 199–201
Poetry, 5, 48, 80, 91, 110, 123, 178
Political Islam, 24, 25. *See also* Extremism, religious; Terrorism
Political theology, 11, 104–5, 199, 210. *See also* Theology
Politics, 127, 145, 175, 199, 200, 209, 220, 228, 232, 237–40, 245; global, 8, 234–35, 247; study of, 49, 118–19, 175, 199, 202, 224, 242; Western, 7–8, 208, 212, 233, 240
Powell, Colin, 4, 234
Practice, religious, 18, 64, 117, 181–82; discipline and, 39–40, 66; diversity among Muslims, 149; embodied, 33, 45–46, 65, 187–88; Islamic law and, 23, 49–50, 55, 118, 238; orthodoxy and, 9, 105; popular, 91, 107; of the Prophet Muhammad, 37, 68, 85, 145, 147; salvation and, 8, 61, 146, 194, 255, 256, 263 (n. 6); scholarship as, 58. *See also* Ethics; Prayer; Ritual; Salvation
Prayer, 10, 39–40, 55, 104, 228; congregational, 37, 41, 166; daily, 19, 31, 32–35, 37, 38, 42, 43, 120, 155, 170, 190, 255, 256; definition of, 37, 38; food and, 42; intention and, 35–36; Sufi, 85; supplicatory, 92
Public sphere, 123, 141, 142, 199–201, 237. *See also* Republic of letters
Purda, 159–60, 162, 173, 174, 256. *See also* Gender segregation
Purity. *See* Ritual; *Wudu*

Qadiri Sufi order, 83, 85
Al-Qaeda, 6–7, 10–11, 207–8, 214. *See also* Extremism, religious; Taliban; Terrorism; War
Qannawji, Siddiq Hasan Khan, 90–91, 195–96, 197
Al-Qaradawi, Yusuf, 236–37, 266 (n. 1)
Qur'an, 54, 68, 79, 90, 106, 146, 155, 170, 179–80, 191, 201, 257; divisions of, 180, 256, 257; exegesis of, 49, 61, 112, 114, 120, 124, 132, 137, 153, 171–72, 181, 192–93, 215, 257; first verse of, 38, 39, 61–63, 64, 68–69; liturgy and, 19–20, 32–33, 37–39, 180, 192; memorization of, 19, 151, 180, 213, 255; Prophet Muhammad and, 148–49, 171–72, 192; reciters of, 151, 256; rhetorical force of, 17, 62–63; Salafi interpretation of, 90, 195; study of, 2, 3, 23, 53, 57, 67, 84, 110, 118, 136, 138, 153, 175, 218; theological controversy and, 106, 113

Qutb, Sayyid, 24, 25, 27
Qutbuddin, 78–83, 113, 130–31

Rakʿa, 31, 37, 256. *See also* Prayer
Ramadan, 19–20, 41, 63, 151, 180
Reason, 79, 80, 106, 128, 134, 175
Religion, 212, 255; in public life, 11, 239; study of, 228;
Republic of letters, 123, 125–27, 141. *See also* Public sphere; Republic of piety
Republic of piety, 139–40, 200. *See also* Public sphere; Republic of letters
Revelation. *See* Qur'an
Ritual, 45–46; controversy surrounding, 93; myth and, 64–65; purity and, 22–23, 36, 119, 155, 156–57, 164. *See also* Practice, religious; Prayer; *Wudu*
Rumsfeld, Donald, 4, 214, 234
Rushdie, Salman, 152

Saints, 91–93, 94, 107
Salafis, 9, 28, 90, 107, 147, 195, 197, 214. *See also* Ahl-i Hadith; Wahhabism
Salah, 33–34, 256. *See also* Prayer
Salvation, 8–9, 48, 176, 182, 183, 194–95, 198–99, 200, 222. See also *Din*; Faith; Knowledge; Practice, religious
Sarodi, Ismaʿil, 151–52, 154–58
Saussure, Ferdinand de, 118
Scholars. *See* ʿUlama
Sciences, 49, 228; instrumental and transmitted, 109–10, 117; natural, 5, 50, 56, 132, 135, 161, 179, 202, 213, 223, 231, 251–52; religious, 44, 102, 184. *See also* Disciplines, academic
Sectarianism, 238–39; intra-Sunni, 101, 135, 165–66, 196, 216; Sunnis and Shiʿis, 27, 87, 210
Secular elites, 10, 11, 225, 234–35
Secularism, 24–25, 74, 136, 140, 176, 177, 200, 222, 226, 256. *See also* Education: religious and secular
Self-formation, 9, 33, 39, 96, 117, 137, 188, 191, 211
Semiotics. *See* Philosophy: language
September 11th, 1, 6–7, 11, 136–37, 150, 209, 215, 233, 240, 247
Sermon, 3, 20, 62, 154, 193, 235, 257. See also *Waʿz*
Sex, 21–22, 119–20, 164, 236
Al-Shafiʿi, Muhammad bin Idris, 30, 63–64, 153, 196
Shafiʿi school, 30, 63–64, 119, 153, 158
Sharh, 153, 257
Shariʿa. *See* Islamic law
Shatibi, Abu Ishaq, 125–26
Shaykhul Hind. *See* Hasan, Mahmud
Shiʿism, 111, 248, 257; law of, 23, 119, 152; madrasas of, 49, 84; Sunnism and, 27, 87, 210; Taliban and, 210
Shirazi, Mir Fathullah, 130
Sin, 21, 46, 47, 60–61, 63–65, 106, 113, 117, 148, 193
Sindhi, ʿUbaydullah, 72, 199
Sirhindi, Ahmad, 85, 102
Skepticism, 59, 176, 224, 252
Soul, 33, 35, 38, 60, 169–70, 186, 198, 229. *See also* Human beings
South Africa, 6, 8, 15–17, 19–20, 24, 26, 52, 56, 139, 241–42; District Six, 16. *See also* Cape Town
South Asia: diaspora from, 2, 8, 56, 100; history of, 170; Islamic law in, 152, 154; madrasas in, 2, 49, 78, 108, 111, 121, 145, 146, 182, 192, 234; scholars, 51, 159; women in, 159, 170. *See also* India; Indo-Pak Subcontinent; Pakistan
Soweto uprisings, 17. *See also* South Africa
Study groups, 16, 43–45
Sufism, 17, 165, 195, 217; lodges, 34, 39, 61, 96; masters, 67, 102, 103, 105, 126, 197; networks, 92; orders, 81, 83, 85, 92, 94; shrines, 168; skepticism of, 195. *See also* Mysticism
Suicide bombings, 164, 166, 209, 214–15, 265 (n. 13), 266 (n. 1). *See also* Terrorism

Sunna, 23, 57, 119, 145, 146–49, 164, 174–75, 192, 195, 213, 252, 257. *See also* Hadith; Islamic law
Sunnism: Hadith and, 132, 147, 149–50, 163, 170; intra-Sunni controversies, 28, 94, 100–101, 104–5; law and, 23, 30, 119, 152, 196; Prophet Muhammad and, 99; Qurʾan interpretation and, 120; Shiʿism and, 27, 87, 111, 210, 248; theologies of, 84, 104, 106, 113–14
Syria, 16, 25, 108, 209, 248

Tablighi Jamaʿat, 16–19, 31–32, 105, 162, 216
Tafsir, 153, 257. *See also* Qurʾan
Al-Taftazani, Saʿd al-Din, 114
Tahawi, Abu Jaʿfar, 152–53, 154–58
Taliban, 1–2, 6–7, 10–11, 25, 105, 163–64, 166, 207–16, 234, 237. *See also* Al-Qaeda; Terrorism; War
Tamerlane, 114
Taqlid, 95, 230
Tarbiyya, 57, 188, 192. *See also* Morality; Self-formation
Tawhid, 116–17, 237, 257
Taʾwil, 153. *See also* Qurʾan: exegesis of
Tawjih, 153. *See also* Qurʾan: exegesis of
Taʿzia, 87, 89
Teachers, 40, 58–60, 67–68, 109, 121, 125–26, 162–63, 181, 187, 190–92. *See also* Curriculum, madrasa; Education
Technology, 56, 59, 123, 128, 132, 183, 231–32, 245, 252
Terrorism, 1, 4, 7, 10–11, 126, 164, 166, 207, 209, 215, 216, 233, 239; madrasas and, 2, 164, 211, 218, 234
Texts, 22, 122, 129–30, 140–41, 256; elucidation of, 152–59; persons and, 58; sanctity of, 134; slavish attachment to, 221. *See also* Curriculum, madrasa; Education
Thanvi, Ashraf ʿAli, 68, 105, 195, 226; biography, 197; pedagogy of, 44, 221–24; publishing record of, 55; social views of, 200–201, 231–32; views of knowledge, 61–63, 197–99
Thatcher, Margaret, 10
Theology, 116, 135, 137, 164–65, 217, 220, 232, 255; controversy over, 82, 92–94, 98–101, 104, 106, 113–14, 166, 260 (n. 4); juristic, 236; mystical, 82, 87; rationalist, 79, 110, 112, 113, 178; reformist, 77, 92–96, 106–7, 238; Shiʿi, 210; study of, 2, 67, 124, 131–32, 138, 182; Sunni, 84, 106, 210
Thomas Aquinas, Saint, 5, 24
Tradition, Islamic, 23, 29, 124–25, 195, 200–201, 220, 250, 252–53; authority and, 9, 22, 174, 192, 222; intellectual, 15, 50, 128, 140, 219, 240
Traditionalists, Muslim, 24, 27, 62, 68, 73–74, 79–80, 122, 136, 145, 199–200. *See also* ʿUlama
Translation, 63, 114, 119, 134, 155, 212

ʿUlama, 33, 124, 146, 151, 164, 224–27, 232, 234, 236–37, 251; authority of, 74; definition of, 20, 179, 255, 257; knowledge and, 56–58; nation states and, 237; obscurantism of, 24, 236; orthodoxy and, 9; political activities of, 51, 133, 234, 236; responsibilities of, 33–34, 220–21, 223, 234–36; uses of media, 235. *See also* Nadwatul ʿUlama; Teachers
ʿUmar (caliph), 68, 88, 210, 261
Unbelief, 100, 113, 117, 198. *See also* Atheism; Beliefs, religious
United Kingdom, 8, 28–29, 56, 139, 165, 213; colonialism and, 17, 19, 24, 61, 68, 72, 88, 89, 97–98, 103, 105, 127, 133; madrasas in, 213
United Nations, 8
United States of America, 96–97, 236–39; critique of, 11–12, 174, 214, 218, 247; education in, 6, 44, 160, 216; madrasas in, 8, 19, 65, 139, 213, 235; Muslims in, 52; public discourse

United States of America (cont.)
in, 209, 212–13, 233–34, 240; war and, 2, 6–7, 12, 164, 207, 211, 235
Universities. *See* Education
Urdu, 27, 93, 138, 154–55, 192; poetry, 45; study of, 20–21, 54–55, 109, 110, 132, 137, 163
ʿUsmani, Muhammad Taqi, 3, 145, 159, 187, 223–24, 225–26, 231, 232
ʿUthman (caliph), 210

Vastanvi, Ghulam, 47–48, 50
Veil, 159–60, 162, 256
Violence. *See* Terrorism; War

Wahhabism, 97, 100
Waliyullah, Shah, 94–96, 97–98, 104, 106, 121–32, 181–82
War, 7, 52, 72, 88, 96, 164, 209–10, 216, 218, 233–35, 240; Islamic ethics of, 10, 61, 97, 118–19, 164, 173–75; on terror, 2–3, 207, 212, 214, 237–38. *See also* Jihad; Terrorism
Waʿz, 55, 193, 257. *See also* Sermon
Women, 231, 256; dress and, 147, 170, 255, 256, 257; Islamic history and, 171, 173, 174; Islamic law and, 210; madrasas and, 140, 146, 159–63, 216; purity, 155, 164; scholars, 80, 159; Taliban and, 210, 237; violence against, 11; war and, 174. *See also* Gender segregation; *Purda*
Wudu, 35–36, 109, 155, 164, 257. *See also* Ritual: purity and

Yemen, 7
Yusufzai, Malala, 210

Al-Zamakhshari, Abul Qasim Mahmud, 112–15
Zoroastrianism, 6, 20

ISLAMIC CIVILIZATION AND MUSLIM NETWORKS

Ebrahim Moosa, *What Is a Madrasa?* (2015).

Bruce B. Lawrence, *Who Is Allah?* (2015).

Edward E. Curtis IV, *The Call of Bilal: Islam in the African Diaspora* (2014).

Sahar Amer, *What Is Veiling?* (2014).

Rudolph T. Ware III, *The Walking Qur'an: Islamic Education, Embodied Knowledge, and History in West Africa* (2014).

Sa'diyya Shaikh, *Sufi Narratives of Intimacy: Ibn 'Arabī, Gender, and Sexuality* (2012).

Karen G. Ruffle, *Gender, Sainthood, and Everyday Practice in South Asian Shi'ism* (2011).

Jonah Steinberg, *Isma'ili Modern: Globalization and Identity in a Muslim Community* (2011).

Iftikhar Dadi, *Modernism and the Art of Muslim South Asia* (2010).

Gary R. Bunt, *iMuslims: Rewiring the House of Islam* (2009).

Fatemeh Keshavarz, *Jasmine and Stars: Reading More than "Lolita" in Tehran* (2007).

Scott A. Kugle, *Sufis and Saints' Bodies: Mysticism, Corporeality, and Sacred Power in Islam* (2007).

Roxani Eleni Margariti, *Aden and the Indian Ocean Trade: 150 Years in the Life of a Medieval Arabian Port* (2007).

Sufia M. Uddin, *Constructing Bangladesh: Religion, Ethnicity, and Language in an Islamic Nation* (2006).

Omid Safi, *The Politics of Knowledge in Premodern Islam: Negotiating Ideology and Religious Inquiry* (2006).

Ebrahim Moosa, *Ghazālī and the Poetics of Imagination* (2005).

miriam cooke and Bruce B. Lawrence, eds., *Muslim Networks from Hajj to Hip Hop* (2005).

Carl W. Ernst, *Following Muhammad: Rethinking Islam in the Contemporary World* (2003).